Presented by
The Arkansas Chapter of the
American Society of Landscape Architects

in observance of
National Landscape Architecture Week 2003

www.asla.org

100 Years of Landscape Architecture:

Some Patterns of a Century

BY MELANIE SIMO

Front cover: Prospect Park
Photograph by Alan Ward

ISBN: 1-888931-20-5

Published by Spacemaker Press ®
for the ASLA Press.

Printed by Palace Press International in China.

CONTENTS

As the American Society of Landscape Architects marks its first one hundred years the word "celebrate" resonates throughout our organization and our profession. We reflect upon the ASLA over the past century, and an incredible story of success unfolds. Indeed, we have much to celebrate.

In 1899 a small group of diverse individuals inspired by a new way of thinking about people, places, land, and life came together to form the ASLA, coalescing and advancing the profession of landscape architecture. Since then, the ASLA has grown into an organization of more than 13,000 members dedicated to enhancing people's lives and creating harmony within their environments. In just one hundred years we have advanced from a profession with a patchwork of education and instruction borrowed from art, architecture, engineering, and horticulture to one with undergraduate- and graduate-degree programs at more than sixty of the most prominent colleges and universities in the nation. During the past century the ASLA has led the profession of landscape architecture in literally reshaping our country and way of life—creating parks, designing new communities, revitalizing the urban core, improving air and water quality, preserving natural areas, planning entire regions, improving social conditions, and creating beauty to sustain our very souls. We have created a new paradigm for the design professions, one that irrevocably links responsible design to the environment.

Against overwhelming odds, in the course of this century the ASLA has led us in obtaining licensure in forty-seven states and has taken the profession from obscurity to wide public recognition of what landscape architects do.

Our past is rich with accomplishments, but what lies ahead for the profession of landscape architecture and the ASLA in the next century? In the early 1960s President Kennedy challenged the nation to put a man on the moon. At the same time he made another challenge: "It is our task in our time and in our generation to hand down undiminished, to those who come after us, the natural wealth and beauty which is ours." As we enter the twenty-first century we have put a man on the moon and explored Mars and Venus. However, President Kennedy's second challenge has gone largely unfulfilled as the world economy and the environment remain on a collision course, and the continued threat of environmental destruction and the misuse of dwindling resources loom heavily on the horizon. At present rates our population will double in the next sixty to seventy years, and under current patterns of consumption, development, and land use growth will come with enormous expansion of urban and suburban areas and the corresponding loss of farm and untouched lands. In the view of one of the founders of Earth Day, Senator Gaylord Nelson, "No war, no revolution, no peril of any kind measures up to the importance of the threat of continued environmental deterioration."

The 1999 Centennial Celebration, then, is not just a time to reflect on our past accomplishments. It is also a time to become active as never before, to redouble our commitment in order to meet the challenges of the twenty-first century.

In the last century landscape architects created a new paradigm for the design professions and the environment. In the twenty-first century we must continue to create new paradigms in which economic prosperity and sustainability go hand in hand, in which livability and the quality of life are primary considerations, and in which beauty and development are one and the same. When creating new archetypes we not only need to understand where to go but we must also commit ourselves to showing others the way. In the words of Plato, "If we are to have any hope for the future those who have lanterns must pass them on to others." As landscape architects we have special lanterns burning with the glow of our unique knowledge and fueled with the energy of our Centennial Celebration. We must help lead the way to a better environment, a higher quality of life, and a secure future.

What must landscape architects do in the future that we have not done in the past? In the words of Oliver Wendell Holmes, "As life is action and passion, it is required of a man to share the passion and action of his time at the peril of being judged not to have lived. It is more comfortable to sit content with the easy approval of friends and neighbors than risk the friction and controversy that come with public affairs." Landscape architects must take action with passion, getting involved in public affairs, in the political process, and in creating the process by which decisions are made—not just settle for a role in partially implementing those decisions. As we enter the new millennium we must diversify our membership and create strength by unifying our entire profession under the ASLA umbrella. We must influence national policy on issues such as zero population growth, national land-use planning, and growth management so that our work and that of our predecessors will not be in vain. We must become the elected and appointed leaders who focus the attention of government on these important issues, imbuing future generations with even greater confidence so they can say in 2099, "Look what the ASLA has done in just two hundred years!"

In 1999 the ASLA has undertaken a series of celebratory programs designed to expand our past accomplishments to meet the challenges ahead. "The 100 Years/100 Parks" program is the profession's anniversary gift to the nation, helping to create or revitalize more than one hundred outdoor spaces across America. The ASLA's "Medallions" program, which recognizes more than 350 significant works of landscape architecture throughout the United States, aims to heighten understanding of our work by the general public. The Frederick Law Olmsted stamp, to be issued by the U.S. Postal Service at the Centennial Celebration in Boston in September 1999, puts the name and image of landscape architecture in the hands of millions of Americans, while the Centennial Summit examines the state of the profession today to articulate our course of action for the future. Finally, the ASLA has produced this book in honor of our centennial. Of all the celebratory projects this—we hope—will provide a lasting memento and a tribute to our profession.

Participating in the creation of *One Hundred Years of Landscape Architecture: Some Patterns of a Century* has been one of the highlights of my service as the ASLA Centennial president. I am confident that you will share in our enthusiasm as you immerse yourself in the pages that follow.

The book begins at the time of the formation of the ASLA, just before the turn of the century, and takes us to the present. Prior to this time the profession began with its roots deeply planted in Old World antiquity. What later became "landscape architecture" in the New World first was practiced here by those who settled the land. And in the early years of our nation the likes of Washington and Jefferson made their mark planning cities, towns, universities, and agrarian landscapes. Indeed, Jefferson, widely revered as an architect, may ultimately be more highly praised for his innate genius in landscape architecture.

In the early nineteenth century such designers of the landscape as W.H.S. Cleveland and Andrew Jackson Downing advanced the concepts that were eventually named "landscape architecture" by Calvert Vaux and Frederick Law Olmsted, Sr. In the late 1860s Olmsted's use of the title "landscape architect" represented the birth and first milestone of the profession as we know it today.

In the next fifty years the profession expanded, attracting a varied group of individuals who rallied around this new way of thinking. While Frederick Law Olmsted, Sr., continued to be the most notable figure, other familiar names of the day included Jacob Weidenmann; John Charles Olmsted; Charles Eliott; Warren Manning; Frederick Law Olmsted, Jr; Henry Vincent Hubbard; John Nolen; O.C. Simonds; Jens Jensen; Charles Platt; Ellen Biddle Shipman; Beatrix Jones Farrand; Frank Albert Waugh; A.D. Taylor; and Arthur Shurcliff. Although most of these individuals adopted the new name "landscape architect," several (including O.C. Simonds and Beatrix Farrand) insisted on clinging to such former titles as "landscape gardener."

In the late nineteenth century came the second milestone for landscape architecture: the formation of the American Society of Landscape Architects on January 4, 1899, in New York City. This, coupled with the creation of the first landscape architecture degree program at Harvard University the very next year, solidified the practice of what had been given its name nearly fifty years earlier into the separate, distinct profession of landscape architecture. The events that have occurred in the one hundred years between the formation of the ASLA and the present are a compelling story of success.

In the following pages historian Melanie Simo begins to tell that story. She takes us on a journey through the past century of landscape architecture, examining the thought, ideology, and trends that have appeared in professional writing, exhibits, competitions, and the ASLA awards program and presenting them in the larger context of the social, political, and artistic movements of the day. Simo weaves a tapestry of the threads that bind one hundred years of our profession into some recognizable patterns that define landscape architecture and the ASLA. In the words of Harvard Professor Emeritus Charles Harris, "What Melanie Simo has [created] is an elaborate brocade, or tapestry, which has many beautiful patterns of emerald, silver, and gold. . . . What she has done is to extrapolate and tie together data about the profession—which has never been done before." As ASLA medal winner John Simonds comments, "Hooray! At last the scope, impact, and history of American land-

scape architecture are being addressed by a scholar and fine writer."

Telling the story of the past, however, can be as elusive as predicting the future, so it is important to note that this work is but one writer's view of our past. This book is not intended to be a definitive history of the last one hundred years of the profession of landscape architecture or of the ASLA. As the subtitle *Some Patterns of a Century* suggests, the book presents a view of our history by an external historian and scholar who has written about landscape architecture and the environmental design professions for many years. It is hoped that this work will stimulate others to recount their own views of our past and to tell more of what Simonds describes as "the highly dramatic yet largely untold saga of landscape architects in America from the time of Vaux and Olmsted," a saga that relates "the immense and telling environmental contribution of this small but rapidly expanding band of educators, practitioners, and agency leaders over the past one hundred years."

As we account for our past we must understand that our history continually evolves, constantly revealing and reinventing itself; it will always be rewritten. As Simo points out, "How landscape architects move into the next century and prosper is a story that cannot yet be told. But one part of that story may depend on how well landscape architects understand where they came from, and how and why."

To complement Simo's work the winners of the ASLA Medal have been asked to give their own personal perspectives, reflections that tremendously enrich our celebration: Garrett Eckbo's profound observations about man and nature; Meade Palmer's modest revelation that working with plants and living things sets us apart; John Simond's outline of the "immense contribution" of our profession; Robert Royston's poetic presentation of his career experience; Ervin Zube's calculated observations of the future; and Ian McHarg's inspirational genius. Sadly, two of these leaders have recently passed away: John Lyle and Ray Freeman. Although they are not here in person to celebrate the centennial, their spirits are with us.

This effort will inspire anyone who reads this book, whether it be the most scrupulous landscape architect or someone outside the profession with only a casual knowledge of what we do. Particular thanks go to Spacemaker Press for its role in producing this book.

For all landscape architects I hope our book will engender a sense of pride, motivation, and recommitment to the mission of our profession. And for those readers who are not landscape architects I am confident that *One Hundred Years of Landscape Architecture: Some Patterns of a Century* will provide insight into the enormous contribution that a small but profoundly dedicated profession has made to the quality of life, the protection of our environment, and the livability of our communities over the past century.

Celebrate the landscape of life!

BARRY W. STARKE, FASLA, ASLA Centennial President

John C. Olmsted 1899–1901, 1904–1905

Samuel Parsons, Jr. 1902, 1906–1907

Nathan F. Barrett 1903

Frederick Law Olmsted, Jr. 1908–1909, 1919–1922

Charles N. Lowrie 1910–1911

Harold A. Caparn 1912

Ossian C. Simonds 1913

Warren H. Manning 1914

James Sturgis Pray 1915–1918

James L. Greenleaf 1923–1927

Arthur A. Shurcliff 1927–1931

Henry Vincent Hubbard 1931–1935

Albert D. Taylor 1935–1941

S. Herbert Hare 1941–1945

Markley Stevenson 1945–1949

Gilmore D. Clarke 1949–1951

Lawrence G. Linnard 1951–1953

Leon Zach 1953–1957

Norman T. Newton 1957–1961

John I. Rogers 1961–1963

John Ormsbee Simonds FASLA 1963–1965

Dr. Hubert B. Owens 1965–1967

Theodore Osmundson FASLA 1967–1969

Campbell E. Miller 1969–1971

Raymond L. Freeman FASLA 1971–1973

William G. Swain FASLA 1973–1974

OWEN H. PETERS FASLA 1974–1975	CHERYL L. BARTON FASLA 1987–1988
EDWARD H. STONE II FASLA 1975–1976	BRIAN S. KUBOTA FASLA 1988–1989
BENJAMIN W. GARY, JR. FASLA 1976–1977	GERALD D. PATTEN FASLA 1989–1990
DEAN LANE L. MARSHALL FASLA 1977–1978	CLAIRE R. BENNETT FASLA 1990–1991
JOT D. CARPENTER FASLA 1978–1979	CAMERON R.J. MAN FASLA 1991–1992
ROBERT L. WOERNER FASLA 1979–1980	DEBRA L. MITCHELL FASLA 1992–1993
WILLIAM A. BEHNKE FASLA 1980–1981	THOMAS PAPANDREW FASLA 1993–1994
CALVIN T. BISHOP FASLA 1981–1982	DENNIS Y. OTSUJI FASLA 1994–1995
THEODORE J. WIRTH FASLA 1982–1983	VINCENT BELLAFIORE FASLA 1995–1996
DARWINA L. NEAL FASLA 1983–1984	DONALD W. LESLIE FASLA 1996–1997
ROBERT H. MORTENSEN FASLA 1984–1985	THOMAS R. DUNBAR FASLA 1997–1998
JOHN WACKER FASLA 1985–1986	BARRY W. STARKE FASLA 1998–1999
ROGER B. MARTIN FASLA 1986–1987	JANICE C. SCHACH FASLA 1999–

THE ASLA MEDAL

The ASLA Medal is the society's highest award. Each year the society recognizes an individual who has made extraordinary contributions to the profession of landscape architecture. The society has a constitutional mandate to advance education and skill in the art of landscape architecture as an instrument of service in the public welfare. One way of carrying out this mandate is to identify those practitioners whose contributions to the profession have had a unique impact on the public welfare nationally or internationally through superior design, planning, writing, and/or public service.

1971	HIDEO SASAKI FASLA	1985	ROBERTO BURLE MARX
1972	CONRAD L. WIRTH FASLA	1986	WILLIAM J. JOHNSON FASLA
1973	JOHN ORMSBEE SIMONDS FASLA	1987	PHILLIP H. LEWIS, JR. FASLA
1974	CAMPBELL E. MILLER FASLA	1988	DAME SYLVIA CROWE
1975	GARRETT ECKBO FASLA	1989	ROBERT N. ROYSTON FASLA
1976	THOMAS CHURCH FASLA	1990	RAYMOND L. FREEMAN FASLA
1977	HUBERT B. OWENS FASLA	1991	MEADE PALMER FASLA
1978	LAWRENCE HALPRIN FASLA	1992	ROBERT S. REICH FASLA
1979	NORMAN T. NEWTON	1993	ARTHUR E. BYE, JR. FASLA
1980	WILLIAM G. SWAIN FASLA	1994	EDWARD D. STONE, JR. FASLA
1981	SIR GEOFFREY JELLICOE	1995	ERVIN H. ZUBE FASLA
1982	CHARLES W. ELIOT II FASLA	1996	JOHN T. LYLE FASLA
1983	THEODORE O. OSMUNDSON FASLA	1997	JULIUS GY. FABOS FASLA
1984	IAN MCHARG FASLA	1998	CAROL R. JOHNSON FASLA

THE LAGASSE MEDAL

The LaGasse Medals are awarded at appropriate times to individuals who through the professional practice or utilization of landscape architecture have made notable contributions to the management of natural resources, the management of public lands, or the management of other lands in the public interest.

The medals are named for Alfred B. LaGasse, who served as executive director of the American Institute of Park Executives and subsequently as executive vice president of the National Recreation and Parks Association. From 1968 until 1976 he was the executive director of the American Society of Landscape Architects and the American Society of Landscape Architects Foundation. Throughout his lifetime LaGasse was concerned with the proper management of the nation's public lands and the judicious use of the country's natural resources. The LaGasse Medal is presented in recognition of his profound concern for excellence in the management of public properties and the management of natural resources for use by the public.

LANDSCAPE ARCHITECT CATEGORY:

1981	CONRAD L. WIRTH FASLA
1982	RAYMOND L. FREEMAN FASLA
1983	RAYMOND E. PAGE FASLA
1984	WILLIAM CARNES
1985	WILLIAM P. MOTT
1986	EDWARD H. STONE II FASLA
1987	DAVID G. WRIGHT FASLA
1988	IAN MCHARG FASLA
1989	JOHN W. BRIGHT FASLA
1995	JERROLD SOESBE FASLA
1996	GERALD D. PATTEN FASLA
1998	MARK ACKELSON ASLA

NON-LANDSCAPE ARCHITECT CATEGORY:

1981	THE HONORABLE LAURANCE S. ROCKEFELLER
1982	THE HONORABLE MORRIS UDALL
1983	LEO DRAY
1984	HOMER WADSWORTH
1985	MARTIN ROSEN
1986	THE HONORABLE JOHN SEIBERLING
1987	EDWARD CLIFF
1988	WILLIAM K. REILLY
1989	WAYNE KENNEDY
1990	ARTHUR A. DAVIS
1991	CARL F. STEINITZ
1995	JAMES P. STORER
1996	JULIA BRODERICK O'BRIEN
1998	WOLF BAUER

THE OLMSTED MEDAL

Award of the Olmsted Medal was instituted in 1990 to recognize important environmental achievements by an individual non-landscape architect or an organization. The award highlights the interprofessional collaboration that landscape architects believe is key to resolving the environmental challenges facing us as we move into the twenty-first century. The medal is named for Frederick Law Olmsted, Sr., founder of the profession of landscape architecture. It represents the profession's commitment to stewardship of the land and through public outreach is intended to advance the mission and goals of the society.

1990   William K. Reilly

1991   The Nature Conservancy

1992   The Honorable Albert Gore

1995   The Honorable Bruce Babbitt

1997   Trustees of the Reservations

1998   1000 Friends of Oregon

"A mere imitation of nature, however successful, is not art, and the purpose to imitate nature, or to produce an effect which shall seem to be natural and interesting, is not sufficient for the duty before us. . . . The combination of art thus defined, with the art of architecture in the production of landscape compositions, is what we denominate landscape architecture."

FREDERICK LAW OLMSTED, SR.

1822 – 1903

In March 1911 at a meeting of the American Society of Landscape Architects (ASLA), the man who was to become the society's first honorary member offered these words of optimism: "If I were asked to mention the most important public movement of the last twenty years, I should say that it was the movement to obtain for all classes of society—indeed, for the entire population—better means of health, rational enjoyment, and real happiness. . . . Successful results in your profession bring health, general well-being, and sweet and wholesome pleasures to mankind. . . . The elements with which you work [trees, shrubs, flowers, lakes, streams, forests, sky, etcetera] are beautiful, wholesome, and winning. . . . The artist may be forgotten, or may be recalled only by the writers and readers of history; but the landscape artist's work will live. . . . So, in spite of the difficulties which attend the development of a young profession whose capacities are not yet fully appreciated, I congratulate you most heartily on the nature of the work to which you have devoted your lives; and I fully believe that your professional lives will be unusually happy, and will bring you durable satisfactions."[1]

The speaker was Charles W. Eliot, president emeritus of Harvard University, "a plain man in a plush age," known for his progressive views of education and society.[2] This former assistant professor of mathematics and chemistry lived into his nineties and continued to attend meetings of the ASLA, offering landscape architects noble, reassuring sentiments just as he provided inscriptions for post offices and other public buildings and monuments across the United States.[3]

But times have changed. We have grown accustomed to portals without inscriptions, monuments without sermons. Nearing the end of a century and of a millennium, people are now looking ahead. So why look back? There are a number of reasons—self-interest, for one. It is in

CENTRAL PARK, NEW YORK, NEW YORK

FREDERICK LAW OLMSTED, SR., AND CALVERT VAUX

PHOTOGRAPH COURTESY OF THE FRANCES LOEB LIBRARY, GRADUATE SCHOOL OF DESIGN, HARVARD UNIVERSITY our own best interests to understand some of the more pressing concerns of the 1890s and the 1900s—for they mirror our own concerns. Rapid technological changes. Waves of acquisitions and mergers among the titans of business and industry. Extremes of poverty and wealth, whether hidden or flaunted. Spreading urban slums, foreclosed family farms, and opulent rural retreats. These are not new phenomena but recurrences. A century ago, as today, the times were deeply troubled, yet some people were hopeful, even confident. In spite of sweatshops and strike riots, depressions and recessions, and ever-unfolding stories of corruption, fraud, and waste, there was some cause for optimism among reformers, educators, journalists, and statesmen. Both Theodore Roosevelt and, later, Woodrow Wilson were activist presidents, Republican and Democrat, who came to be associated with progressive movements for political and social reform. And each in his own way, whether proclaiming the Square Deal, the New Nationalism, or the New Freedom, embodied the Progressives' confidence in the future.[4]

Was it, then, an auspicious time to institutionalize a new profession in 1899? Will it be an auspicious time to enter that same profession in 1999? Some clues—rather than some pat answers—lie in the historical record, from which this account of patterns and turning points, defeats and triumphs has been drawn. The specific conditions for practice, teaching, and research have changed, of course. But, as evident in the brief historical sketch that follows, concerns about the *pace* of change and the *scale* of operations have been remarkably durable over time.

Following the accelerated growth of industrialization, urbanization, and immigration in the post-Civil War decades, the pace of modern life was still quickening in the new century. Between 1900 and 1910 an unprecedented 8 million immigrants were admitted into the United States. And these newcomers—along with the telephone, Standard Oil, the powerful trade unions, and Sigmund Freud—were all components of a new, larger-scaled, more complicated world that was, in the words of Walter Lippmann, "full of stirring and confusion and ferment."[5] To the journalist Herbert Croly this "increased momentum of American life" appeared to be the only possible beginning for a better life, both for individuals and for society as a whole.[6] What is more, the movement for social and environmental improvements of which Charles W. Eliot was so serenely confident was broadening its base of support. As one observer wrote in a 1913 article in *Landscape Architecture* magazine that discussed the economics of town planning, "unless the mass of the people are convinced, there is no hope; for the driving force of political action in our time is not the beliefs and aspirations of a few intellectuals, but those of the great body of the people."[7]

Despite the materialism and short-term self interest encouraged in a rapidly industrializing society, the turn of the century showed signs of a shift in the general tone and content of public discourse. Particularly among the younger generation of literate and articulate people, whatever their social backgrounds, there was a growing sense that a new set of goals was needed in American life: not so much the entrepreneur's ideals of expansion and material success as the citizen's ideals of honest government, a fairer distribution of the nation's bountiful resources, and progress achieved through cooperation and planning, even through cultural refinement. "The American people were melting down old heroes and recasting the mold in which heroes were made," recalled William Allen White, owner of a newspaper in Kansas and author of the book, *The Old Order Changeth* (1910).[8]

This was the Progressive Era, its spirit first apparent on a local and regional scale in the 1890s. William Jennings Bryan, whose emotionally charged speeches defended small farmers' interests in the American heartland, and Wisconsin's Robert M. La Follette, whose pragmatic political reforms included direct primaries, regulation of the railroads, and taxation of corporations, were both exemplars of that era of ferment and change. By the early 1900s the impulse for progressive reforms had swelled to a national movement and even, for a brief moment in 1912, to a new national political entity, the Progressive Party.[9]

One general-interest magazine that spanned this period was *The Craftsman* (1901–1916), in which reports on garden cities, improved tenement houses, and city planning mingled with essays on art, craft, and political reform. Editor Gustav Stickley frequently quoted or extended the ideas of John Ruskin and William Morris, who stressed the interdependence of art, craft, and social conditions. Similarly, Jane Addams's *Twenty Years at Hull House* (1910) showed that art and cultural experiences could be as meaningful to the working poor of Chicago's West Side

as to the leisure class. Although only a small pioneering effort, the social settlement of Hull House brought together people of different social classes (including Italian, Greek, and Russian-Jewish immigrants who worked in shops and factories by day) to learn crafts and attend concerts and art exhibitions in the evenings and on weekends. It was at Hull House, in 1901, that Frank Lloyd Wright gave his famous lecture, "The Art and Craft of the Machine." Over time, then, the mingling of different sorts of people that Frederick Law Olmsted, Sr., had envisioned for New York's Central Park took place here and there, not only in urban parks but also in some pockets of the nerve-jangling inner city.

Meanwhile, a growing interest in the conservation of natural resources brought together different impulses toward progressive reform. As president in the early 1900s Theodore Roosevelt not only set aside millions of acres of conservation land. He also appointed as head of the new federal Division of Forestry the ambitious young Gifford Pinchot, whom Olmsted had earlier interviewed for the new position of forester at the Biltmore estate in North Carolina. Further, Roosevelt raised conservation to a national cause when, in 1908, he called his Conference of Governors and appointed a National Conservation Commission. In 1909 with Gifford Pinchot as chairman this commission produced the nation's first inventory of natural resources (or "national wealth").[10] There would, of course, be setbacks to the conservation movement and sharp differences of opinion among those initially committed to the broad concept of conservation. The beauty and recreational value of national parks and forest reserves would not always survive competing claims for the commercial value, or "wise use," of these resources. But in 1911 Charles W. Eliot and his landscape architect friends could look forward to a bright future.

Eliot's emphasis on electives for undergraduates and on specialized studies in the new graduate and professional schools would influence both the course of American higher education in general and the development of landscape architecture in particular. As president of Harvard, he accepted Nelson Robinson's substantial gift, not only for studies in architecture but also for the establishment of the country's first degree program in landscape architecture in 1900-1901.[11] Nevertheless, landscape architects would probably not recognize Eliot's name today were it not for his son, the less robust and more introspective Charles Eliot, who died in 1897 of a sudden illness in his thirty-eighth year. This young Eliot was one of the most promising among the younger generation of American landscape architects in the 1890s. Before joining the elder Olmsted and his stepson John Charles as a partner in the new firm of Olmsted, Olmsted and Eliot in 1893, Eliot had envisioned a complete system of regional parks and parkways for metropolitan Boston. And he wrote voluminously—journals, park reports, book reviews, and many letters to the editors of local newspapers, advocating public improvements such as the damming of the Charles River, a tidal estuary. Regarding this watercourse, effectively an open sewer, he argued that not only its neighbors but all the citizens of Boston should carefully consider the current proposals for eliminating pollution and creating a riverside park, parkway, and playgrounds.[12]

Having absorbed the idealism of John Ruskin, John Stuart Mill, William Morris, and other towering nineteenth-century figures, Eliot would not detach issues of beauty from their wider contexts—cultural, social, scientific, and spiritual. Without reducing a problem to merely utilitarian components, he could still pursue the "greatest good for the greatest number." A quiet confidence and reasonableness pervaded his balanced arguments. In one essay, "What Would be Fair Must First be Fit," Eliot cited both the scientific evidence of natural selection and the rational arguments of Humphry Repton as authorities for his belief that function, or fitness to purpose, must lie at the heart of any attempt to alter a landscape "for the use and delight of men."[13]

It is not surprising that Charles Eliot should be asked for his opinion about the formation of a professional society to represent the field of landscape architecture in the United States. What is perhaps surprising is that he said, in effect, "No." When Warren H. Manning, a long-time colleague of the elder Olmsted, circulated this sort of query among several distinguished individuals in the winter of 1896-1897, Eliot emphasized the dearth of professionals then in the field and their lack of widespread public recognition. Rather than some sort of "trades union or professional league" he recommended a broad-based association of individuals interested in the advancement of landscape art—something along the lines of an association for the advancement of science. Amateurs, writers, park superintendents, land owners, engineers, foresters, gardeners, and anyone else willing to contribute perhaps two dollars a year could be brought together, he suggested, along with members of village improvement societies and others.[14]

Eliot was not alone in hesitating to endorse the formation of a professional association of landscape architects in the 1890s. His partner John Charles Olmsted would also have preferred to form a kind of "grassroots" organization in the still formative years of landscape architecture when the number of professionals was very small and regular academic training in the field did not exist. Nevertheless, the ASLA was formed before the century's end—in 1899. The fact that today, a hundred years later, this society has grown to a body of some 13,000 members and associates suggests that history has proven these two distinguished forebears wrong. But the matter is not so easily settled. Consider just one of J. C. Olmsted's reservations: "Until the public is educated to the idea that they should employ a landscape architect corresponding in mental capacity, education, and experience to the architects which they employ for their houses, there will be little hope of any considerable number of suitable men taking up the profession."[15]

Would a professional society, formed in the absence of widespread public understanding and interest, resemble a cart before the horse? Who, in fact, would be most likely to provide the horsepower, the "drive" needed to advance a movement for the creation of well-designed public parks, parkways, gardens, subdivisions, city and regional planning studies, rural cemeteries, golf courses, forest reserves, and other amenities for use, beauty, and general well-being? These were the sorts of questions that seem to

have engaged several respondents to Manning's query.

The man who had done as much—if not more—than anyone else to establish the profession of landscape architecture in the United States was unable to comment on Manning's proposal. By the late 1890s Frederick Law Olmsted, Sr., had succumbed to a debilitating illness—senility, it was called—in the wake of the physical and mental stresses he had endured during a lifetime of extraordinary accomplishments. And, as his biographer Laura Wood Roper has pointed out, landscape architecture was not his only profession; his contributions to the cultural and social life of the United States ultimately transcended that profession.[16] But there does survive the response of Olmsted's elder colleague, H.W.S. Cleveland, who wrote from Chicago, "Such an association as you suggest seems to me not only desirable, but imperatively demanded as the only means of maintaining the dignity and respectability of the profession." And he advised that "none but strictly professional men" be allowed to become members.[17]

Responses to Manning's query tended to favor either an exclusively professional society or a more broad-based association of people. Charles Sprague Sargent, director of the Arnold Arboretum in Jamaica Plain, Massachusetts, thought the association an "excellent thing to organize," but he referred to its potential members as "landscape gardeners." This was the term that his former protegee Beatrix Jones (later Farrand) continued to use in describing her own work. O. C. Simonds, known for his design of Graceland Cemetery near Chicago, also preferred the term "landscape gardener." Into the proposed society he would welcome professional landscape gardeners, teachers in the field, superintendents of public grounds, and editors, writers, and patrons who might be able to influence public taste "in the right direction." The only group Simonds would not admit to such a society were those involved in commercial enterprise.[18]

When asked for his views on the forming of a society of landscape architects, Liberty Hyde Bailey, professor of botany and horticulture at Cornell University, raised the specter of "combinations" (or trade unions), an emerging counterforce to the combinations of business enterprises, or "trusts." The Sherman Antitrust Act of 1890 was beginning to be seen as a tool to curb not only the power of monopolies but also the power of labor unions. And in the eyes of some critics both kinds of power on a large scale were potential threats to a democratic nation. Accordingly, Bailey welcomed the idea of "a society of landscape gardeners or landscape art improvers" but thought, on the one hand, that the inclusion of teachers and writers as members would perhaps allay any suspicion of an attempt to form a combination. On the other hand, recognizing the professional's reluctance to join in with "this more popular element," Bailey thought they might just as well organize alone. Mariana Griswold Van Renssalaer, a critic of architecture and landscape design and author of a profile of Frederick Law Olmsted, shared Bailey's interest in a society that might include people other than professionals. "It should be formed of genuine artists and of amateurs of the art," she suggested. But she, too,

would exclude people whose interests were mainly commercial.[19]

The society that was in fact formed at a meeting in New York on January 4, 1899, laid the foundation for an exclusively professional society—which would, however, include some who called themselves "landscape gardeners," such as founding members Beatrix Jones and O. C. Simonds.[20] This society would not admit nurserymen, builders, or others engaged in commercial enterprises, and for many years its honorary and corresponding members and associates (that is, nonprofessional landscape architects) were very few in number. As late as 1926—the year Charles W. Eliot died—there were only two honorary members: Professor Bailey and Mrs. Van Rensselaer, who received her honorary membership that year. By then some of J. C. Olmsted's initial reservations would have been allayed by the existence of several professional degree programs in landscape architecture, at Harvard, Cornell, the University of Pennsylvania, and several of the land-grant colleges that would emerge as major universities. In 1910 the magazine *Landscape Architecture* was begun to serve as the ASLA's "official organ." And gradually, through such venues as illustrated books and magazines, traveling exhibitions, and national and international design competitions, the work and thought of landscape architects became better known to a broader public.

At first glance the precautions voiced by a few landscape architects in the early years of the profession may seem insignificant. But surveying the spectrum of opinion about forming a professional society of landscape architects is useful for two main reasons. First, the public's dim understanding of landscape architecture is a problem that has not diminished over time; the need to explain the profession to the public, a recurring theme throughout these pages, has continued to haunt many landscape architects to this day. The second reason is that the final, collective decision to form a professional society in 1899 represents the thinking of the time. The emerging Progressive Era was significant not only for a surging interest in social and political reforms, "trust-busting," and natural-resource conservation, but also for the rise of a new major player in the life of the nation—the professional. This was an expert, someone presumably above the fray of politics who could be expected to act from motives higher than self-interest or mere profit. Above commercialism, above favoritism, highly trained for a role in society perhaps hitherto unrecognized, the professional was emerging as an indispensable contributor to society.

The rise of the professional is one important development traced in Samuel P. Hays's study of the Progressive Era, *Conservation and the Gospel of Efficiency* (1959). "The direction of change was toward centralization," Hays observes. And the spirit of progressivism—"efficiency, expertise, order"—was critical.[21] No longer could an individual with merely entrepreneurial instincts or a generalist's competence be expected to solve all the problems of the new, larger scale of things—from banking houses and oil conglomerates to metropolitan areas, universities, and labor unions. The size and complexity of these emerging centers of power called for a new form of organization with a higher degree of coordination and co-operation. People were needed at the middle levels of a hierarchy—managers, administrators, researchers, and technicians—people who could analyze, synthesize, and deal with abstractions. Closer to the top of that hierarchy, people were also needed to take charge of great collective undertakings, working either within a large organization or from the outside as professional consultants. There was, then, an increasing need for people with graduate training in economics, business administration, law, medicine, and engineering, just as in the many new specialties developing among the natural sciences.

In landscape architecture there was not initially the same generally recognized need to specialize within a profession. It is true that some inclination to focus on, say, town planning or "landscape engineering" was apparent before the outbreak of World War I. But specialization would not become a critical issue for the whole profession until after World War II. In the early 1900s landscape architecture was still a kind of specialized field in itself, focused on aspects of land development that had previously been managed (or ignored) by architects, engineers, and horticulturists.

The event that had recently brought members of all these professions together, along with sculptors and painters, was the 1893 World's Columbian Exposition in Chicago. There, a new, larger scale of undertaking in physical planning and design called for a higher level of cooperation. At a banquet honoring the exposition's designers the presiding architect Daniel Burnham had high praise for the absent Frederick Law

Olmsted, Sr. "Each of you knows the name and genius of him who stands first in the heart and confidence of American artists, the creator of your own parks and many other city parks. He it is who has been our best adviser and common mentor. In the highest sense he is the planner of the Exposition. . . . As artist, he paints with lakes and wooded slopes; with lawns and banks and forest-covered hills; with mountainsides and ocean views."[22]

In keeping with Burnham's metaphor, landscape architects, for many years thereafter, would insist on the artistic foundation of their profession. And, as will become evident, the foil for this claim to artistic expertise was not science, but commercialism. In the early years most landscape architects would take for granted the need for at least some grounding in the natural sciences. Their real challenge seemed to come from the realm of commerce—from nurserymen and contractors who might compete with them for commissions. Hence the need for landscape architects to convince the client and the public at large that they were artists, not merely businessmen "in trade." At the same time a few among them, notably Warren Manning, came to insist on the increasingly larger scale that needed to be addressed by landscape architects.

Manning's role in the development of the profession was critical. The son of a prominent nurseryman near Boston, he could not look upon tradesmen with the remoteness cultivated by many of his fellow landscape architects. The elder Olmsted had frequently depended on Manning for his knowledge of plants, and the two had often worked together

on such major projects as the Chicago Exposition and the Vanderbilt estate, Biltmore. In 1899 Manning became a founding member of the ASLA. In 1914 he served as ASLA president. Yet despite these signs of solidarity with his fellow professionals he was developing a vision for the profession and the nation that would set him apart from others in the field.[23] With the elder Olmsted, it is true, Manning shared a keen interest in planning and design at an increasingly large scale. Both men also made a point of communicating in professional and popular forums. But Manning, who outlived Olmsted by thirty-five years, pursued that vision of long-term, large-scale planning and design through the heyday of the Progressive Era.

William Grundmann, curator of the Manning Collection at Iowa State University, has written that Manning "was a driving force in founding [the ASLA] in 1899."[24] Manning was also apparently optimistic about the centralizing tendencies of modern American society. In one early article on village improvements, published in Stickley's *Craftsman* magazine in 1904, he drew connections between different scales of planning, from the setting aside of a village commons to the elder Olmsted's systems of urban parks and parkways, Charles Eliot's plans for a metropolitan park system, and the national park system that would probably emerge as modern transportation systems made more accessible "every nook and corner of our vast domain." The focus of this article was on small-scale local improvements, but the vision was grand: a "movement to make our whole country a park."[25]

Later Manning would write about a scale of planning that could not be accomplished without a centralized planning body of some sort. In 1916 appeared Manning's article "National Parks, Monuments and Forests," which contained a list of 190 items, all keyed neatly into a U.S. postal map. Seven years later, in 1923, appeared Manning's remarkable "National Plan Study Brief," in which the same base map was used repeatedly to designate natural resources and infrastructure: crop regions, original forest acres, rainfall, soils, coal, water power, railroads, population, even a composite map of "commercial and recreation areas and connecting ways." As Charles Beveridge has noted, Manning's comprehensive plan dealt with natural resources and communications in a way that recalls the elder Olmsted's plan for improvements on Staten Island, New York, back in 1871. But here, again, the scale was vastly enlarged—to span a whole continent.[26]

In keying his information to maps derived from the same base map Manning became a pioneer of the "overlay" mapping techniques that were further developed in the 1960s.[27] And with this national plan he outlined briefly the kind of survey that Ian McHarg has been longing to undertake with technological tools that Manning could hardly have anticipated.[28] In these respects Manning was ahead of his time. But in his conceptual thinking he was also very much *of* his time, the Progressive Era. In his plan of 1923, an "executive summary" of his still unpublished report, Manning observed, "Our government is gradually establishing a control that is checking the economic exploitation of the majority by a minority and bringing natural resources, such as forests and water powers, under government control. A more centralized control of our resources and industries is also leading to a more equitable sharing of profits between capital and labor. . . . There should be a nation-wide plan devised for locating, securing, and recording accurately such data as are essential for the development of our country. . . . With a definite coordinated plan for the development of our resources and peoples, in which we all can take part, we shall enter a new era of progressive growth."[29]

Manning's views on national planning, having evolved over many years, were beginning to crystallize when he published his listing of national parks, monuments, and forests in 1916. By then, however, the Great War was raging in Europe, and President Wilson and his cabinet were forced to turn from domestic issues to foreign affairs. Questions of war and peace, of engagement or isolationism were then more pressing than planning for America's natural resources and for highways to connect commercial and recreation areas. Still, Manning may have found confirmation of his views in a book that appeared shortly after the outbreak of war, Walter Lippmann's *Drift and Mastery*, which was published in the United States in 1914. There, confronting the promise as well as the confusions of modern American life, the young journalist Lippmann wrote, "You have to make a survey of the natural resources of the country. On the basis of that survey you must draw up a national plan for their development. You must eliminate waste in mining, you must conserve the forests so that their fertility is not impaired, so that stream flow is regulated and the waterpower of the country made available."[30]

Lippmann went further, writing of scientific agriculture, cooperation, collaboration, professionalism, efficiency, the larger scale of organizations, the loss of certitudes, the "chaos of a new freedom," and the need for a "conscious mastery of experience." It was an energizing, affirmative book, the precocious product of a young man just a few years out of college. It was also a product of the Progressive Era, along with Charles Eliot's metropolitan planning, Warren Manning's national planning, and the collective decision to form an American Society of Landscape Architects.

The Progressive Era did not survive World War I. After American troops came home Wilson did not garner support for America's participation in the League of Nations, and in 1920 the new president-elect Warren G. Harding spoke in vaguely reassuring tones of a "return to normalcy." These developments, along with periods of prosperity and recession, world war, cold war, and undeclared war, will enter into the main story of landscape architecture and its development, although sometimes only in passing. The need for some wider context should be self-evident; landscape architects can accomplish little that is not grounded in, or influenced by, the realities of the larger society—its organization and its available resources and technologies. But also evident is the need to distill. Many details must be eliminated in order to clarify a few major developments, some main currents or directions, some influential individuals, and a few seminal projects.

In addition to main currents we will also be conscious of undercurrents. Just as the great wave of forces in our time has yielded modernization, standardization, mechanization, and centralization, so the currents beneath the surface have yielded some small, but ultimately important counterforces. In the face of late-twentieth-century modernism there arose a renewed interest in historic restoration and a curiosity to learn from the past; in the face of standards and machines, a revived interest in craft and personal expression; in the face of centralization, a recognition of the importance of the small-scale "grassroots" effort. More aware of such shifts in recent decades, we are now inclined to recognize both the mainstream and the eccentrics.

This attitude is not merely contemporary. It was evident in a speech given only a few weeks after the fateful crash of the stock market in 1929. In January 1930 ASLA President Arthur A. Shurtleff (later Shurcliff) assured his fellow landscape architects, "Of calm, deliberate, and even cold men, we have our quota. Some of us are comforted by the belief that we attain the happy medium of tranquillity and balance, but none of us, I think, could be really happy without the presence of the extreme men. They give a thrill and zest which is needed in any live group of men. The extreme men are often nearest the truth. Our Society also embraces all ages, many nationalities, all tastes, all the United States, most points of view, and two genders. Evidently the bond which unites our Society must be strong if it can hold in thrall such a group of variants."[31]

Something of this attitude may survive among landscape architects today, despite familiar concerns over a lack of focus, a fear that the profession is stretched in too many directions with no common core of skills and convictions to pass on to the next generation. Today landscape architects are concerned about new directions for the profession, its future, and its immediate prospects, now that powerful economic and technological forces are changing the rules of the game. These forces seem to be giving a considerable edge to engineers, financial managers, and masters of electronic communications in the struggle to control the shaping of the physical environment.

In the August 1997 issue of *Landscape Architecture* magazine "A Profession in Peril?" by landscape architect Patrick A. Miller laid out in stark detail a selection of critical issues identified in a survey of distinguished fellows of the ASLA. Miller quotes such concerns as the following: "Landscape architecture continues to fight defensive actions in that practitioners spend too much time explaining the profession," (James C. Stansbury); "Many people do not understand the scope of landscape architecture. ASLA has spent considerable money on this, and we must keep trying," (Raymond L. Freeman); "We require critics, a dialogue, a philosophical position, and a system of discrimination. Without this we are not much more than a collection of individuals with specific points of view and style and not a profession," (M. Paul Friedberg).[32] More questions arise from the diversity of landscape architects' interests and agendas. Can landscape architects maintain the self-image that ASLA

Fellow William H. Roberts described—that of being both specialists and generalists—and still communicate the breadth of their profession to the public?[33] Today, the public is not only confused about what it is that landscape architects do. Many people still do not understand the professional's claim to "landscape" when the materials are of brick and concrete or fiber optics and plastic. And they cannot fathom the claim to "architecture" when they see nothing resembling a structure that could shelter a human being.

The frustration with the term "landscape architecture" dates back at least to the elder Olmsted's own ambivalence in the 1860s. He and Calvert Vaux had been appointed "Landscape Architects & designers" to the commission that was overseeing the development of New York's Central Park. Vaux, trained as an architect, had no problem with the term. In fact, he saw it as a means of asserting the artistic content of their work, a "tangible something to stand on," a basis from which to command respect and wield authority.[34] In time Olmsted would assert his claims to an art of design. Yet later in life he still felt uncomfortable with the term "landscape architect." It was not only a certain vagueness that disturbed him, but also the lack of a comprehensive definition of the responsibilities of a landscape architect.[35]

From time to time there have been calls to jettison "landscape architecture" and adopt something simpler, like "site planning," "land planning," or "environmental design." But could the field's diversity and breadth of vision survive a change of name? This question is not yet settled. "The split between those who build and those who regulate and theorize has turned what I sincerely feel is a fine diversity into a separation by 'article of faith,' a litmus test of goodness," ASLA Fellow Peter Walker wrote recently in response to Miller's questionnaire. "If this issue is not resolved, many fine minds will redefine themselves and cease to relate professionally to the title. The tragedy is that this is completely unnecessary."[36] Some readers agreed. ASLA Fellow John O. Simonds, for one, refused to lose the field's "illustrious heritage" for the sake of a new name. Meanwhile Rick G. Spalenka of Cedaredge, Colorado, urged his colleagues to "quit beating our heads against a romantic and outdated wall" and identify more closely with "holistically minded civil engineers."[37]

The issues of self-image and losing ground to other design professionals may be around for a long while. Whether the best "markets" for the services of landscape architects lie in aesthetic contributions or something closer to civil engineering is a concern that was first forced upon landscape architects' consciousness during the Great Depression. And as the issues persist, the old debates of the 1890s, the 1930s, and the 1960s no longer seem remote. Suddenly relevant, they may even glow with light reflected from another era. With some knowledge of the past a dialogue between the present and the past becomes not only possible but useful. The perspective of a century can reveal continuities, turning points, and moments of decision when one road was taken, another declined, usually with only a dim sense of what lay in the future. Predicting the future is hazardous, of course. As one ASLA president remarked in 1934, "Never prophesy anything until after it has happened."[38] President Henry Vincent Hubbard could not have known for certain that the worst years of the Depression had passed. We know—in hindsight. But this retrospective of landscape architecture over the past century aspires to more than hindsight—or prophecy. Acknowledging a bias toward whatever can illuminate the situation of landscape architects here in the United States in the year 1999 we will try to understand the forces that have shaped the profession. Along the way we will identify some influential individuals and projects that have helped to define new directions. And we will recognize some of the currently rising tides. Sometimes individuals and groups have been inclined to move against the tide in order to maintain a particular identity or agenda. For example, should landscape architects have insisted on their identity as fine artists? Well into the 1940s, some did, in the face of mounting forces that favored science, technology, standardization, efficiency, systems, and increasingly sophisticated functional organization. Was this a failure of perception? Or a lingering preference for the identity that the elder Frederick Law Olmsted ultimately chose—once he accepted the title "landscape architect" and its artistic implications? In effect Olmsted resisted forces that might have led him to become mainly an organizer and administrator of great undertakings. As a journalist and as executive secretary of the U. S. Sanitary Commission during the Civil War, he had shown promise as a leader and manager. But as a shaper of the physical landscape of parks and communities he also demonstrated what a landscape architect/artist with a powerful vision of society and civilization could contribute.

At this point the main threads of the story must be secured. Chapter One focuses on the kinds of people who were first drawn to the field of landscape architecture. What they had studied and accomplished before coming into contact with landscape architects is significant—as are the professional interests and avocations that they maintained while external forces were changing their conditions of practice. Also in Chapter One two major threads running throughout this history are raised for the first time: the concept of wholeness and the relationships between the arts and the sciences. Chapter Two continues to examine landscape architects' professional identity as it evolved through the years of prosperity, depression, and war. By the end of World War II claims to fine art had largely subsided, while claims to a more pragmatic art of design, closely allied with site planning and engineering, had gained some credibility.

The pivotal Chapter Three describes the transition from decades of underemployment among landscape architects to decades of unprecedented opportunity and promise. Chapter Four examines the roots of divisions that still haunt the profession of landscape architecture. The sometimes conflicting concerns of imaginative design, social responsibility, and ecological relationships are seen through the eyes of some of the field's leading figures, including Garrett Eckbo, Hideo Sasaki, Philip Lewis, Ian McHarg, and Neil Porterfield. Here, two other strong threads running through this history are identified: The first is the ASLA awards program, which has served for nearly half a century as a barometer of opinions and values upheld by a selection of landscape architects and their colleagues in allied fields; the second is the landscape architect's tradition of criticism, including opposition to the status quo, which has roots much deeper than the cries of resistance heard in the 1960s.

The remaining chapters piece together some longer historical narratives. Chapter Five traces the relations between process and product from the time of the anti-Communist probes of the early 1950s through the first inklings of postmodernism in landscape architecture. In Chapter Six a variation on the theme of art and science returns as developments in both artistic exploration and environmental planning are traced from the 1970s through the end of the 1980s. In Chapter Seven the thread of wholeness, visible now and again throughout this history, reappears in the context of a profession that remains if not "in peril," then in tension among its many strengths. Here, the two historical narratives introduced in the previous chapter are brought up to date—the sometimes intertwining developments in artistic exploration and environmental planning. In addition, there is a brief historical narrative concerning technology and the media. And one challenge remains to the profession—to use the latest tools of technology and the media so effectively, and so wisely, that landscape architects can resist becoming the tools of their tools.

How landscape architects move into the next century and prosper is a story that cannot yet be told. But one part of that story may depend on how well landscape architects understand where they came from—and how and why.

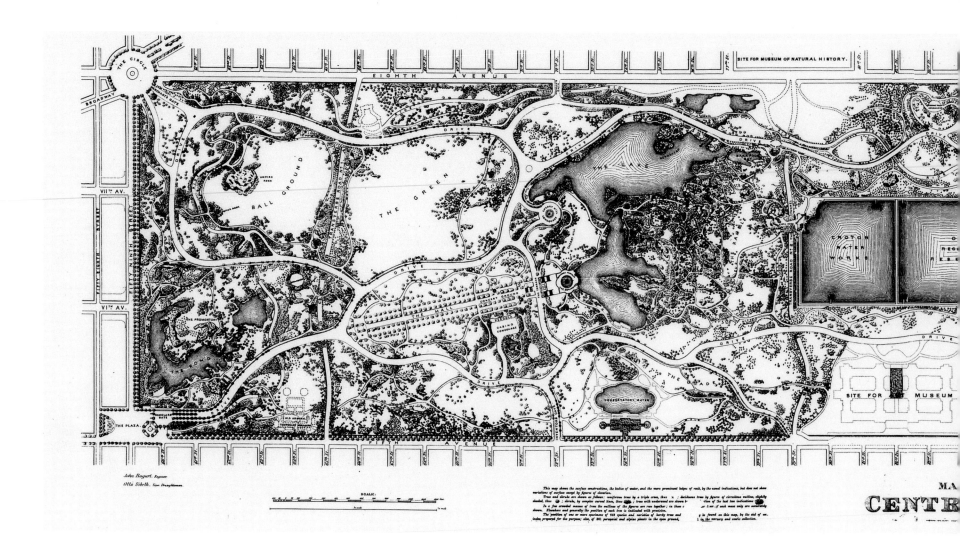

"Seeing the decorous, law-abiding, rule-respecting throngs which now fill Central Park of a Sunday afternoon in spring—throngs much larger and of much more motley composition than were anticipated in the fifties—it is amusing to know that when the plan of Messrs. Olmsted and Vaux was accepted, some of our influential citizens cried: 'Such a park is too aristocratic to be sanctioned in America, too artistic to be respected by the American populace.' "

MARIANA GRISWOLD VAN RENSSELAER (1893)

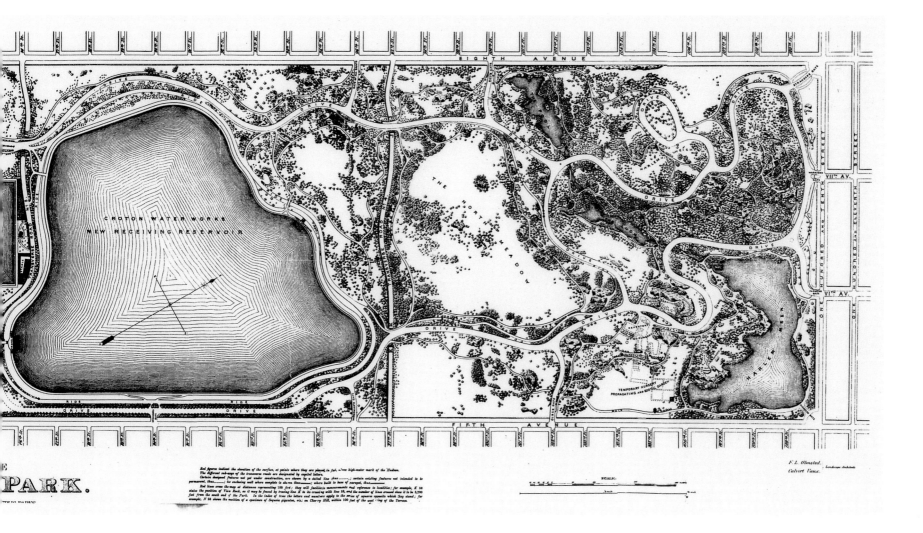

PARK.

MAP OF THE CENTRAL PARK

NEW YORK, NEW YORK

DESIGNED BY FREDERICK LAW OLMSTED, SR.

AND CALVERT VAUX, FROM 1858

PUBLISHER UNKNOWN

COURTESY OF THE NATIONAL PARK SERVICE

FREDERICK LAW OLMSTED NATIONAL HISTORIC SITE

" 'What is the ideal cemetery?' . . . A parklike area as beautiful as it can be made;

as beautiful, indeed, as we in our belief imagine the Garden of Eden to have been."

O. C. SIMONDS (1930)

GRACELAND CEMETERY

NEAR CHICAGO, ILLINOIS

DESIGNED BY O. C. SIMONDS, FROM 1878

PHOTOGRAPHER UNKNOWN

COURTESY OF THE FRANCES LOEB LIBRARY

GRADUATE SCHOOL OF DESIGN, HARVARD UNIVERSITY

"No impression upon the youthful mind exerts a more powerful and lasting influence than that which is made by daily familiar intercourse with scenes of simple natural beauty, and the man whose boyhood was passed amid such scenes will find that he recurs to them in after life with a keener sense of their loveliness, as he contrasts them with the magnificence and ostentatious display which mark a more artificial condition of life."

H. W. S. Cleveland (1873)

ROGER WILLIAMS PARK

PROVIDENCE, RHODE ISLAND

DESIGNED BY H.W.S. CLEVELAND IN 1878

"If people generally get to understand that our contribution to the undertaking is that of the framing of the scheme rather than the disposition of flower beds and other matters of gardening decoration . . . it will be a great lift to the profession—will really give it a better standing than it has in Europe."

FREDERICK LAW OLMSTED, SR. (1892)

WORLD'S COLUMBIAN EXPOSITION

CHICAGO, ILLINOIS

FREDERICK LAW OLMSTED, SR., AND COLLEAGUES

LANDSCAPE ARCHITECTS, 1893

PHOTOGRAPHER UNKNOWN

COURTESY OF THE NATIONAL PARK SERVICE

FREDERICK LAW OLMSTED NATIONAL HISTORIC SITE

"You may melt your metals and cast them into the most beautiful molds you can; they will never excite me like the forms which this molten earth flows out into."

HENRY DAVID THOREAU (1854)

PROSPECT PARK

BROOKLYN, NEW YORK

DESIGNED BY FREDERICK LAW OLMSTED, SR.

AND CALVERT VAUX, 1866–1867

"A million sunsets will not spur on men towards civilization. It requires Art to evoke

into consciousness the finite perfections which lie ready for human achievement."

ALFRED NORTH WHITEHEAD (1933)

THE RIVERWAY

BOSTON, MASSACHUSETTS

DESIGNED BY FREDERICK LAW OLMSTED, SR.

1880S AND 1890S

PHOTOGRAPH BY THOS. ELLISON

COURTESY OF THE NATIONAL PARK SERVICE

FREDERICK LAW OLMSTED NATIONAL HISTORIC SITE

"This is a difficult and novel question, the beach being the first thing that I know of

to be set aside and governed by a public body for the enjoyment of the common people."

CHARLES ELIOT, ON REVERE BEACH, MASSACHUSETTS (1897)

REVERE BEACH

REVERE, MASSACHUSETTS

FORMING PART OF ELIOT'S CONCEPT OF A METROPOLITAN PARK SYSTEM FOR BOSTON,

THIS BEACH IS SHOWN AS IT WAS BEFORE IMPROVEMENTS WERE MADE—THAT IS, BEFORE 1896.

PHOTOGRAPHER UNKNOWN

COURTESY OF THE FRANCES LOEB LIBRARY

GRADUATE SCHOOL OF DESIGN, HARVARD UNIVERSITY

CHAPTER 1

ART AND SCIENCE, BEAUTY AND WELL-BEING

1899–1924

The people who identified themselves as landscape architects and landscape gardeners at the turn of this century were a varied lot. Among those who founded the American Society of Landscape Architects in 1899 two had degrees in civil engineering—O. C. Simonds and Charles N. Lowrie—and one, John Charles Olmsted, remained a member of the Boston Society of Civil Engineers for thirty-three years. Like Lowrie, J. C. Olmsted and Samuel Parsons, Jr., had studied at Yale's Sheffield Scientific School, but they earned the Bachelor of Philosophy degree. Other charter members of the ASLA, Warren H. Manning and Samuel Parsons, Jr., were sons of successful nurserymen, and Manning had studied at a business school. Among the eldest of these founding members was Nathan F. Barrett, born in 1845, a Civil War veteran who had been a sailor and an assistant to his brother, a nurseryman, before striking out on his own. A garden designer during the Gilded Age, Barrett had also

laid out the grounds of railroad stations and in 1872 planned the town of Pullman, Illinois, for George Pullman, the railroad-car manufacturer.

These notes begin to suggest a pattern. Many of these men had backgrounds in the natural or applied sciences, yet for some reason they were drawn into a new, not yet established profession associated with art. Some charter members of the ASLA had had unique training in both the arts and the sciences. Twenty-six-year-old Beatrix Jones had had private instruction in botany, horticulture, and landscape design from Charles S. Sargent, director of the Arnold Arboretum near Boston. After completing these studies and traveling in Europe, she had set up her own practice as a landscape gardener in New York around 1895. (In 1913 she became Mrs. Farrand). J. C. Olmsted had been a partner with his stepfather, the elder Olmsted. And Downing Vaux had worked with his father, the English architect Calvert Vaux, who

"DUMBARTON OAKS," WASHINGTON, DC

BEATRIX JONES FARRAND, LANDSCAPE ARCHITECT, FROM 1921

PHOTOGRAPH COURTESY OF DUMBARTON OAKS, STUDIES IN LANDSCAPE ARCHITECTURE, PHOTO ARCHIVE had been an assistant to Andrew Jackson Downing and, later, a partner with the elder Olmsted.[1]

Frederick Law Olmsted, Jr., whose training was closely monitored by his father, happened to be absent from the ASLA's first meeting; but since he was liable for the $10 "fine," or dues, along with the ten others present, he has traditionally been considered a charter member. George F. Pentecost, Jr., and Samuel Parsons, Jr., hosted that first meeting at their office in New York City. Also present was Daniel W. Langton, "a southerner with a true artist's temperament," who had served as both a public official and a designer, working on parks, playgrounds, and country residences.[2]

In the next several years, with formal training in landscape architecture still fairly rare, people continued to be drawn to landscape architecture from other fields. Arthur Shurtleff had earned a bachelor's degree in mechanical engineering at the Massachusetts Institute of Technology (MIT) before moving on in 1895-1896 to the Lawrence Scientific School at Harvard, where Charles Eliot was his advisor. Charles Downing Lay, one of the three founding editors of the quarterly, *Landscape Architecture* in 1910, had spent four years at the School of Architecture at Columbia before entering the new program in landscape architecture at Harvard. In 1902 he became the second graduate of that program; the first had been his fellow founding editor, Henry Vincent Hubbard, who graduated in 1901. (Hubbard had previously spent one year studying architecture at MIT.) One ASLA president, James L. Greenleaf, had been an adjunct professor of civil engineering at Columbia for four years in the 1890s. And Ferruccio Vitale, born in Florence, had studied engineering and architecture in Florence and Turin and worked with his father, an architect, before working with George F. Pentecost, Jr., in New York and becoming a landscape architect.[3]

These facts help to explain why landscape architects seem to have felt relatively little antagonism between the arts and the sciences in the early 1900s. At that time a well-educated person would have had some familiarity with both areas of knowledge—not necessarily a specialist's command of a subject, but at least a generalist's broad comprehension. Some landscape architects with solid technical training, including Shurtleff, Greenleaf, and Lay, found time for painting or wood engraving. At his home in Connecticut Lay, the son of a painter, covered the walls of his studio with his own frescoes, while Greenleaf exhibited his landscape paintings at the National Academy of Design in New York. Today, after more than a century of specialization in the arts and sciences, this fluidity of movement between different ways of knowing seems remarkable.

It is not always clear exactly what drew someone toward landscape architecture, but a few personal glimpses survive. Arthur Shurtleff, who changed his name to Shurcliff in 1930, recalled why he had turned away from mechanical engineering: "My interest in country scenery, landscape sketching and painting, natural history, touring-a-wheel, camping, mountain climbing, and in a fondness for farms, the poetry of Wordsworth, Emerson, and the journals of Thoreau—these influences led me away from mechanics toward scenery, toward planning and construction for the scenes of daily life." And Beatrix Jones Farrand recalled her reasons: "It is work—hard work and at the same time it is perpetual pleasure. With this grand art of mine I do not envy the greatest painter, or sculptor or poet that lived. It seems to me that all arts are combined in this."[4]

In the 1890s people could have learned about landscape architecture through a variety of means: the popular writings of Mariana Griswold Van Rensselaer; the professional reports and writings of the Olmsteds and Charles Eliot; the magazine *Garden & Forest*, directed by Charles S. Sargent; the American Park and Outdoor Art Association, founded in 1897 in Louisville, Kentucky; and the Massachusetts Forestry Association.[5] They were also exposed to such examples as the splendid grounds of the 1893 World's Columbian Exposition in Chicago and the parks of the new National Park Service (established in 1916) to which they had increasing access by train and touring car. Such exposure may help to explain a growing interest in landscape architecture. But there may have been more specific reasons for architects, engineers, and horticulturists to turn toward a less established, still developing field. Some may have been attracted by the public-spirited, noncommercial stance of the new profession. Some may have been intrigued by landscape architects' involvement with art and scenic beauty. For some, ambivalent about the forces in modern industrial society that were leading toward centralization and specialization, landscape architecture may have offered both adventure and a haven, "a place of grace" set apart from marketplace,

bureau, and factory.[6] Landscape architecture may even have held out the promise of unity—or wholeness—as it did in Chicago in 1893. Although ephemeral and dazzling in its surface opulence, the exposition may have offered some sensitive souls a vision of wholeness.

In the early twentieth century the concept of wholeness that is now found in the science of ecology was not yet generally recognized. As Robert Wheelwright, one of the three founding editors of *Landscape Architecture* magazine, recalled of Harvard's graduate program in landscape architecture in 1906–1908: "The science of ecology was undeveloped when we studied plant materials, but the early twentieth century was a time when the influence of nineteenth-century naturalists was felt. The writing of Burroughs, Thoreau, and others was still strong and was reflected in examples of landscape design that had matured, created by such men as Downing and Olmsted. A definite understanding of the relation of plants to environment and site, an appreciation of the beauty in natural plant associations, was acknowledged without attempt at scientific explanation." Moreover, the appreciation of this kind of beauty did not derive only from literature or lectures on botany. Wheelwright recalled that the countryside was still accessible and largely unencumbered by signs of human occupation. So the beauty of natural plant associations was not merely an abstract concept for him and his fellow designers; it was "inspiration."[7]

Wheelwright, who founded the first degree program in landscape architecture at the University of Pennsylvania in 1924, was a genial, lighthearted yet astute observer of people and events in the profession of landscape architecture. In fact, his recollections on the absence of a scientific ecological theory in his field during the 1900s flesh out in concrete detail what was generally expressed in a multivolume work of philosophy that appeared in 1905–1906, George Santayana's *The Life of Reason*. Investigating some differences and interrelations among the arts, the sciences, and religion, Santayana, a Harvard professor of philosophy, noted the absence of wholeness in contemporary scientific thought. "Indeed the conception of a natural order, like the Greek cosmos, which shall include all existences—gods no less than men, if gods actually exist—is one not yet current, although it is implied in every scientific explanation and is favoured by two powerful contemporary movements [evolution and speculative idealism]," he wrote. "The sciences have not joined hands and made their results coherent, showing nature to be, as it doubtless is, all of one piece."[8]

As the sciences were developing along paths toward ever greater specialization, some theorists—professors and graduate students mainly—might contemplate the whole of something. But most young people setting out on a career in the natural or applied sciences in the early 1900s could not enjoy the luxury of time and financial support for disinterested contemplation. During their working lives, at least, they would tend to focus on practical, useful work, based on what was generally considered "trustworthy knowledge." Santayana held no absolute faith in this kind of knowledge. He considered science—like art or like reli-

gion—to be a system or construct that might be useful for present-day purposes yet someday prove invalid. Santayana suggested that science was "tentative, genial, practical and humane, full of ideality and pathos, like every great undertaking." Far from being an antithesis of art, science was, in his view, "the mental accompaniment of art."[9]

Born in Madrid (1863) and reared from adolescence in Boston, Santayana had at least a modest influence on landscape architects' work and thought. He is occasionally quoted in such writings as *Introduction to the Study of Landscape Design* (1917) by Henry Vincent Hubbard and Theodora Kimball, for he was one authority, along with the Italian philosopher Benedetto Croce, to whom Hubbard and Kimball could turn in their efforts to explain unity, beauty, and ideal types in landscape architecture. Although not their final arbiter in matters of aesthetics, Santayana was a force to be reckoned with at a time when landscape architecture first emerged as an organized profession, mainly in New York and Boston. His writings also represented a middle ground between mid-nineteenth-century romantic views of art and nature and early-twentieth-century modernist views of art and architecture.[10]

Santayana may have struck a sympathetic chord with landscape architects. He wrote about the freedom and creativity of artists, who make over the world rather than merely consider how it came to be or what it would consent to be. But he also believed that art, like science, required a "faithful study of the world." Artists were not meant to play the fool or to cut capers, he noted, but rather to build well, to speak well, with great sanity and vision. "Art, in its nobler acceptance, is an achievement, not an indulgence," he wrote. "It prepares the world in some sense to receive the soul, and the soul to master the world; it disentangles those threads in each that can be woven into the other."[11]

If this is not a concept of wholeness, it comes close. And for landscape architects who aspired to achieve unity among the parts of a whole composition, these insights would be welcome. Santayana also recognized that "happiness is the ultimate sanction of art. . . . Art springs so completely from the heart of man that it makes everything speak to him in his own language; it reaches, nevertheless, so truly to the heart of nature that it cooperates with her, becomes a parcel of her creative material energy, and builds by her instinctive hand."[12]

In the early 1900s these were words that landscape architects would have been pleased to hear as they entered a field in which a main concern was to link the natural world, with its evanescent materials of living things, to the world of art and permanence. By the fall of 1903 the "somewhat new and still undifferentiated art" of landscape architecture in the United States had lost many leading figures: Andrew Jackson Downing, H.W.S. Cleveland, Calvert Vaux, Jacob Weidenmann, Charles Eliot, and most recently Frederick Law Olmsted, Sr. The legacy of these forebears remained largely in their built works. The urban parks and park systems of New York, Boston, Chicago, and other cities, the picturesque grounds of the Mall in Washington, D.C. (soon to be entirely redesigned along the lines of Pierre L'Enfant's original scheme), academic campuses, residen-

tial subdivisions, and some large private estates were their salient projects, all subject to alteration by human will or by natural processes.

Most of these designers were also writers, who preserved for posterity some plans and some general ideas. But by the early 1900s some of their relevant published works were difficult to find or somewhat dated. Olmsted's collected writings would not begin to appear in book form until 1922. Charles Eliot's papers, which his father had lovingly assembled in a thick volume in 1902, were, however, readily available, and so it was largely through Eliot's writings, as well as through personal memory, oral tradition, and a few other books, that the principles of landscape architecture were first handed down to Americans in the new century.[13]

The elder Olmsted confided in an 1890 letter to an old friend, Mrs. William Dwight Whitney, "I know that in the minds of a large body of men of influence I have raised my calling from the rank of a trade, even of a handicraft, to that of a liberal profession—an Art, an Art of Design."[14] As ideas such as this filtered down—through Eliot or the Olmsted brothers or Manning—the next generation reiterated them. In 1896, while acknowledging the many scientific and technical studies encompassed in his field, Eliot emphasized that landscape architecture was an art of design that ought to be taught in a school of design.[15] In 1910, in the first issue of *Landscape Architecture*, Eliot's father, then the emeritus president of Harvard, asserted that landscape architecture is "primarily a fine art" with the dual functions of creating and preserving beauty and promoting comfort, convenience, and the health of urban populations.[16]

In 1912 Warren Manning reiterated this claim to the status of a fine art.[17] In 1915 the first three-year fellowship in landscape architecture at the American Academy in Rome was awarded. And for many years thereafter landscape architects would reassert their claim to art, even fine art. In themselves, these facts may be of passing interest. But together with a commonly shared appreciation of scenic beauty and landscape composition, these repeated identifications with artists suggest the mental climate in which the small band of professional landscape architects would begin to face some grave challenges just before the outbreak of war in Europe.

In 1910 Henry Vincent Hubbard noted that people were showing more interest in landscape beauty—not as a luxury, but as a "practical necessity."[18] A few months later an unsigned review of Frank Waugh's *Landscape Beautiful* (1910) also suggested that beauty was somehow essential to human well-being. In Waugh's book the reviewer detected an implicit message—that "beauty in landscape is a fundamental need of our intellectual existence." Again, the issue was not extraordinary beauty, but the beauty of common landscape, "a national asset of almost inconceivable value, as yet practically undeveloped."[19]

Waugh, a professor of horticulture and landscape gardening at what was then Massachusetts State Agricultural College (now the University of Massachusetts, Amherst), was an independent-minded, versatile fellow who had studied etching at the École des Beaux-Arts in Paris, played the flute, made a plan for Grand Canyon Village, Arizona, in 1918, and wrote articles on roadside ecology in the 1930s. In 1910 he was also sufficiently interested in aesthetics to read George Santayana's highly theoretical work, *The Sense of Beauty* (1896).

Waugh and his colleagues were trying to understand landscape beauty in all its social, psychological, and aesthetic ramifications. These were not disinterested intellectual inquiries. Landscape architects wanted to understand how the experience of beauty in the landscape might affect people on many different levels. Often perceived as purveyors of luxuries, these professionals wanted to convince clients and the public that beauty, an essential quality of human experience, could be found in many environments, but especially in restful, unobtrusive, even humble settings. The frontispiece of Waugh's *Landscape Beautiful* was a Millet-like photograph of a woman in a cultivated field, bending to fill a basket of potatoes (or some such vegetable). And when landscape architect Harold A. Caparn wrote about Central Park as a work of art in 1912, it was not the Mall or the great central fountain with its Angel of Bethesda that he focused on, but rather the motives from which the park was originally derived—that is, rural (often agricultural) and pastoral landscapes.[20]

What distinguished Central Park from the common landscapes that inspired it, Caparn noted, was skillful composition, a series of pictorially composed scenes that conveyed an "impression of unity" to the mind. He granted that within "our own world of artists" there were some who would have preferred to find in this great urban park more clarity and logical sequence, less aimlessness and a greater sense of the grand scheme. But against these reservations Caparn posed the example of anatomical studies, which, seemingly vague and shapeless, were actually portions of the most complete whole imaginable—a living organism. Central Park, he noted, was not created for the beauty of its plan, nor was it conceived only for people within the park—but also for those above, looking down from the upper stories of buildings on Fifth and Eighth avenues and Fifty-ninth and 110th streets. In the end Caparn returned to the interests of the park's admirers: "The fact remains that few people can enter Central Park without becoming sensibly happier. . . . Surely, for a man to be able by his creation to arouse in innumerable others who come after some such sense of [the] beautiful in nature as has inspired himself, to instill into them something of his own spirit, is a great achievement; and the means by which he does it is entitled to be termed in a very high degree a Work of Art."[21]

This defense of naturalism in Central Park, against the views of neoclassical designers who would have preferred something more grand and clearly structured, reflected the opposition between "formal" and "informal" design that had troubled landscape designers for years. Controversies over these two qualities had erupted sporadically since the early eighteenth century in England and would continue to divide some landscape architects long after Harold Caparn's day. Yet in this opposition lay a source of creative tension that was more interesting than the simple dichotomy implied. Later such landscape architects as Garrett Eckbo would transcend this dichotomy and play one quality off the other in the mod-

ern landscape. Meanwhile, among landscape architects and their fellow artists in the early 1900s "formal" and "informal" would represent two quite different ways of thinking about landscape and art.

The first great challenge for landscape architects in the new century was the controversial proposal to dam the Tuolumne River in the Hetch Hetchy Valley at Yosemite in California. Ever since the 1880s officials in San Francisco had been looking toward the High Sierra for sources of water for a burgeoning urban population. But beauty—rare, scenic beauty of national importance—had been the major impetus for passage of the Yosemite Act of 1864, signed by President Lincoln. Initially set aside expressly for "public use, resort and recreation" and administered by the state of California, Yosemite reverted to federal control, first as reserved forest lands in 1890 and, finally, as a national park in 1905. Within this park, after the boundaries had been redrawn in 1890, was Hetch Hetchy Valley, a configuration of mountains, meadows, and a river of extraordinary beauty. After the terrifying earthquake of 1906 San Francisco secured permission to dam this valley for its own pressing (and prospective) needs. The controversy that raged for many years thereafter pitted formerly congenial people into two main camps: the conservationists, including the former chief forester of the United States, Gifford Pinchot, who viewed the proposed reservoir and hydroelectric plant as components of "wise use," and the preservationists, including John Muir, who passionately argued for the recreational and spiritual values of the park as scenic wilderness.[22] The elder Olmsted had been appointed a commissioner of Yosemite Park back in 1864, and in his report of 1865 he emphasized the total experience of that magnificent scenery, viewed as a continuous landscape of both stupendous and gentle, even playful, scenes.[23]

At that time, in 1865, there was no immediate threat to the integrity of the Yosemite Valley. But a half century later the threat to a portion of that continuous landscape, Hetch Hetchy Valley, was immediate and potentially precedent-setting. Landscape architects had good reason to be concerned about the valley's fate. The master printer who was producing *Landscape Architecture* four times a year was J. Horace McFarland, president of the American Civic Association and, ultimately, the leader of the preservationists' opposition to the dam. The younger Frederick Law Olmsted, who had not yet been born when his father was commissioner of Yosemite Park, took a stance as well. At issue was not a simple choice between active preservation or laissez-faire, but a tangle of interests ranging from economic benefits and basic human needs to concepts of "wise use" and different kinds of beauty in the landscape. For a while the younger Olmsted tried, behind the scenes, to mediate between McFarland and Gifford Pinchot, his father's old colleague.[24] But eventually he made his own views public.

The younger Olmsted's survey of the issues involved at Hetch Hetchy was so scrupulously fair that his own predilections were not immediately obvious. "In most of the objects with which we are concerned beauty is, and ought to be, an absolutely incidental factor," he wrote. "We want only that sort and degree of beauty which is compatible with a high degree of utilitarian efficiency. . . . Beauty of scenery is ordinarily and properly an incident, a by-product in man's use of the earth." Nevertheless, he asserted, some kinds of beauty in the landscape are so rare in their totality that they become incompatible with ordinary economic uses. To the concept of "full economic use" he contrasted the idea of "highest recreative values," which was becoming more important with the "intensifying strain of our civilization." In the end Olmsted argued that the entire Yosemite National Park should be preserved for the enjoyment of future generations because of its rare beauty. To do otherwise, he wrote, would set a precedent for abandoning the original purpose of a park whenever it conflicted with "any considerable utilitarian interests."[25]

These arguments appeared in print barely a month before President Wilson signed into law a bill granting San Francisco the rights to Hetch Hetchy—on December 19, 1913. In effect, the preservationists (including landscape architects) lost a battle for recognition of the psychological and spiritual benefits of landscape beauty in the face of powerful economic and social interests, while the nation and the world lost an irreplaceable wilderness. The fate of Hetch Hetchy also revealed the power of a cluster of concerns that would increasingly conflict with landscape architects' traditional aesthetic ideals—efficiency, "scientific management," and technocracy, or rule by experts. These were concerns that the younger Olmsted, a skillful planner and administrator like his father, would not disparage. Nevertheless, outliving his father by more than half a century, the younger Olmsted would struggle to reconcile aesthetic, social, and scientific claims during an era when artists were slipping away from the overlapping circles of power in which Daniel Burnham and the elder Olmsted had once maintained a foothold.

Working in comprehensive, often regional-scaled planning, the younger Olmsted was, as Shary Page Berg has explained, "devoted to order and the public good in a more abstract sense" than his father had been.[26] This tendency toward abstraction was itself a sign of the times. All the more refreshing, then, were Olmsted's occasional admissions of strong emotions that could move him. Addressing the American Civic Association in 1921, Olmsted admitted that he had only recently had more than a "tripper's glimpse" of the national parks and forests—a full two months at Yellowstone and in the southern Sierra. There, his deepest sensation had been one of freedom.

The second great challenge to the young profession of landscape architecture was widely shared. From the summer of 1914 onward Europe was embroiled in the War to End All Wars, and by early April 1917 the United States had finally joined the Allied cause. A few weeks later the younger Frederick Law Olmsted, the architect/planner George B. Ford, and the engineer E. P. Goodrich made their way through the military hierarchy to a sympathetic architect who had just assumed the rank of major and become head of the Committee on Emergency Con-

struction for the U. S. Army's General Munitions Board. Olmsted and his colleagues had just arrived in Washington from Kansas City, fresh from the ninth National Conference on City Planning. These planners wanted to offer their services in designing cantonments for the troops and housing for the workers in war industries. Their offer was accepted, and in a matter of days Olmsted was made a member of the committee that developed a prototype plan for cantonments and also advised on selecting the necessary town planners and engineers.[28]

In 1918 Olmsted became manager of the Town Planning Division of the United States Housing Corporation, and under his direction, in the government's belated efforts to provide adequate housing for workers in war industries, many landscape architects served as planners. Among ASLA fellows alone were A. F. Brinckerhoff, Harold Caparn, Stephen Child, J. F. Dawson, A. S. De Forest, John L. Greenleaf, G. D. Hall, Henry Vincent Hubbard (as assistant manager), H. J. Kellaway, Charles Downing Lay, Charles N. Lowrie, Warren Manning, E. T. Mische, A. R. Nichols, John Nolen, R. A. Outhet, Carl R. Parker (another assistant manager), T. G. Phillips, James Sturgis Pray, C. H. Ramsdell, Arthur Shurtleff, A. D. Taylor, Loring Underwood, Ferruccio Vitale, and Phelps Wyman. Fletcher Steele, a captain in the American Red Cross, served in England, France, and Russia. Some younger men, including Gilmore Clarke and Philip H. Elwood, Jr., served on the front lines. Meanwhile, such older men as Arthur C. Comey, George E. Kessler, S. Herbert Hare, and Robert Wheelwright served as camp planners, town planners, and supervisors. In all, over three quarters of the ASLA's members were active in the war effort.[29]

For some of these men the focus on engineering and the technical aspects of planning in wartime was a continuation of their prewar practices. Several had already become active in the American City Planning Institute, which was formed in 1917 at the instigation of the younger Frederick Law Olmsted and a colleague, attorney Flavel Shurtleff. In that organization—later known as the American Institute of Planners—fifty-two charter members had been drawn together in what was clearly a complex, multidisciplinary, collaborative effort. Among these charter members the fourteen landscape architects outnumbered all other professionals—including thirteen engineers, six attorneys, five architects, and a few writers, publishers, economists, educators, and public officials.[30] Landscape architects shared with all these kindred spirits a concern for the long-term development of cities, towns, and their outlying regions in a safe, convenient, economical, and harmonious manner. But the great challenge for landscape architects in the planning effort—which was furthered and strengthened by the war effort—came from people whose priorities were radically different.

Describing landscape architects' contributions to planning during the First World War, the planning historian Mel Scott singles out in particular Nolen, Hubbard, Child, and Arthur Shurtleff. In their war housing projects Scott recognized considerable skill, aesthetic sensitivity, and social consciousness. Their street systems followed the contours of the land.

They knew how to lay out the land and group structures, while preserving natural features and providing many areas for recreation. Ironically, this high quality of physical planning later came under fire from some members of Congress who complained that the war housing was "too good." Behind these complaints, Scott explains, were probably fears of socialism, which could be raised by any substantial, permanent housing financed and owned by public-sector agencies. But with or without the ideological overtones, there remained the old conflict between aesthetic and utilitarian interests, dramatized so poignantly in the controversy over Hetch Hetchy. And intensifying the conflict was the growing fascination for statistical data, zoning, minimum standards, and the kind of efficiency found in a book that appealed particularly to businessmen and efficiency experts, Frederick Winslow Taylor's *Principles of Scientific Management* (1911).[31]

Given their experience of planning during the war and the forces of change in society that favored efficiency and scientific method, many landscape architects could have reverted to the more technical and pragmatic roots of their hybrid profession. No doubt some did. Nevertheless, among members of the ASLA—still a fairly small band of about 173 people in 1926—there were many attempts to achieve a balance between aesthetics and efficiency, personal expression and what the younger Olmsted called "self-subordination" in the public interest. Serving on the U. S. Senate's McMillan Commission, the federal Commission of Fine Arts, the National Capital Park and Planning Commission, and in such other capacities as honorary vice-president of the Sierra Club, Olmsted continually tried to maintain a balance among competing interests. Hubbard, his trusted assistant during the war, continued to practice after the war while he also taught courses in landscape architecture and chaired Harvard's new department of city planning. For many years Hubbard was editor and publisher of both *Landscape Architecture* and *City Planning*, the official organ of the American City Planning Institute. In addition, *An Introduction to the Study of Landscape Design*, which Hubbard and his future wife Theodora Kimball brought out in 1917, remained a standard text for decades.

Depending upon our point of view, these stalwarts of the profession and the ASLA either upheld the highest standards of professional practice in the face of drastic economic, social, and cultural changes—or prevented the profession from keeping pace with those changes because of a certain inflexibility of mind and parochial views of their members' and society's interests.[32] For the first quarter century of its existence the annual meetings of the ASLA were held in New York or Boston. Although this arrangement may have been convenient for members who lived in the Northeast it did not acknowledge the importance of trustees and regional chapters in such distant cities as Kansas City and Portland, Oregon. Then, too, the society's lack of an annual full-scale physical presence in other regions of the country tended to exacerbate regional differences in practice and in philosophical and social views. Nevertheless, with their strong social and institutional connections Olmsted, Hubbard, and their close colleagues could hope to influence the direction of the society through leadership and advocacy or by using the pages of its official organ of communication, *Landscape Architecture*, as a forum for debate.

One particular focus for landscape architects during the period was the growth of cities, which was occurring on such a large scale that a new word was coined to describe them—"megalopolitan."[33] In the early 1900s the response to megalopolitan growth might be some version of The City Beautiful. Daniel Burnham's 1905 plan for San Francisco with its grand radiating avenues, its axially aligned civic center, and its underlying expectations of inevitable growth represented planning on a grand scale, yet it was soon surpassed by his 1909 plan for Chicago, which was on a truly regional scale.[34] These plans have since been faulted for "aristocratic" assumptions and a focus on visual and spatial concerns. In contrast, the regional-planning studies that emerged during and shortly after World War I, in both Britain and the United States, were more pragmatically conceived and based on surveys of natural resources and industrial, economic, and social conditions, all compiled with some approximation of scientific method. Again, underlying these plans was an assumption that urban growth was inevitable. As Thomas Adams argued, "We cannot stop the dispersal of industries into rural areas, but we can assist in planning and directing it in the right way."[35]

Adams, the founder of the British Town Planning Institute, also directed the ten-year, ten-volume *Regional Plan of New York and its Envi-*

rons (1921–1931), which Lewis Mumford severely criticized for its "routine" assumption that urban aggrandizement was inevitable.[36] A writer and critic of enormous importance for both architects and landscape architects, Mumford looked forward to the gradual dispersal of metropolitan cultural and social amenities to smaller cities and towns by way of modern technology and astute planning. He had come into a circle of planners and designers, including the architect and landscape architect Henry Wright, shortly after the war. And among the major achievements of this group, known as the Regional Planning Association of America (RPAA), were such small-scale experiments in housing as Sunnyside Gardens on Long Island and Radburn, New Jersey. These garden-city prototypes were viewed as contributions to a whole network of garden cities—which would offer an alternative to metropolitan growth.[37] In the 1920s, however, it was not Mumford, but his fellow RPAA member, the forester Benton MacKaye, who contributed a few potent ideas to the magazine, *Landscape Architecture*.

In 1927 MacKaye emphasized a certain balance in regional planning that Aldo Leopold (not yet a household name) was talking about. In the interests of balance, MacKaye argued, people should oppose the ruthless "metropolitan invasion" that was taking over the earth like the invasion of glaciers in prehistoric times. Spreading globally from a single-nerve center—the worldwide industrial system—the metropolitan invasion was rapidly absorbing the land beyond city limits and penetrating into the hinterland. To oppose this invasion and achieve a balance between work and recreation, city and wilderness, MacKaye argued for what he called "a Barbarian invasion" of explorers—members armed with charts and surveys who would set out like pioneers on a "quest for harmony." In the end this exploration would yield a counterforce to the spreading metropolis—a continuous Appalachian Trail, made up of villages and wilderness, the artificial and the natural, from which would spring true "outdoor culture."[38]

Here was an admittedly Utopian scheme that was achievable in small increments, yet grand in the aggregate. The Appalachian Trail was to extend from Georgia to Maine. Its story cannot be told here, but some of the ideas that MacKaye stimulated—about the Appalachian Trail and rural and regional planning generally—will reappear in the following chapter.

The third great challenge for landscape architects in the early 1900s was less clearly defined than the struggle over Hetch Hetchy or the outbreak of World War I: the modern movement in art and architecture. Ironically, landscape architects formed their first professional society in this country and declared themselves to be artists at a time when many artists in other fields had already moved beyond a profoundly romantic view of the world, a view which had once readily encompassed the designer of romantic landscapes in parks and gardens as a true artist. Around the turn of the century, more rapidly in Europe than in the United States, artists were developing other views of nature and culture, views not entirely coherent, that would eventually reflect some of the tremendous changes in the modern world, including the demise of aristocracies and the rise of science and technology. Eventually landscape architects would have to absorb what Frederick Karl has called "slow shifts in modes of perceptions, really cultural earthquakes."[39] But in the first few years of the new century they did not perceive this challenge.

In the early 1900s one related challenge was easier to recognize, and landscape architects discussed it a great deal. This was the need to achieve and maintain recognition as professionals and as artists rather than as tradesmen or technicians. In a variety of ways, then, landscape architects tried to communicate who they were and what they could do. As early as the spring of 1902 the ASLA held an exhibition of members' work in the St. James Building at 26th Street and Broadway, New York City. Most of the work exhibited by Parsons, Pentecost, and Beatrix Jones among others consisted of private residences. But also shown were institutional grounds, the Hampton Normal & Agricultural Institute in Virginia by Manning Brothers—along with the West Side Park in Newark by Olmsted Brothers, a subdivision by O. C. Simonds, and a park and the grounds of a "Home for the Friendless" in Scranton, Pennsylvania, by Downing Vaux. Five years later, in March 1907, a larger number of ASLA members exhibited their work at the Sixth Annual Exhibition of the Municipal Art Society in New York City. And more exhibitions would follow. Meanwhile, the ASLA would occasionally meet at the National Arts Club in New York to discuss such

proposals as a pending bill to create an interstate park along the Palisades of the Hudson River. (They supported the bill, and it passed.)[40]

The conservative tone of most American art in those years is now legendary. The City Beautiful movement was still on the rise, encouraged by what has been called the American Renaissance in painting, sculpture, architecture, and landscape design, a rebirth that owed a great deal to the art of the Italian Renaissance.[41] At the same time the stirrings of profound changes in the contemporary art of Western Europe—like tremors of the cultural earthquake that Karl has recognized—could be felt in the New York City lofts and attics[42] as well as at such memorable exhibits as the Armory Show in the spring of 1913.

However, it was not until the 1930s that landscape architects would discuss in print the works of art that, in hindsight, would be considered the most forward-looking of the past one hundred years. Apart from occasional unenthusiastic references to Whistler or Turner and the warmer responses to Poussin and Claude Lorrain American landscape architects in the 1910s and 1920s did not write about paintings per se. They were more interested in the general effects of light, color, atmosphere, and, above all, unity in their landscape compositions. For Beatrix Jones Farrand and Henry Vincent Hubbard the focus was, typically, upon pictorial composition or on a sequence of scenes experienced as one moved through space.[43] These designers recognized the difference between painting in two dimensions and composing in three dimensions. But it was *Landscape Architecture* editor Charles Downing Lay who underscored the difference.

In his 1918 essay "Space Composition" Lay got beyond the pictorialism found in the works of Claude, Poussin, and the Hudson River School but not as far as the space-time concepts of Einstein's physics or Picasso's cubism. Lay's position, like that of Santayana, was the middle ground of rational, penetrable, three-dimensional space. "Nature allows herself to be accurately conceived only in spatial terms," Lay quoted from Santayana. With this emphasis on spatial design Lay could compare works as vastly different as the Baroque gardens of Le Nôtre and the romantic or "naturalesque" parks of the Olmsteds and Charles Eliot. Lay also mentioned Julius Meier-Graefe and Adolph von Hildebrand, whose writings on art had already been translated into English. But the heart of Lay's argument was all of a piece with the ideas, the terminology, and the passions of the Lithuanian-born, Boston-educated Bernard Berenson.[44]

Contemplating works by the Central Italian painters of the Renaissance—the greatest of whom was, arguably, Piero della Francesca—Berenson articulated several points that Lay could apply to landscape architecture. In Berenson's concept of "space-composition" Lay found something so valuable for landscape design that he repeatedly paraphrased the master. Berenson had written, "Space-composition . . . woos us away from our tight, painfully limited selves, dissolves us into the space presented, until at last we seem to become its permeating, indwelling spirit. . . . This wonderful art can take us away from ourselves and give us, while we are under its spell, the feeling of being identified with the universe, perhaps even of being the soul of the universe." For Berenson, as for Lay, such an experience seemed to be the essence of religious emotion. And this, in turn, could amplify in heightened language the more modest justification that Charles Eliot had given for urban parks and for "the quiet and peculiar refreshment which comes from contemplation of scenery." Lay made connections between the experiences of landscape that Eliot and Berenson had described, then let the art critic and connoisseur have the last word: "Believe me, if you have no native feeling for space, not all the science, not all the labor in the world will give it you, and yet, without this feeling, there can be no perfect landscape—for space composition is the bone and marrow of the art of landscape."[45]

This emphasis on spatial design represented a development beyond the American Renaissance and The City Beautiful. It freed the landscape architect from the perceived boundaries of historic styles. And if it did not keep pace with the avant-garde of the art world, it prepared younger designers, such as Fletcher Steele, to wrestle with new concepts of space-time and modernist abstraction in the years to come.

In 1923 Lay recognized that a new animosity was rising in his field, a conflict more serious than that between the professional and the tradesman. In effect it stemmed from the rise of science and technology. "We suffer professionally, as do most artists, through inadequate public support," he observed. And for this Lay blamed not society but landscape architects themselves. Although landscape architects had a dual function—to serve society's practical needs and to create something of beauty—the real justification for the profession, he argued, was to create a thing of beauty. He disagreed with Charles Eliot's idea that fitness, or "perfect adaptation to use," constituted beauty: "Else would the dam or the factory become beautiful and the engineer be an artist. Absurd, isn't it?" Lay asserted that artists, including landscape architects, should demand employment—and judgment—on the basis of the artistry that they add to practical things. In parks and city planning, as in other work, grace and beauty should be considered first and cost, last. And, as technical problems became simplified, Lay predicted that landscape architecture, the "most artistic of the professions," would take the lead. "We and not the scientist have the greater sensitiveness to natural beauties," he concluded, "and we should lead everyone to an understanding of the esthetic aspect of all out-of-doors, whether it be unspoiled nature or man-made art."[46]

This was no longer the voice of the leading editor of *Landscape Architecture*, for Lay and Wheelwright had both stepped down around 1920, leaving Hubbard to shoulder the financial and editorial burdens.[47] And Hubbard, whose sympathies were increasingly turning toward the practical aspects of planning, would chart his own editorial course, while leaving the pages of the "official organ" of the profession open to the younger landscape architects who would begin to discuss modern art and landscape design in the 1930s.

Meanwhile, in 1924, the year the ASLA reached its first quarter of a century, one long-term project, originally conceived around 1916, then delayed by the war, was finally completed. This was *American Landscape Architecture*, a sumptuous portfolio of professional photographs edited by landscape architect P.H. Elwood, Jr. An ASLA committee of three—Frederick Law Olmsted, Jr., Charles N. Lowrie, and Noel Chamberlin—had sifted through the submitted projects and selected the images. Private residences outnumbered public projects by about six to one, yet the range of project types was impressive. There were gardens by a few architects—Charles Platt, Wilson Eyre, and Welles Bosworth (who had designed gardens for J.D. Rockefeller in Pocantico Hills, New York). One stunning image of the road that winds around the sheer rock cliffs of Storm King Mountain at the Palisades Interstate Park, New York, depicted the work of landscape engineer W.A. Welch. But most of the work was by landscape architects: O.C. Simonds's curving drives and intimate woodland scenery at Graceland Cemetery in Chicago; private residences by Beatrix Farrand, Marian C. Coffin, Jens Jensen, Charles Downing Lay, Fletcher Steele, and A.D. Taylor among many others; parks by Warren Manning, Charles Lowrie, George E. Kessler, and Olmsted Brothers; a botanical garden at Ohio State University by Elwood; an open-air theater at Vassar College by Loring Underwood. It was for such a broad range of useful and elegant work, carried out with a fine attention to craft, that landscape architects in the 1920s wanted to be known.[48]

"The value of Yosemite was that of any fine passage of scenery: There must be indefiniteness,

mystery, subtlety, and variety. Indeed, Olmsted's most enthralled descriptions of the valley were of

times when he saw the mountains obscured by clouds or made mysterious by the light of camp fires."

CHARLES E. BEVERIDGE (1995)

HETCH HETCHY VALLEY

YOSEMITE NATIONAL PARK, CALIFORNIA

THE VALLEY WAS THE SUBJECT OF A DEBATE OVER ITS SELECTION AS A SOURCE OF WATER FOR THE

CITY OF SAN FRANCISCO, 1909 – 1913.

"His clients invariably became his friends and he was always a welcome guest at their homes. By nature truly an artist in all that the word means, his mind was free from sordidness of any kind, and his 'art' was to him the greatest thing in the world."

RICHARD SCHERMERHORN, JR., REMEMBERING NATHAN FRANKLIN BARRETT (1920)

"NAUMKEAG," RESIDENCE OF JOSEPH CHOATE

STOCKBRIDGE, MASSACHUSETTS

THIS PORTION OF THE GARDENS WAS DESIGNED BY NATHAN F. BARRETT, 1886.

PHOTOGRAPH BY JESSIE TARBOX BEALS

COURTESY OF THE FRANCES LOEB LIBRARY

GRADUATE SCHOOL OF DESIGN, HARVARD UNIVERSITY

"At best it takes time for trees to come to full maturity and to give an adequate idea of the designer's original intention, but fortunate is the tree, in this era of change, that is allowed to live so long!"

MARIAN CRUGER COFFIN (1940)

"HILLWOOD," RESIDENCE OF

EDWARD F. HUTTON

WHEATLEY HILLS, LONG ISLAND, NEW YORK

GARDENS DESIGNED BY MARIAN C. COFFIN 1922

PHOTOGRAPHER UNKNOWN

COURTESY OF THE FRANCES LOEB LIBRARY

GRADUATE SCHOOL OF DESIGN, HARVARD UNIVERSITY

"Our ideal gardens are yet to come. The task is too great for one mind. All forces of American art must unite harmoniously, and then the garden of the Middle West will rise in a new and more beautiful form. We are but dreaming of what the future will bring to us—listening to the invigorating winds that sweep down from the lofty peaks of the western mountains, brushing across the Great Valley of the Father of Waters; listening with keen interest to what they have to say from hills and valleys, lakes and plains. But we also rise on tiptoe to look over the Alleghenies, and the Rocky Mountains, for inspiration from the very cradles of civilization."

JENS JENSEN (1908)

ROSENWALD ESTATE

RAVINIA, ILLINOIS

LANDSCAPE AND GARDENS DESIGNED BY

JENS JENSEN 1907

"Photographs of landscape scenes have many disadvantages as compared with the sight of the scenes themselves, but one advantage they certainly also possess. They can seize and record the best aspect, the most favorable light, the best composed point of view. And they can judiciously omit incongruities which in the scene itself so often bear witness to the impossibility of parts of the problem—or sometimes, alas! to the insufficiency of the designer. Not infrequently, therefore, photographs can carry, better even than the actual scene, the ideal toward which the designer strove through difficulties on the ground."

HENRY VINCENT HUBBARD (1932)

"THE COTTAGE," RESIDENCE OF

H. H. HUNNEWELL

WELLESLEY, MASSACHUSETTS

LANDSCAPE AND GARDENS DESIGNED BY

HENRY VINCENT HUBBARD 1923

UNDER THE EMPLOY OF THE OLMSTED BROTHERS

PHOTOGRAPH COURTESY OF THE NATIONAL PARK SERVICE

FREDERICK LAW OLMSTED NATIONAL HISTORIC SITE

"The modern landscape architect has in the examples of the styles of the past a treasury of inspiration and information to aid him in his present work; but he should study these styles not as an archaeologist, not as a copyist, but as a workman providing himself with tools for future original use."

HENRY VINCENT HUBBARD (1917)

"MARIEMONT," RESIDENCE OF

MRS. J. T. EMERY

NEWPORT, RHODE ISLAND

GARDENS DESIGNED BY

PRAY, HUBBARD & WHITE, BEFORE 1924

PHOTOGRAPHER UNKNOWN

COURTESY OF THE FRANCES LOEB LIBRARY

GRADUATE SCHOOL OF DESIGN, HARVARD UNIVERSITY

"Is there any life more real than the life in the garden for those who actually take

part in its creation and nurture it carefully week by week and year by year?"

Louise Shelton (1915)

Residence of Ruth Dean

East Hampton, Long Island, New York

Gardens designed by Ruth Dean

Before 1917

Photographer unknown

Courtesy of the Frances Loeb Library

Graduate School of Design, Harvard University

"The work of Art is a fragment of nature with the mark on it of a finite creative effort, so that it stands alone, an individual thing detailed from the vague infinity of its background."

ALFRED NORTH WHITEHEAD (1933)

"BROOKSIDE," RESIDENCE OF

WILLIAM HALL WALKER

GREAT BARRINGTON, MASSACHUSETTS

GARDENS DESIGNED BY FERRUCCIO VITALE

ABOUT 1918

PHOTOGRAPHER UNKNOWN

COURTESY OF THE FRANCES LOEB LIBRARY

GRADUATE SCHOOL OF DESIGN, HARVARD UNIVERSITY

"Conservative always, an archaeologist never, he follows the old forms, both in garden architecture and in country house work,

filling them with a vigorous new life. Refined and delicate in detail, the masses are bold and simple, but throughout them there

is a quality of reserve which marks perfection in design—an unstudied grace which is the end and aim of study."

ARCHITECTURE MAGAZINE, ON PLATT'S WORK (1909)

"FAULKNER FARM," RESIDENCE OF

MR. & MRS. CHARLES F. SPRAGUE

BROOKLINE, MASSACHUSETTS

GARDENS DESIGNED BY CHARLES A. PLATT, 1897

"And herein lies the paradox of Gwinn: Platt's geometry was conceived as a foil for the lake, the grandest force of nature at Gwinn; Manning's wild garden plantings, as one family member remarked, ' [were] extraordinary, just as one might expect in painting, rather than nature alone.' Each designer had ultimately embraced the antithesis of his own passion, and made it his own."

ROBIN KARSON (1993)

"GWINN," RESIDENCE OF WILLIAM GWINN MATHER

CLEVELAND, OHIO

LANDSCAPE AND GARDENS BY

WARREN MANNING, CHARLES A. PLATT,

AND ELLEN SHIPMAN, FROM 1907

PHOTOGRAPH BY A. G. ELDREDGE

COURTESY OF THE FRANCES LOEB LIBRARY

GRADUATE SCHOOL OF DESIGN, HARVARD UNIVERSITY

"For the roughness of the earth and of man encloses as much

as the delicatesse of the earth and of man,

And nothing endures but personal qualities."

WALT WHITMAN (1856)

"WYCHWOOD," RESIDENCE OF

CHARLES L. HUTCHINSON

LAKE GENEVA, WISCONSIN

GARDENS DESIGNED BY OLMSTED BROTHERS

1901 – 1902

TAKEN BY AN UNKNOWN PHOTOGRAPHER IN THE FALL OF 1905

COURTESY OF THE FRANCES LOEB LIBRARY

GRADUATE SCHOOL OF DESIGN, HARVARD UNIVERSITY

"Here as in many other spatial compositions, Greenleaf employed carefully placed trees with seemingly

random spacing to remove all signs of harshness from an essentially rectilinear plan. In the opinion of

most of his contemporaries, [this] Green Garden was Greenleaf's finest single achievement."

NORMAN T. NEWTON (1971)

"KILLENWORTH," RESIDENCE OF

GEORGE D. PRATT

GLEN COVE, LONG ISLAND, NEW YORK

GARDENS BY JAMES L. GREENLEAF

ABOUT 1914

PHOTOGRAPHER UNKNOWN

COURTESY OF THE FRANCES LOEB LIBRARY

GRADUATE SCHOOL OF DESIGN, HARVARD UNIVERSITY

"Any mind with sufficient imagination to grasp it must be stimulated by this conception of the city as one great social organism, whose future welfare is in large part determined by the actions of the people who compose the organism today, and therefore, by the collective intelligence and will that control these actions. The stake is vast, the possibilities splendid."

FREDERICK LAW OLMSTED, JR. (1916)

MARIEMONT

GENERAL PLAN FOR A NEW TOWN, CINCINNATI DISTRICT, OHIO

PREPARED BY JOHN NOLEN, 1921

COURTESY OF THE MARIEMONT PRESERVATION FOUNDATION

MARIEMONT, OHIO

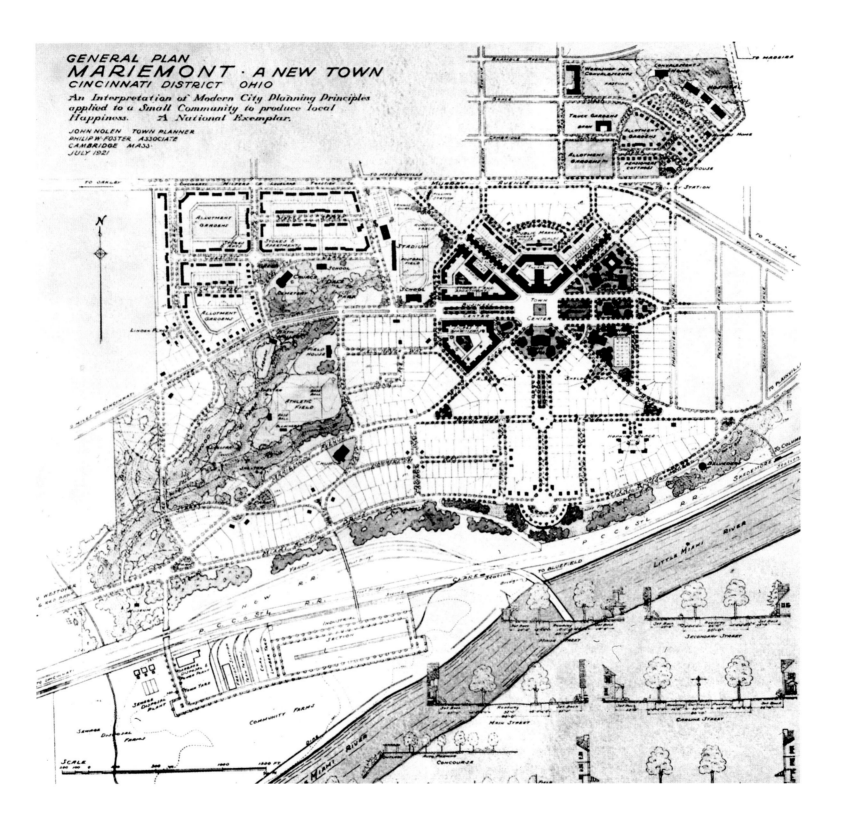

GENERAL PLAN
MARIEMONT · A NEW TOWN
CINCINNATI DISTRICT OHIO

*An Interpretation of Modern City Planning Principles
applied to a Small Community to produce local
Happiness.   A National Exemplar.*

JOHN NOLEN   TOWN PLANNER
PHILIP W·FOSTER ASSOCIATE
CAMBRIDGE MASS·
JULY 1921

"Why Rome? Because all this uncounted wealth, this endless store heaped up by the hands, the passions and the minds of all that long procession of the generations, this still undiminished fountain men call Italy—all this belongs to no one people, to no group nor class nor nation. It is yours and it is mine; it is there for all who would seek."

C. Grant LaFarge (1920)

Section and Elevation of the

Villa Papa Giulio

Rome

Measured and drawn by Clarence D. Platt

Charles Eliot Traveling Fellow in Landscape Architecture

Harvard University, 1924 – 1925

Courtesy of the Frances Loeb Library

Graduate School of Design, Harvard University

LONGITUDINAL SECTION ON THE MAIN AXIS
Scale: One Inch Equals Twenty Feet

TERMINAL FEATURE ON MAIN AXIS
Scale: 1/8" = 1'

SECTION AND ELEVATIONS OF

VILLA PAPA GIULIO

BEYOND THE PORTA DEL POPOLO

ROME

MEASURED & DRAWN BY CLARENCE D. PLATT
CHARLES ELIOT TRAVELLING FELLOW IN
LANDSCAPE ARCHITECTURE · HARVARD UNIVERSITY
1924 · 1925

GARDEN FAÇADE OF CASINO
Scale: 1/8" = 1'

CHAPTER 2

FROM ART TO SERVICE: PROFESSIONAL IDENTITY IN TIMES OF PROSPERITY, DEPRESSION, AND WAR

1925 – 1945

"When you understand all about the sun and all about the atmosphere and all about the rotation of the earth, you may still miss the radiance of the sunset." Alfred North Whitehead was writing about the development of modern professionalism, which was leading toward ever greater specialization and abstraction. The year was 1925, and the English mathematician was disturbed by some results of professionalism: "It produces minds in a groove. . . . The leading intellects lack balance. . . . The specialised functions of the community are performed better and more progressively, but the generalised direction lacks vision. . . . The whole is lost." In a sense these results were inevitable, for Whitehead saw within the innumerable scientific discoveries of the nineteenth century a natural direction toward professionalism. In turn this led to a one-sided form of education with its "center of gravity" in the intellect. As a counterbalance, then, he advocated a greater emphasis on intuition, values, and

qualitative experience—concrete, directly perceived, and precious. "What I mean is art and aesthetic education," he explained.[1]

Whitehead's book, *Science and the Modern World* (1925), could not have appeared at a better time for landscape architects. Still claiming art and aesthetics as their justification for being, by the mid-1920s they already had to reckon with shifts in practice, from primarily private commissions—mainly residential—to an increasing number of public-sector and commercial jobs with greater emphasis on efficiency and economy. From within the profession there were mounting pressures to standardize teaching practices, for in 1925 there were more than eighty schools in the United States in which something resembling landscape architecture was taught. (Few, however, granted degrees in the field.) At the same time, there were pressures from outside the profession. In 1925 ASLA President John L. Greenleaf noted that "the practical man, the park promoter, the engineer are very self asser-

BLUE RIDGE PARKWAY, 469 MILES IN VIRGINIA AND NORTH CAROLINA

STANLEY ABBOTT, PARKWAY RESIDENT LANDSCAPE ARCHITECT, FROM 1935

PHOTOGRAPH BY ALAN WARD

tive." And Greenleaf, a former professor of civil engineering at Columbia, had at least some credibility when he spoke with misgivings about "the engineering point of view." In his view landscape architects and engineers could both claim technical competence in, say, park design. "But in the appreciation of scenery and the development of sheer landscape beauty our profession ought to reign supreme," he wrote. "Let us remember that Landscape Architecture is essentially a fine art, not primarily applied science, above all not a trade."[2] This last sentence would resonate in landscape architects' writings for more than a decade—long after the worst years of the Great Depression. For all their claims to fine art, landscape architects have always been to some extent businessmen and businesswomen. And in the generally prosperous 1920s many of their clients were businessmen. Nevertheless, as professionals, they continually tried to shield themselves from any taint of commercialism—no simple matter at a time when the president of the United States proclaimed, "The business of America is business."[3]

Ironically, Vermont-born President Calvin Coolidge, legendary for his silence, once went so far as to speak of industry and commerce as a moral high road: "The man who builds a factory builds a temple, the man who works there worships there, and to each is due not scorn and blame, but reverence and praise," he insisted. "We are all members of one body. . . . Large profits mean large payrolls. . . . We do not need more government, we need more culture."[4] Accordingly, Coolidge reduced personal income taxes and tended to limit the government's involvement in people's lives and livelihoods. He may not be remembered for his contributions to American cultural life, but in 1927 he did appoint a landscape architect of wide experience and dedication to his art, Ferruccio Vitale, to the Federal Commission of Fine Arts. And at about the same time Coolidge alerted the National Conference on City Planning to developments in "the art of city planning" in Washington. What particularly intrigued the president was the principle of "far-sighted and comprehensive planning" applied to the administration of the nation's business—as well as to the development of the nation's rapidly growing cities and towns.[5]

To appreciate landscape architects' collective stance in the prosperous 1920s—identifying themselves as professionals and artists above the fray of the business world—it helps to recall more than the wit of Mencken and the satires of Sinclair Lewis, whose novel *Babbitt* (1922) gave a new word to American and British dictionaries. On the surface, landscape architects were lining up against the forces of Babbittry, a stereotype of the middle-class businessman's mentality in which material success was everything while art and intellectual pursuits counted for little, if anything. But something else was slipping into the common culture. It was a kind of idealism that landscape architects would soon find themselves identifying with—in spite of their self-image as artists.

A new wave of "business idealism" was lapping American shores in the 1920s. "If the business of America was business, then business meant much more to Americans than the making of money," writes the eminent historian Arthur M. Schlesinger, Jr. The businessman's virtues—thrift, efficiency, hard work, and material success—came to be seen as the basis of a kind of secular religion. Overlaid on the nineteenth-century concept of Social Dar-winism—competitive struggle in industry, commerce, finance and human relations—was a new gloss of business responsibility. Henry Ford reasoned that he had to keep prices low enough and wages high enough to maintain demand for all those mass-produced black cars. Some of his peers were indignant, but Ford also won praise for his generosity and noble conscience. Schlesinger identifies the official philosophy of this new era as a faith in "character, service, and high wages," and if this faith was not entirely con-vincing when examined by the light of everyday business practices, still it could appeal to people whose "idealism needed an outlet," as Schlesinger puts it. For a brief moment in 1927, he notes, the brave young Charles A. Lindbergh, Jr., who flew alone across the Atlantic, provided a symbol of deeper, higher motives than private gain. But hovering less spectacularly throughout the 1920s were ideas such as those found in a little book that appeared the same year as Sinclair Lewis's *Babbitt*.[6]

In *American Individualism* (1922) Herbert Hoover, a Quaker, offered a way of reconciling private interests with public responsibility. As Schlesinger explains, there were two moral principles at stake here, and Hoover, just back from several years of humanitarian service and diplomacy in Europe during the Great War, considered them to be defining principles of a particularly American form of individualism. They were, first, equality of opportunity and, second, a "rising vision of service." Thus, in a decade of increasingly aggressive sales promotions, the relaxation of the Sherman Antitrust Act, and increasing speculation on the largely unregulated stock market, there emerged

an alternative ethos, a self-regulating philosophy of community responsibil-ity and cooperation among businessmen, who flocked to Rotary Clubs and other service organizations. As it happened, Hoover, as Secretary of Com-merce under presidents Harding and Coolidge, then as president from 1929 through early 1933, had the chance to test his idealistic philosophy at the highest levels of government—in times of prosperity and depression.[7]

Landscape architects, too, would have their idealism tested. In the land of go-getters like George Babbitt, they asserted some artistic purposes that were being ignored for the most part. Later, at a time when banks were closing and soup kitchens were opening, landscape architects reconsidered their own capacities for public service. It is no surprise that their work and thought were influenced by the business climate within which they had to function, even as they struggled to share with clients and the general public some cherished, noncommercial values. In the absence of any commonly shared philosophy of organic wholeness in design, however, landscape architects spoke with many different voices. And so, before attempting to characterize their collec-tive professional identity, we should acknowledge their diversity and listen for those softer voices that would otherwise be lost in the chorus.

"Warm, generous, gentle, and . . . fatherlike" is the way Robin Karson re-cently described Warren Manning, a dependable family man and a mentor to younger landscape architects such as Fletcher Steele, Albert D. Taylor, and Marjorie S. Cautley.[8] But Manning also seems to have had an instinct for what would "sell" in a given political and economic climate. As noted earlier, he was developing his ambitious comprehensive national plan for natural resources and infrastructure during the Progressive Era. But by the time he published a brief summary of that plan, the "National Plan Study Brief," in July 1923 Warren G. Harding was in office and the mood of the nation had shifted. The revolution in Russia had instilled in this country not only a fear of Bolsheviks but also a vague suspicion of centralized planning of any kind. Appealing, then, to the values upheld in a flourishing system of free enterprise, Manning characterized his plan as definite, logical, practicable, and nonpolitical. Moreover, it would be handled by experts who would eliminate waste and secure the "best use" of material, human, and aesthetic resources. Beauty was one value of his proposed "National Public Reservation System." But there were other benefits that surely would appeal to social workers, doctors, and shrewd employers. Manning noted, "Universal out-doors recreation for adults to make them more fit for longer periods of efficient service is fast coming to be regarded of equal importance with properly directed recreation in the mental and physical training of children."[9]

In 1925 Frank Waugh believed that the great range of work then being done by landscape architects kept the profession from slipping into "deadly monotony." In designing clean and beautiful factory villages that might "save the lives of women and children," in laying out land subdivisions for real estate men, or in planning "princely" estates for the wealthy, landscape architects were upholding their own personal ideals. He nevertheless hoped that all landscape architects, whatever their specializations, could uphold three outstanding ideals: "to make a snug, comfortable and beautiful suburban home; to make a clean, healthful, convenient city; and to protect and interpret the native landscape."[10]

Arthur Shurtleff may have been the first landscape architect to speak publicly about migrant farm workers—in 1926. Addressing the American Federation of Arts in Washington, D.C., Shurtleff lingered over two migrations in American history: the covered wagons moving westward in the mid-nineteenth century and the new covered wagons—black ones—bulging with bedding, bundles, and tools and carrying seasonal migrants to work in the fields. Some observers thought these overburdened black cars out of place on the road. But Shurtleff thought they had come to stay, like countless other black cars that were beginning to compete with the scenery at the national parks. It was a long, idiosyncratic speech typical of Shurtleff, father of six children, composer of verses, whimsical, yet deeply in earnest. Speaking of slow time and fast time, he remarked, "Men try now to keep pace with the piston-rod and the cam-shaft. We are said to think fast. We seem to act fast and to build fast, but posterity will, of course, decide that." In the end he asked his fellow artists to help create a sense of responsibility for the "loveliness of the earth" as exemplified in the national parks and forests.[11]

In the mid-1920s ASLA President Greenleaf encouraged landscape architects to participate in conferences—for their own personal development, for good publicity, and for the opportunity to extend landscape architects' collective influence. In 1924 he reported that one ASLA representative, S. Herbert Hare, had spoken at the American Federation of Arts, while others had attended the National Conference on State Parks

(Charles N. Lowrie) and the International City Planning Conference at Gothenburg, Sweden (John Nolen).[12] Of course, any publicity derived from these appearances would be welcome. At that time the ASLA was still a small, fairly exclusive body committed to upholding high standards. As noted earlier, membership leveled off in 1926 at 173 individuals. The 1920 U. S. Census, however, had reported 4,462 "landscape gardeners."[13] The discrepancy is remarkable, even considering the fact that not all highly skilled and talented landscape professionals sought ASLA membership or chose to remain affiliated with the society.

In his long annual report of 1927 Greenleaf revealed a dry sense of humor in the midst of troubling developments. The "usual rumblings and internal readjustments" he compared to tremors of land masses in the formation of continents. Signs of discontent in one region or another he likened to crosscurrents or rocks that momentarily interrupt the strong currents of a river. (These signs will be considered below). But otherwise he spoke plainly, with feeling. He believed that a solid education in landscape architecture should include a cultural foundation and the ability to write well. Moreover, the landscape architect should harbor an inner flame, a passion that would ultimately lead to fine results. Although executive skills and a good business sense were financially rewarding, Greenleaf warned of the architectural offices that were becoming efficient factories for turning out large buildings overnight. Rather than become executives or business "go-getters," he urged landscape architects to hold aloft the torch of the fine arts. Finally he urged upon them the practice of collaboration, which was already on the increase as private clients, architects, and Fine Arts commissioners were recognizing the value of landscape architects. And so he reasoned that collaboration ought to be a "living, vital principle" among all practitioners of the fine arts.[14]

Here, explicitly and between the lines, Greenleaf recommended one collective stance from which landscape architects could try to resist some of the commercialism in their midst without renouncing the material rewards of a satisfying practice—whatever the proportion of private and public or commercial commissions. It was not, of course, the only stance available. In the Midwest Jens Jensen had found his own way. And in the Connecticut River Valley and among the Berkshire Hills of Western Massachusetts there were landscape architects whose passions were less identified with the fine arts, per se, than with a wider view of the wilderness, the farm, and human settlement. These things cried out for attention from landscape architects at a time when a booming economy and a fascination for the motor car were threatening destruction of a kind of beauty not always celebrated in art.

Jensen's case was exceptional. Born in Denmark in 1860, he had a cultural upbringing somewhat comparable to that of Charles Eliot, who was born ten months earlier. Both families cultivated a love of the outdoors and a respect for learning. A feeling for subtleties in nature and a vision of whole networks of parks, reservations, and forests were common to both men. But there the similarities end. After Jensen immigrated to the United States he had to learn a new language and assume a range of menial jobs at first, despite considerable education, travel, and military service. And whereas Eliot died in 1897, Jensen lived until 1951. A designer of parks, an artist in the garden, and a teacher at his home, "The Clearing," Jensen was honored as a prophet in his adopted Midwest.[15] Yet a gulf separated him from many of his colleagues on the East Coast. In 1927 he resigned from the ASLA, having been a member since 1923. He had published two brief essays in *Landscape Architecture* (both focused on trees).[16] And he had also given the opening address, "The Design of Home Grounds," at the first session of the first annual ASLA meeting in the Midwest—in 1926 in Chicago. This much can be gleaned from public records.[17]

But there is an underlying story, recently fleshed out in Robert Grese's biography of Jensen. Speaking to his colleagues in Chicago, Jensen had emphasized an approach to design that he had developed over more than three decades of practice. Given the "manner of life of our people," he reasoned, native plants and the development of a native or regional style were more appropriate than imports, including formal gardens. Ultimately, he argued, the home landscape influences "the soul of the people." After the talk ended President Greenleaf thanked Jensen but doubted that all the members of the society would share his views. There followed an inconclusive debate over the merits of "formal" versus "informal" design.[18] A transcript of that debate could be illuminating and yet miss a profound difference in sensibility between Jensen and some arbiters in the field.

In 1918 an anonymous reviewer had regretted the old-fashioned concepts, "spirit of the landscape" and "soul of the landscape," in *The Natural Style in Landscape Gardening*, a book written by Frank Waugh, a professor at Massachusetts Agricultural College. Decades later, in 1940, Otto G. Schaffer,

a professor at the University of Illinois, would gently criticize Jensen's book *Siftings* (1939) for a sensibility that was old-fashioned compared with the "progressively changing and broadening point of view" of most landscape architects.[19] More examples would be needed to prove beyond a doubt what can already be sensed. An impatience with emotional, poetic evocations of relationships in the natural world was developing in some circles, while landscape architects were generally on the defensive with their claims to fine art in an increasingly commercial, technological world. It was as if landscape architects were being pressed from two sides—from the "sincere" but seemingly old-fashioned naturalists among them, such as Jensen and the Midwestern-born Waugh, and from the efficient, businesslike, quantitatively oriented people who represented the forces of change.

Yet another stance was taken by one contributor to *Landscape Architecture*, Walter Prichard Eaton, who for years lived quite removed from cities and great institutions yet played a role in shaping a regional landscape. Eaton disliked billboards. He also disdained the motor roads that led up to the summits of otherwise fairly pristine mountains. He didn't mind tourists. In the 1920s tourism was one of the major industries in his home territory of Berkshire County, Massachusetts, just as it is today. But in the absence of planning Eaton could foresee the attractive, neat little country towns of Lenox and Stockbridge squandering their cultural inheritances and missing their chances to represent a "summer civilization of grace and charm and prosperity." And so he put his faith in regional planning, "a hand on the rudder of evolution," a "hopeful defiance of chaos and blind chance." Working to make Mt. Everett part of the Appalachian Trail, he argued for better coordination of various public trusts and reservations of wilderness lands. Living on an old farm, with pastures and a rye field reverting to pine and gray birch, Eaton was the only one among his fellow commissioners to traverse that entire 800-acre domain of the Mt. Everett Reservation on foot.[20]

An amateur designer, Eaton encouraged landscape architects to question the status quo. Quietly working against the forces of metropolitan "invasion" that Benton MacKaye had warned of, he roused his neighbors, sat on committees, and, when not busy designing gardens and garden ornaments, found time to write a little book on landscape architecture and garden design. Appearing in 1932, this was an engaging collection of essays, *Everybody's Garden*.[21]

Writing, speaking, setting up exhibitions, and entering competitions were all ways in which landscape architects could contribute to the cultural life of their time. These were also forms of self-promotion that landscape architects could seek with the blessing of their professional society, the ASLA. Promotion, or the broader concept of public relations, was a major consideration for that small, still fairly exclusive body of some 200 landscape architects in the late 1920s. In addition to the exhibitions sponsored by the ASLA in the early 1900s the Boston and New York chapters held their own exhibitions, beginning in the spring of 1915 in Boston. Also that year a group of students from the Harvard School of Landscape Architecture was awarded a gold medal at the Panama-Pacific Exposition in San Francisco for their exhibition of plans and freehand drawings of private residences, parks, land

subdivisions, and city-planning studies.[22]

In 1920 James L. Greenleaf became vice president of the Architectural League of New York. And in the League's exhibition that year the firm of Vitale, Brinckerhoff and Geiffert won the League's first gold medal in landscape architecture. An award not given out lightly, this medal went to eleven landscape architects and firms between 1920 and 1934. Apart from indicating fairly good relations among these allied professionals in New York City, the medal also recognized the talents of women landscape architects at a time when their own society, the ASLA, had no women among the officers and trustees and very few women working on committees. Thus, the Architectural League honored Ruth Dean, Marian Coffin, and Annette Hoyt Flanders, along with their male colleagues: the Vitale firm, James L. Greenleaf, Olmsted Brothers, Harold Hill Blossom, O.C. Simonds & Co., Bremer W. Pond, Gilmore D. Clarke, and Alfred Geiffert, Jr.[23]

These awards gave a certain credibility to the landscape architects' claims to fine art. Other awards indicated that landscape architects were, in fact, recognized among their fellow artists—that collaboration among equals in the fine arts was not merely an article of faith. Alfred Geiffert, Jr., an associate of the National Academy of Design, received the gold medal of the National Sculpture Society as well as the president's medal from the Architectural League of New York. And in 1937, while serving on the Board of Design for the New York World's Fair of 1939, Gilmore Clarke was made an honorary member of the American Institute of Architects (AIA).[24]

Exhibitions and competitions received good coverage in *Landscape*

Architecture. In 1920 readers learned of the recent British Housing Competition, sponsored by the Royal Institute of British Architects and the Local Government Board; the competition for a city plan for Paris; and the American Housing Competition, conducted by the *AIA Journal* and *Ladies' Home Journal*. In 1921 the Art Institute of Chicago held an exhibition based largely on a series of competitions that involved architecture, the applied arts, and landscape and garden design.[25] And with every announcement of these competitions and their results in the professional journals designers and planners had the opportunity to reflect on some of the most critical issues of the time. Sometimes the results appeared in more popular magazines and major newspapers. At the very least the names of successful competitors, their talents, their services, and their profession remained in the public eye. Yet it seems that landscape architects, chronically dissatisfied with their modest level of recognition in the larger world, were reluctant to organize their own professional competitions.

There were, of course, occasional competitions and "landscape exchange problems" open to students of landscape architecture (a project initiated by Stanley White at the University of Illinois). And there was the prestigious Rome Prize competition in landscape architecture, initially open only to those unmarried young men, not over thirty years of age, who had the required educational or professional experience along with a suitable character, physical fitness, and artistic ability. In 1915 the first Rome Prize went to Edward Lawson for his solution to a given problem—a country estate in suburban New York. As a sign of the times, perhaps, the second Rome Prize

winner, Ralph E. Griswold, was honored in 1920 for his solution to a less rarefied problem—a public park in a residential district of a large city.[26]

In the early years the projects of Rome Prize winners were exhibited at various schools of landscape architecture, just as, in the 1920s, the ASLA sometimes let an exhibition of members' work travel to schools and arts institutions. But for many years, perhaps because its members were few, the ASLA did not organize its own competitions. Then, too, in the climate of outlandish real estate promotions and increasingly bold advertising (at a time when more than one landscape architect railed against billboards) there was a line to be drawn between publicity, or public relations, and advertising. "Shall the ASLA Undertake Publicity?" asked ASLA Fellow Earle S. Draper, in an article published in January 1929. As chairman of the society's publicity committee, Draper surveyed the possibilities and concluded with a qualified "No." Publicity, he believed, was better left to individuals or to the local chapters of the ASLA. His main concerns were the ethics of advertising and the fundamental reason for the profession's existence.[27]

A responsible professional should not emulate commercial advertising campaigns, Draper argued. Although most campaigns increased consumption and sales, he saw two major drawbacks: First, they stressed volume, and, second, they were competitive. He also noted that the cycle of artificially stimulated demand and consumption must be continually fed by growth—or else fail. Moreover, there were fundamental differences between commerce and landscape architecture. "Modern advertising is usually competitive, directly or indirectly, and is most concerned with the increased sale of a commodity or a 'tangible,' " he reasoned. But landscape architecture was deeply concerned about intangibles. "Our main claim for professional existence," he asserted, "is artistic perception. . . . We, as a profession, are going to get proportionately more work as the love and appreciation of the artistic in life increases in the public at large." And so he urged landscape architects to help create in their communities an interest in many art forms—paintings, sculpture, the symphony, theater. They would then have more work than they could find in a community preoccupied with business. And what if the individual felt the need for some sort of promotion or advertising? The ethics of advertising, he believed, was largely a question of good taste.

Before the end of that year, with the crash on Wall Street in October 1929, some of the tasteful and idealistic assumptions of landscape architects like Draper would begin to be challenged. The Great Depression and World War II would not entirely eradicate these assumptions, but the scope and the needs of the profession would have to be reconsidered.

In 1930 and 1932 two presidents of the ASLA offered two different visions of landscape architecture. Each was a vision based on personal values, which one man hoped to locate at the center of his colleagues' own sense of professional identity. And while each implied a mission, only the more pragmatic vision had a chance of success in the larger world.

In January 1930 ASLA President Arthur A. Shurtleff tried to explain the bond that held together the diverse group of designers, planners, and conservationists, among others, who considered themselves landscape architects. If there were no "compelling force of urgent human need," he reasoned, the bond between these professionals would be weak. But the bond was strong because, in the long process of human alteration of the surface of continents, something was in jeopardy—"the loveliness of the earth." This quality could be found in a city, in a park, on a mountain, in a garden, along a river or by the shore of the sea. It could be recognized in wilderness or in places shaped by human will. What mattered was that it was fragile. Landscape architects might explain their work in terms of mechanical fitness or engineering economy, he noted, but "loveliness of the earth" was the larger, more compelling vision. And now that this loveliness was in peril ("Increasing fears for it are on every tongue," Shurtleff wrote), landscape architects should do their part in saving, protecting, and creating it.[28]

Evidently this vision was too delicate for the hard times that followed. Today it could be dismissed as wishful thinking, yet it represents an acute feeling for essentials. In the language of a Jensen or a Waugh, Shurtleff made a plea for the kind of environmental responsibility later found in Ian McHarg's *Design with Nature* (1969). With none of the scientific justifications of McHarg's work Shurtleff was intuitively aware of what was appropriate in the landscape. This is clear in *New England Journal* (1931), the little book that Shurtleff brought out after he had changed his name to Shurcliff. In two different passages the loveliness of pastures, fields, orchards, roads, bridges, dams, and mills is recognized as the product of both human effort and natural processes. The people who created these things (among them Shurcliff's ancestors) "were partners with the sky and earth as the birds who build nests of grass with the faith of birds are partners with the heavens and the ground." Or again, "to look upon a good field is to bear witness to the loveliness of the earth, to the rewards of frugality, and to the partnership of the sun."[29]

Henry Vincent Hubbard respected his predecessor's point of view. In his own president's report of 1932 he acknowledged Shurcliff's concern for the loveliness of the earth as a concern of any artist. But Hubbard faced a different combination of threats. One was economic—although the problems of unemployment were perhaps so obvious that he did not even mention the Depression. Another was aesthetic—the modern movement, which posed a challenge to any traditional landscape architect's view of the world. A third was professional—the fact that engineers and architects were still much better known and appreciated for what they did. Thus, in an attempt to justify the existence of landscape architecture as a separate profession (and indirectly to deal with the other two threats), Hubbard made the case for the "public service" that landscape architects provided. While the engineer excelled in useful, economical works and the architect provided man-made form for use, stability, economy, and beauty, the landscape architect served in a different capacity: "As Landscape Architects, we know best, and so come to love best, that beauty which nature offers to us," he insisted, "rather than that beauty which we create in man-made forms as an expression of man's originality and his dominance over natural materials."[30]

In hindsight we know the winning concepts. "Public service" was the most useful thing that landscape architects could offer during the Depression and

World War II—particularly services based on technical expertise and attention to pragmatic results. Modernism was the dominant point of view among planners and designers in the United States from the late 1930s through the 1960s. And technological control over the vagaries of nature, not the "loveliness of the earth," has remained a dominant motive of human efforts for many years, both before and since Shurcliff's cry from the heart.

The story of how landscape architects survived the Depression has been told elsewhere, with emphasis on the many programs begun during the administration of the indomitable Franklin D. Roosevelt. Earle S. Draper was appointed director of the Division of Land Planning and Housing of the Tennessee Valley Authority (TVA). Later he took charge of all the TVA's regional planning studies. Such landscape architects as Jacob L. Crane, Elbert Peets, Hale J. Walker, and University of Illinois Professor Stanley White worked with architects and engineers on the government-sponsored new towns. Others worked for the U.S. Park Service, the U.S. Forest Service, the Civilian Conservation Corps (CCC), the Farm Security Administration, the Works Progress Administration, as well as other agencies. All told, according to Albert D. Taylor, some ninety percent of the landscape profession was employed by the government at some point during these years.[31]

By the spring of 1935 Albert D. Taylor, the new ASLA president, could report that the "stress of the extreme emergency period" of the Depression was past. In the coming years of recovery he expected to see more employment of landscape architects as consultants—which would allow them to return to private practice. In some cases, however, landscape architects were passed over in favor of other professionals with other skills. For example, the TVA's Land Planning Division hired more geographers than landscape architects, as the TVA's emphasis shifted from physical town planning to the broader field of regional land planning.[32] Thirty years later landscape architects could rightly expect to compete successfully against geographers for jobs in regional planning. But in the mid-1930s they still hoped to be judged on both technical and aesthetic grounds. As Hubbard put it in 1935, the essential condition for good work in landscape architecture was the freedom to evaluate all the requirements of a problem and then crystallize a design in order to produce "an aesthetic unity embodying an economic unity."

These are some of the views of the ASLA's leadership during the Great Depression. In general they represent a sober, conservative outlook—with a determination to maintain an aesthetic component in whatever work landscape architects might perform as a public service. But other views of art and design also emerged in those lean years.

In 1930 ASLA Fellow Fletcher Steele wrote about the pioneering ideas of a few European modernists in garden design—Tony Garnier, Le Corbusier, Pierre Le Grain, Robert Mallet-Stevens, Gabriel Guevrekian, among others. Nothing like their work had ever been featured in *Landscape Architecture*, and it caused a stir not only among the young Harvard students who would begin to write manifestos in the late 1930s (Garrett Eckbo, Dan Kiley, and James Rose), but also among some of the fellows and members of the ASLA. Steele's attitude was refreshing—not revolutionary, but free of prejudice. "We must search a new point from which to view art," he suggested. If the "dead axis of the past" is shattered in a garden by Le Grain, so be it. "We are made to think and to feel, whence must come understanding."[34] The striking photographs and plans he selected for commentary were probably sufficient to confirm readers in their own views, for or against modernism. The text was engaging, open-minded, but not a manifesto.

Two years later Steele offered a shorter, more penetrating essay without images. In "Landscape Design of the Future" he picked up on an idea from his older colleague Charles Downing Lay.[35] "I believe that successful space composition will be the next serious preoccupation of landscape architects," Steele ventured. Like Lay, he found in spatial relations a spiritual quality that, at its most intense, could seem almost mystical—as if one were part of the space itself. The composition of space is intangible, Steele noted; it has nothing to do with styles. It is a question of feeling, not seeing, and therein lies the spirit, the charm of a place. "Those who live in a well composed space day by day never tire of it nor want to get away," he wrote in 1932. He refers, perhaps, to the old family homestead he had known as a child in upstate New York. He would write about it again, with more acute feeling, some thirty years later.[36] But Steele was not simply looking backward. He was, instead, looking to artists—people who could "see farther than others into the significance of the world around us." He predicted a fusion of those old polar opposites, "formal" and "informal" styles. He was deeply moved by the power of nature's story, but that was not the main story for him. "We are human and the story of man must always come first," Steele insisted. It was a vote of confidence for the modern landscapes to come, not prefigured in images but rendered convincingly by a few words that stirred the imagination.[37]

These thoughts surfaced in a symposium held at the ASLA's annual meeting in Philadelphia in 1932. Steele may have been more intrigued by modernism than most of his colleagues, but some were at least curious. Malcolm H. Dill, ASLA, viewed modern art as important in its spirit—its insistence on honesty in materials, craft, and construction. ASLA Fellow Ralph E. Griswold emphasized creative principles and warned that landscape architecture might deteriorate through "stupid adherence to rules," for the times were changing—fast. He also differentiated between professional success and artistic advancement. "Our future as Landscape Architects depends altogether on the creative quality of our work," he concluded.[38] ASLA Fellow Richard Schermerhorn, Jr., was willing to reconsider the basics— what to teach, how to describe the field, how to define it, and to what extent it was a fine art. Plants, he felt, were slipping in importance, while a knowledge of city planning and zoning was becoming more critical. He sensed that great opportunities for landscape architects lay in a field much wider than country estates and gardens. "I actually believe Landscape Architecture need not eventually suffer in its standing as a fine art," he asserted, "if it enters more fully this wider arena of stern realities."[39]

And so the discussions among landscape architects of a certain age—over thirty, at any rate—continued sporadically in *Landscape Architecture*, while the younger generation of designers found other outlets for their ideas. From September 1937 onward, while still a student at the GSD, Garrett Eckbo vented his impatience with formulas, rules, axes, and focal points in such periodicals as *Pencil Points* (the forerunner of *Progressive Architecture*) and *Magazine of Art*. In the late 1930s, imagining an era when science might become an integral part of landscape development, James Rose mulled over the relations of space and time, materials and people, first in *Pencil Points* and later in *California Arts and Architecture*, for which Thomas Church served as an editor in the 1930s. In 1939 and 1940 *Architectural Record* published three articles that Eckbo, Rose, and their Harvard classmate Dan Kiley wrote together, exploring the possibilities for "environmental equilibrium" in the urban, rural, and primeval landscapes of the modern world.[40]

This was the sort of experimental work and thought that did not appear in *Landscape Architecture*. Maybe it was a plus. What a pleasure it is today to find that Eckbo's early explorations of organic relationships between sculpture and landscape architecture led to a spirited exchange of views in *Magazine of Art* and that this exchange appeared alongside a response to an interview with the conductor Eugene Ormandy and a note on *Burlington Magazine* editor Roger Fry and Postimpressionist painting! These chance juxtapositions at least hint at the cross-fertilization that could have occurred among the arts at that time.[41] Meanwhile, the potential links among landscape architects, planners, architects, and engineers were not always evident in print. The architectural journals did not always credit the contributions of landscape architects. And in the 1920s, as Henry Vincent Hubbard began to edit *City Planning* and its successor, the *Planners' Journal*, he included relatively few articles on planning in his other magazine, *Land-*

scape Architecture.[42] Some landscape architects, notably Henry Wright, John Nolen, and Hubbard himself, would look to many societies and periodicals to satisfy their own broad professional interests in planning and design. But anyone who chanced to pick up *Landscape Architecture* in the late 1930s would not immediately sense, among the generously illustrated articles on estate gardens and national parks, that landscape architecture encompassed a much wider field.

Thus it happened that although Eckbo worked in the San Francisco office of the Farm Security Administration (FSA) in the late 1930s, his collaborative work with architects and engineers on migrant farm workers' communities was never published in *Landscape Architecture*. He did, however, include images and discussions of these communities in his later writings. In 1941 the architectural historian and critic Talbot Hamlin also wrote a long article on these FSA communities illustrated with unattributed plans and renderings, some of which Eckbo had drawn up, having learned from experience in the field about designing for "real" people and dire needs.

Hamlin, too, knew something about migrating "Okies" and referred to the depiction of their plight in John Steinbeck's novel, *The Grapes of Wrath* (1939). Hamlin understood the hardships caused by industrialized one-crop farming, compounded by drought, erosion, and the Depression. He was also familiar with problems of site planning and building. Looking over some construction details, he was moved to write, "Could we but learn to study these human needs as freshly and independently as they have been studied in these communities, if we could but analyze the purposes of

each building part with as little dependence on convention or past usage, . . . [thinking] in as powerful a manner of the necessary integration of form and use and structure, there would be no limit to the architectural progress we might make. . . . These communities . . . are beautiful because designed by artists, to whom creation was not limited by any economic deadline." Whether the problem was a privy or a community center, he noted, the designers had approached it as a means to a physical product and also to a "new and beautiful creative form."[43]

Years later Eckbo reflected on the migrant workers' communities: "This I still look back to as the best collaborative design team experience I have had. There have been many others, but none have lasted as long or been as productive."[44] In seven years the San Francisco office of the FSA built temporary communities for about 12,500 migrant families and permanent housing for about 1,750. By 1942, when these efforts ended, landscape architects were, for the most part, preoccupied with the nation's efforts to win a second world war.

For landscape architects the decade of 1935–1945 was a time of ferment. As the economy gradually recovered and the federal government's emergency programs were phased out, more opportunities did, in fact, allow landscape architects to return to private practice. In the late 1930s the pages of *Landscape Architecture* were filled with large photographs of estate gardens, national parks, parkways, the malls and monuments of Washington, D.C., and the New York World's Fair. At first glance it might appear that not much had changed in landscape architecture since the late 1920s. But the changes were evolutionary. Increasingly landscape architects were venting their frustrations over the name, the content, and the direction—or lack of it. One unsigned article in 1939 noted that in the United States physical planning had come to be considered "a most important function of the profession"—although the name "landscape architecture" was unfortunate.[45] A few years later, while landscape architects were again serving their country in military and civilian capacities, some of them paused to reflect on what they were really doing— camp planning, site planning, land planning, and civil engineering. Landscape architect and planner Arthur C. Comey recommended a new name for the ASLA—the American Society of Land Planners. Another landscape architect, who happened to relocate his office, simply put his name on the door but neglected to indicate what profession he practiced.[46]

Great expectations were stirred by two world's fairs in 1939. "Building the World of Tomorrow" was the slogan of the New York fair. The fair on Treasure Island in San Francisco Bay was, for some, a "magic city" like its predecessor in Chicago in 1893. And if no single landscape architect rose to the prominence that the elder Olmsted had achieved in Chicago, there were several who made notable contributions: in New York, not only Board of Design member Gilmore Clarke, but also Alfred Geiffert, Jr., Umberto Innocenti, Richard K. Webel, and Clarke's partner, Michael Rapuano; in San Francisco, Harry W. Shepherd, Elmer G. Gould, Tamura Takeshi (from Tokyo), and the landscape engineer Julius L. Girod, who served as chief of the fair's Bureau of Horticulture.[47] Yet these fairs did not add up to "landscape" or "art" in the public eye. In Flushing Meadow, New York, on the site

of a former tidal marsh and refuse dump, the overwhelming motif of the fair was technology. It was a spectacular triumph over nature by human ingenuity, symbolized by the vast geometric forms of a trylon and perisphere. The artificial island in San Francisco Bay was a more romantic, dreamlike world. Neither wholly futuristic nor nostalgic, it was a celebration of what the fine and applied arts could offer in concert. Still, one observer, art critic Eugen Neuhaus, missed something. He knew what a landscape architect could accomplish in other circumstances, but on Treasure Island, where architects were in charge, the landscape architect's main contribution was "horticultural display."[48]

At the same time landscape architects could also look back on a more traditional world—the recently restored Colonial Williamsburg. Underwritten largely by John D. Rockefeller, Jr., the restoration was unprecedented in scale and complexity, involving extensive archaeological and bibliographical research. The head of the landscape restoration and planning, Arthur Shurcliff, found that the early designers had not only chosen excellent sites for building but had also laid out the gardens and the whole town with acute attention to the ratios of proportion. One of the leading architects, William G. Perry of Perry, Shaw and Hepburn, noted that architecture—if it was to achieve harmony with nature—could not stand alone. It needed the "resource and appreciative skill" of the landscape architect and the gardener. In the end these allied professionals brought something of eighteenth-century Williamsburg back to life. And in that homage to the nation's heritage in Virginia, Shurcliff found what young Eckbo was finding among the windswept sites for migrants' communities at the other end of the continent—a deep satisfaction in collaboration.[49]

In 1937 the San Francisco Museum of Art held an exhibition that may have encouraged collaboration. Entitled "Contemporary Landscape Architecture and its Sources," the exhibition catalog featured essays by architect Richard Neutra, architectural historian and critic Henry-Russell Hitchcock, Jr., and landscape architect Fletcher Steele. There were photographs and models of work by Steele, Neutra, Thomas Church, R. M. Schindler, Frank Lloyd Wright, Le Corbusier, Mies van der Rohe, and Gabriel Guevrekian among others. And collaborators were credited: architects William Wurster and Hervey Parke Clark with Church, for example, and landscape architect Helen Van Pelt with Frank Lloyd Wright. In his essay Steele further pursued ideas about creative space composition. But a close reading of Hitchcock's and Neutra's essays reveals that the architects were seeking simple, seemingly natural settings for modern buildings with the kind of native (or at least unobtrusive) plants that Jensen might have provided. They were not particularly interested in space compositions in the landscape—modern or otherwise. In effect, they wanted a landscape that would more or less disappear. Neutra even called it "landscaping."[50] This attitude would linger among architects for decades. Landscape architects who wanted to make the landscape recognizably modern often had to provide a quiet setting for exquisite objects in space. Some architects were more willing than others to include landscape architects in their own artistic quests. But sometimes

"service," whether for the public good or for more narrowly conceived private interests, was the very best that landscape architects could offer. In 1946, when landscape architect Edward H. Laird presented to the first postwar annual ASLA meeting his site planning for the General Electric Company's new "Electronics Park" in Syracuse, New York, the work was considered one of several "Opportunities for Service in 1946."[51]

But that takes us into the postwar era. Here, the last word will be given to younger people who, before the war, scorned old boundaries and sought new directions. ASLA Fellow John O. Simonds once recalled the late 1930s, when he was in graduate school at Harvard, as a time of searching. Setting out on a quest for a new philosophy of planning, Simonds eventually found that what counted was not the designed shape or space or form—but the quality of experience. It gave him new insights into the planning theories of Le Corbusier, as well as a finer appreciation of the crystalline, the organic.[52] Vincent Merrill, a junior associate of the ASLA in 1941, was also intrigued by new notions of planning and design, beyond the "rare and almost unsought luxury" that they once were. Determined to remain self-critical and open-minded, this future partner in the stalwart Boston firm of Shurcliff, Shurcliff and Merrill urged that his elders remember their elders, the rebels. "These makers of history whom we revere so highly were, without exception, engaged in reexamining, and in some cases in rebelling against, the accepted life and thought of their times," Merrill wrote. "Strange how highly we reverence the memory of these men and yet seem to forget entirely, indeed to controvert, the spirit in which they lived."[53]

"In art we must feel the form underlying everything: the human form under drapery, the form of the earth under the greenery. In everything we have continual need of realizing the permanent qualities, the underlying truth, and nowhere more than in the landscape that we live with day by day."

ALLEN TUCKER (1920)

RESIDENCE OF J.E. LEWIS

FOX CHAPEL, PENNSYLVANIA

GARDENS DESIGNED BY RALPH E. GRISWOLD

1920S

COURTESY OF THE FRANCES LOEB LIBRARY

GRADUATE SCHOOL OF DESIGN, HARVARD UNIVERSITY

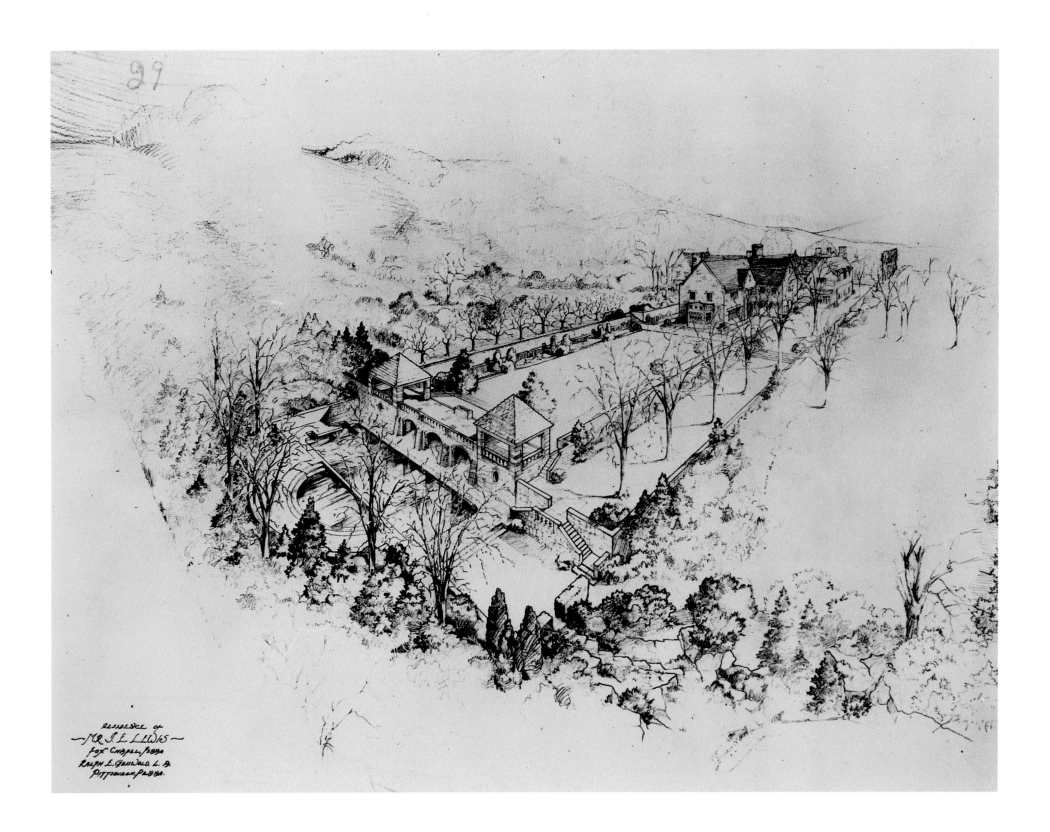

RESIDENCE of
—MR J.E. LEWIS—
FOX CHAPEL, PA
RALPH E. GRISWOLD L. A.
PITTSBURGH, PA. U.S.A.

"The Classic Spirit is the disinterested search for perfection; it is the love of clearness and reasonableness and self-control; it is, above all, the love of permanence and of continuity. . . . It does not consider tradition as immutable or set rigid bounds to invention. . . . It wishes to add link by link to the chain of tradition, but it does not wish to break the chain."

KENYON COX (1911)

RESIDENCE OF DR. HARVEY S. MUDD

BEVERLY HILLS, CALIFORNIA

EDWARD HUNTSMAN-TROUT, 1920S

"Fleming's work was extremely individual and unorthodox, at times

challenging all rationality, often guilty of the most whimsical exaggeration,

yet somehow invariably delightful.

NORMAN T. NEWTON (1971)

RESIDENCE OF BURT EDDY TAYLOR

GROSSE POINTE, MICHIGAN

BRYANT FLEMING, 1920S

PHOTOGRAPHER UNKNOWN

COURTESY OF THE FRANCES LOEB LIBRARY

GRADUATE SCHOOL OF DESIGN, HARVARD UNIVERSITY

"The best European and American town planners make the same differentiation between wheel and foot traffic as Olmsted did: Indeed, in Radburn, N. J., Mr. Henry Wright has laid out a town in this fashion, with an internal park system completely out of the range of traffic. This modern design only adds to one's appreciation of Olmsted's power as an inventor."

Lewis Mumford (1931)

Radburn

New Jersey

Planned and designed by

Henry Wright, Clarence Stein,

and others, in the late 1920s

Photographer unknown

Courtesy of the Frances Loeb Library

Graduate School of Design, Harvard University

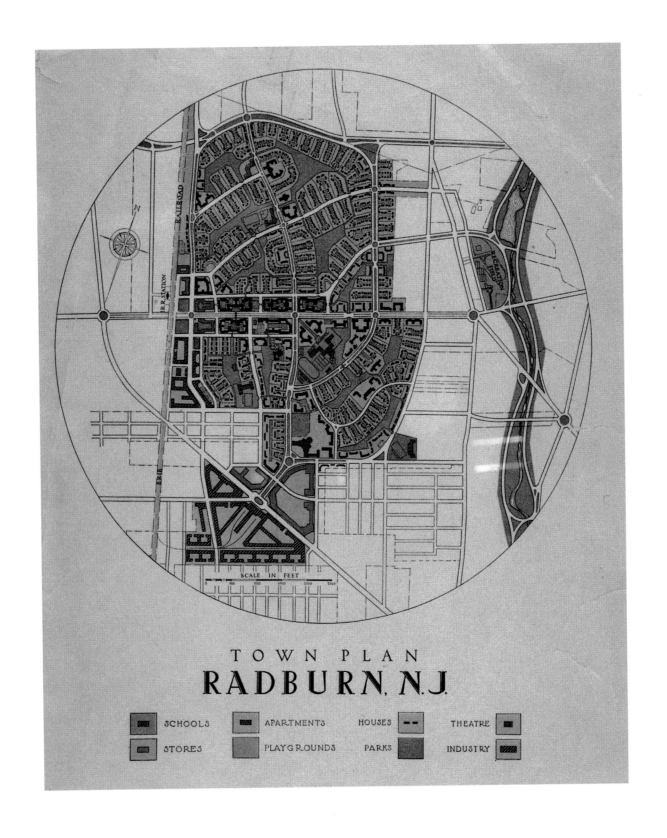

TOWN PLAN
RADBURN, N.J.

SCHOOLS		APARTMENTS		HOUSES		THEATRE
STORES		PLAYGROUNDS		PARKS		INDUSTRY

"The classic architecture demanded a formal type of development, and as the site was rugged, something more than one hundred thousand yards of excavation were required. However, the Rockhill District in which the grounds are located, on account of its rolling wooded slopes and picturesque native dry stone walls, made necessary an informality of treatment around the outside borders. Beautiful groves of existing trees helped to accomplish this, although some three hundred trees, moved in with derricks, added to the wooded support."

S. HERBERT HARE (1939)

NELSON-ATKINS MUSEUM OF ART

KANSAS CITY, MISSOURI

LANDSCAPE DESIGN BY HARE & HARE

LATE 1930S

COURTESY OF THE FRANCES LOEB LIBRARY

GRADUATE SCHOOL OF DESIGN, HARVARD UNIVERSITY

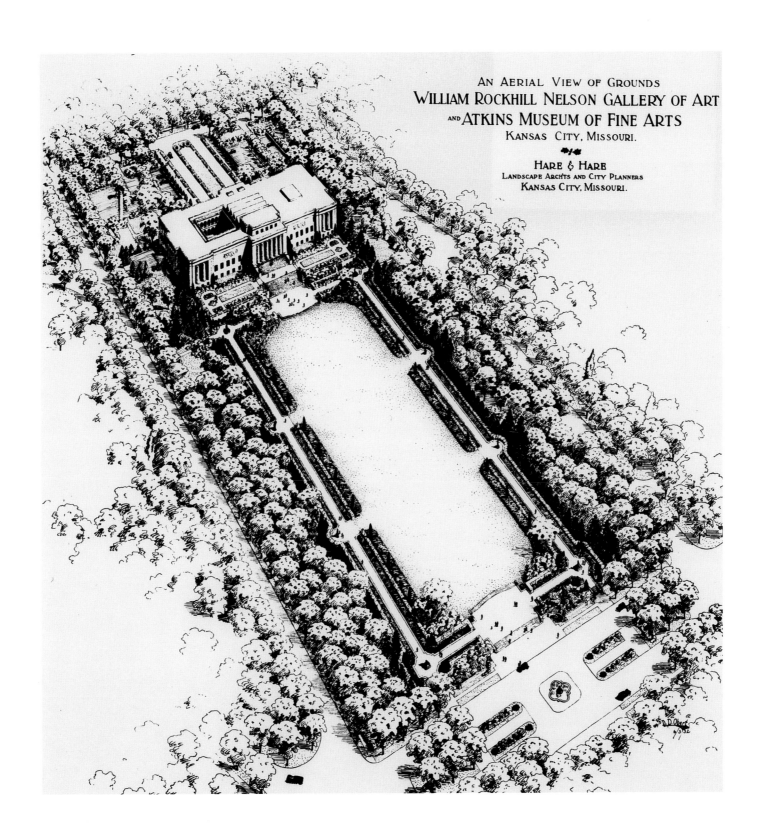

An Aerial View of Grounds
WILLIAM ROCKHILL NELSON GALLERY OF ART
and ATKINS MUSEUM OF FINE ARTS
KANSAS CITY, MISSOURI.

HARE & HARE
LANDSCAPE ARCHTS AND CITY PLANNERS
KANSAS CITY, MISSOURI.

"He made a great contribution here in Washington. He laid out the entire Montgomery County [Maryland] streamline park, including Rock Creek. Once I took him there and he showed me a boundary change I had often wondered about. It turns out there was a landowner that wouldn't sell."

ROCK CREEK PARK

WASHINGTON, DC

PLANNED AND DESIGNED BY CHARLES ELIOT II,

OLMSTED BROTHERS, AND OTHERS

PHOTOGRAPHER UNKNOWN

COURTESY OF THE FRANCES LOEB LIBRARY

GRADUATE SCHOOL OF DESIGN, HARVARD UNIVERSITY

"You know the exultant feeling with which you behold ground ample enough and free enough for your roaming spirit. . . .

You exult that you can be free at last in 'God's own open.

' Where the occupants of tens of thousands of black-covered wagons exult in this way . . .

the park soon begins to look like an 'open' which the Almighty would hardly recognize for His own."

ARTHUR A. SHURTLEFF (LATER SHURCLIFF) (1926)

MOUNT RAINIER NATIONAL PARK

PUBLIC CAMP GROUNDS, PARADISE VALLEY, WASHINGTON

PHOTOGRAPHER UNKNOWN

COURTESY OF THE FRANCES LOEB LIBRARY

GRADUATE SCHOOL OF DESIGN, HARVARD UNIVERSITY

"These communities are human and attractive because their designers understood people and their needs and insisted that all of those needs—intellectual and emotional as well as physical—should be taken care of. . . . What was necessary was not mere shelter but rather the creation of a new pattern of community life."

TALBOT F. HAMLIN (1941)

FARM SECURITY ADMINISTRATION

HARLINGEN, TEXAS

PARK AND COMMUNITY BUILDING BY

GARRETT ECKBO, 1940

DRAWING COURTESY OF THE GARRETT ECKBO COLLECTION (1990 – 1991)

DOCUMENTS COLLECTION, COLLEGE OF ENVIRONMENTAL DESIGN

THE UNIVERSITY OF CALIFORNIA, BERKELEY

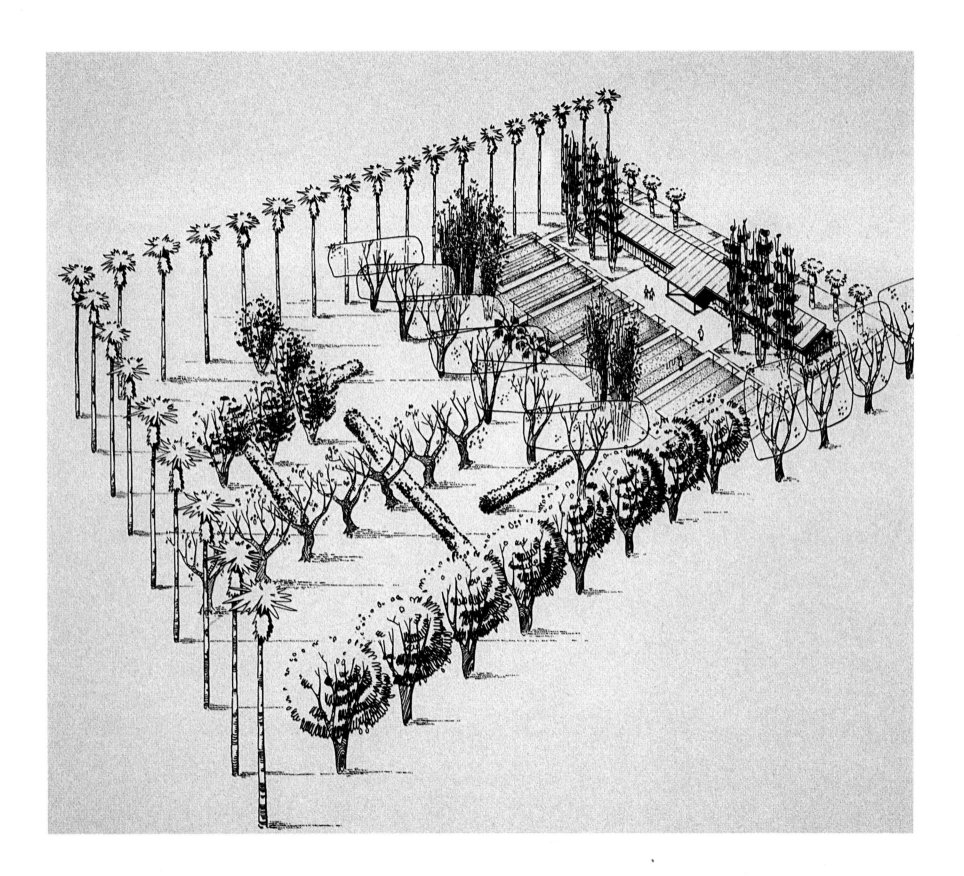

"The glow of much old beauty is fading before our hungry eyes from the very

excess of our interest and the inevitable changes in our modern life and

thought. We must search a new point from which to view art."

FLETCHER STEELE (1930)

GARDEN AT "NAUMKEAG"

STOCKBRIDGE, MASSACHUSETTS

DESIGNED BY FLETCHER STEELE

FROM LATE 1920S

PHOTOGRAPH BY ALAN WARD

"Henry Adams saw in the great dynamo of the Chicago Fair of 1893 the hope of the world. Were he alive today he would probably spend most of his time in this part of the Fair [the 'foreign section.'] For it is not the simple wonder of the miracle of modern production that today challenges intelligence and imagination, but the deeper questions of who shall use these powerful instruments, by what policies and to gain what ends."

FREDERICK A. GUTHEIM (1939)

WORLD'S FAIR

FLUSHING MEADOW, NEW YORK, 1939 (AERIAL VIEW)

GILMORE D. CLARKE, MEMBER

BOARD OF DESIGN

PHOTOGRAPHER UNKNOWN

COURTESY OF THE FRANCES LOEB LIBRARY

GRADUATE SCHOOL OF DESIGN, HARVARD UNIVERSITY

"The design of the building itself featured a spiral ramp for the demonstration of automobiles. Inspired by the sense of movement and simplicity inherent in this feature, the landscape design grew to emphasize direction. The simplicity of architectural line was carried out in plant material and accomplished by the use of very few varieties, mostly red cedar and hedges of hemlock."

GILMORE D. CLARKE (1939)

LANDSCAPE OF THE NETHERLANDS PAVILION

NEW YORK WORLD'S FAIR, 1939

DESIGNED BY RICHARD K. WEBEL

OF INNOCENTI & WEBEL

PHOTOGRAPHER UNKNOWN

COURTESY OF THE FRANCES LOEB LIBRARY

GRADUATE SCHOOL OF DESIGN, HARVARD UNIVERSITY

"The manner in which science, technology, and 'business' are permitted to displace both art and religion is a strong argument at any time for the 'decline of the West.' There are many others. For this very reason it is all the more needful that we keep our vision clear to those instances in which the human spirit still soars and art still has her triumphs."

FRANK A. WAUGH (1935)

LANDSCAPE OF THE

FORD MOTOR COMPANY BUILDING

NEW YORK WORLD'S FAIR, 1939

GILMORE D. CLARKE AND

MICHAEL RAPUANO, LANDSCAPE ARCHITECTS

WALTER DORWIN TEAGUE, DESIGNER

OF BUILDING AND EXHIBIT

PHOTOGRAPHER UNKNOWN

COURTESY OF THE FRANCES LOEB LIBRARY

GRADUATE SCHOOL OF DESIGN, HARVARD UNIVERSITY

CHAPTER 3

A PROFESSION IN TRANSITION

1945 – 1965

Every era may seem transitional to those who live through it. Even so, there is something extraordinary about the first two postwar decades, and historians, economists, and cultural critics are still trying to make sense of them.[1] Were they an aberration, a period of unprecedented growth and prosperity in the United States while much of the developed world was still recovering from the devastating effects of the Second World War? Or was there a Golden Age in all developed countries worldwide? Were these decades somehow favored with just the right conditions to nurture the creativity of a melting pot of people? Or were they years of an unusually broad-based consensus in political, economic, and cultural spheres—when subtle differences of opinion were reconciled in the interests of such larger goals as building an interstate highway system, expanding opportunities for higher education, and landing a man on the moon? So simply stated, none of these explanations is satisfying in itself. Yet together they begin to suggest why these two postwar decades, seen through veils of time, now appear like a favored transition between eras that unquestionably did try men's souls.

For landscape architects these years were a critical period of transition. With an unprecedented amount of development, redevelopment, and economic expansion landscape architects were faced with opportunities they had never had—and have not had since. Also unprecedented were the challenges to plan and build on a scale not conceivable since the park systems of the elder Olmsted, Eliot, Manning, and George Kessler and The City Beautiful plans of Daniel Burnham. But even more challenging than the volume and scale of work was the modernist viewpoint that now prevailed among the planners and designers of the Western world. This entailed much more than an aesthetic of flat roofs, smooth surfaces, and expansive planes on which to place a few objects in space. It meant that landscape architects who wanted to help shape the new large-scale developments—urban renewal, suburban workplaces, campuses, airports, housing, shopping malls—had to work with designers who did not appreciate land and landscape as they had commonly been appreciated before the First World War. While the legacy of both the romantic and the neoclassical periods still offered examples of coherent landscapes, rural and urban, some designers might be inspired to seek wholeness. But in the modernist world of the 1950s and 1960s wholeness—a widely appreciated, satisfying integration within the larger environment—became increasingly difficult to achieve.

Today landscape architects can point to a few early postwar modern landscapes that did manage to achieve a degree of wholeness. In 1955 in the small town of Columbus, Indiana, Dan Kiley worked with two sympathetic architects, Eero Saarinen and Kevin Roche, to integrate a modern house into a modern landscape. The result—the Miller garden—did not intrude upon its comfortable, traditional residential neighborhood on the fringes of town; nor was the garden entirely walled off, for staggered masses of hedges allowed glimpses into the garden from the street. In 1948 in Sonoma County, California, Thomas Church employed a young architect, George Rockrise, and a few young landscape architects, including Lawrence Halprin, to work on a project that ultimately stood out from his many other fine modern gardens. It was not only the serenity of the exurban site, but also the masterly way in which a pool, a pool house, and a few boulders and existing live oaks were

integrated to form a new whole, fused with the earth, the distant salt marsh, and the sky. Other exceptional works of the 1940s and 1950s, public as well as private, could also be mentioned, works that sometimes went unnoticed for years in official circles of landscape architects.

The explanations for this lack of awareness of seminal works in the field are varied, but one important, complicated reason has to do with the ways in which the official professional society, the ASLA, viewed its traditional mission, its reasons for being. The conservative tendencies of the society vis-à-vis the modern movement have already been touched upon. But one tendency needs to be considered in greater detail—an ambivalence about seeking publicity for and critical examination of the work of its members. Ultimately, the issues of criticism, competition, publicity, and professional stature in the public eye would be brought out into the open and widely debated among ASLA fellows and members. But in the early postwar years more immediate issues of competition for employment—even the survival of the profession itself—were more pressing.

In 1947 ASLA Fellow Gilmore Clarke surveyed the critical issues facing both society as a whole and the small profession of landscape architecture. He spoke of the spreading ugliness in the cities and the countryside and called attention to devastated forests and polluted streams. Recognizing a changed economy, he was interested in new, more flexible patterns of professional practice that might rise to the enormous challenges at hand. "Beauty must ever be the watchword," he asserted, "but there seem to be new and fresh ways of achieving beauty." Clarke was somewhat apprehensive about the future of landscape architecture, particularly in light of the "thinning ranks" of students in the field. (He believed many of the best qualified students were studying architecture and engineering.) "As I look about, I see no Frank Lloyd Wrights or Le Corbusiers of landscape architecture," he observed, "and I am at a loss to know whether this lack is a liability or an asset. These two men have occasionally shaken the foundations of their profession—not, however, without profit to themselves! Perhaps we might with profit admit one or more practitioners of the exotic to call public attention to our professional offerings!"[2]

In 1949 the 542-member ASLA was fifty years old. Looking back on those years, ASLA Fellow Bremer Pond noted that the profession of landscape architecture was still somewhat dependent on government-sponsored projects in the aftermath of World War II. Lately, private development had been hampered by the inflated costs of labor and building materials, while income taxes remained relatively high. In this context Pond asserted, "As a Society now in direct competition with others tending to encroach on our field we need all the publicity we can possibly devise." Earlier in the ASLA's history, Pond noted, exhibitions (including ones that traveled) and press notices were "most successful" in securing publicity for the profession. During the Great Depression the exhibitions had died out, but now they were being revived—on the Pacific Coast.[3]

During the 1950s occasional exhibitions of professional work, displayed at annual ASLA meetings and briefly mentioned in *Landscape Architecture*, would publicize some of the members' current work. But evidently some of the more innovative projects of that time were not submitted. A member in the early 1930s, Thomas Church had had some photographs of his early, tentative efforts in modern garden design published in the ASLA's large folios of members' work. Later, however, as he began to work more or less as his own contractor, employing skilled craftsmen whose opinions he valued, his practice did not follow the ASLA's guidelines for professional practice that distinguished landscape professionals from tradesmen and commercial entrepreneurs. There were times in its history, then, that the ASLA did not have the active participation of some leading landscape architects, while it continued to uphold its exacting professional standards and mount exhibitions of its members' work from time to time.[4]

Out of these exhibitions and the occasional prizes for displays would emerge the regular annual ASLA awards program. This development from somewhat amateurish exhibition to well-publicized professional competition is a transition that will be followed closely throughout these pages. In the process, however, one long-term change of enormous importance might be missed, so gradually did it slip into the common culture and gain ascendancy. This was the transfer of importance from the word to the image. ASLA annual meetings in the late 1940s and the 1950s featured speeches, panels, round-table discussions, field trips, and presentations of members' work—often without slides or images. The profession was part of a culture in which the written and spoken word were heeded. Even the results of the ASLA's first postwar competition in 1954 were communicated in words alone, in fact by mere lists. This is not to say that landscape architects were not visually oriented. Nor does this transition involve a steady growth in sophistication. Rather, it involves a transition from verbal modes of communicxation to visual ones—while the overall level of sophistication varied a great deal.

Another transition in the 1950s was equally far-reaching and difficult to fathom at the time. It was the growing awareness that a new kind of professional would be needed to be truly effective in the postwar era. The Great Depression and the Second World War had fairly well exhausted landscape architects' claims to being fine artists. Many would settle for a tacit claim to "artist," while a few, including Ian McHarg and Philip Lewis, soon realized that the science of ecology and scientific methods would become increasingly powerful bases of operations. Frustrations with the title "landscape architect" became a moot issue as more and more professionals began to use multiple titles, including "land planner" or "city and regional planner." Moreover, some offices with strong ties to academia, including those led by Hideo Sasaki and Ian McHarg, became multidisciplinary, like some successful forerunners in architecture, Skidmore, Owings and Merrill (SOM) and The Architects Collaborative (TAC). And increasingly the old boundaries and turf wars among design professionals became less relevant than the abilities to manage projects efficiently and to orchestrate different kinds of talents, skills, and understandings.

This is roughly the sort of development that ASLA President John L. Greenleaf had urged his fellow landscape architects to avoid back in 1927. He had seen its early signs in the landscape architect/planner who was eager to be sought out as a man of "business efficiency" and to be known as a great executive—and also as a designer. Rather than condemn this development outright, Greenleaf had suggested that "the tendency toward town planning as an executive business proposition [may] tend to blind our eyes to the finer phases of our profession." And he ended with reminders of both duty and joy in the profession of landscape architecture as a fine art.[5] So—why unearth these presumably forgotten sentiments in the midst of postwar expansion and the transition toward new kinds of professionals and offices? It is not only to note how far landscape architects had come in the quarter century since Greenleaf's time. It is also to prefigure a similar warning that would be sounded in the midst of postwar prosperity—in 1965.

But first the context of postwar developments needs to be sketched in. By the end of the 1950s many articulate and forceful practitioners and educators were assuming major responsibilities for planning and shaping new kinds of postwar landscapes. These civic, institutional, and industrial landscapes were often indirect products of the federal interstate highway program, the G.I. Bill of Rights, the National Science Foundation, the National Defense Student Loan program, and the defense industries that continued to thrive during the Cold War. After fifteen years of depression and world war, not only was the volume of work expanding rapidly, but the problems were also more complex, requiring changes in the way landscape architecture was taught and practiced. On the rise were interdisciplinary studies, specialization, and research aided by sophisticated new technologies and supported by foundations and the federal government. As offices grew, taking on more disciplines, they became more hierarchical in organization. And among these changes none was more critical than the return to the larger scale of work and the broader social and environmental goals of Olmsted and his colleagues in the nineteenth century. But this awareness of the profession's original ambitions was also part of the transition; only gradually would a sense of history begin to inform and invigorate current practice.

Before the war there had been some upheavals in practice and underlying assumptions. In their manifestos of the late 1930s Eckbo, Kiley, Rose, and landscape architect and planner Christopher Tunnard had emphasized flexibility, economy, and more intensive human uses of parks, gardens (communal as well as private), airports, old canal and railway corridors, and other ignored or underused outdoor spaces. Among these landscape architects the interest in conservation of natural resources was intuitive, its importance often implied, while hu-

man needs and social purposes were underscored. It was a time for reflection and rethinking, while opportunities to plan and build in the old, familiar milieux of the private sector were scarce.[6]

After the war a scattering of somewhat younger landscape architects began to explore a wider range of purposes—environmental, social, artistic, and institutional. Exuberant manifestos gave way to more sober descriptions of work in progress, for clients with specific needs and substantial budgets. Along with new forms—some expressing new functions and materials—there also arose a new consciousness of the interrelations among things. An interest in human ecology, as well as in the ecology of flora and fauna, was growing, along with pollution, congestion, urban redevelopment, suburban development, the loss of farmland, and the gain of technological tools.

Some might assume that the assimilation of ecological ideas in landscape architecture was for many years inhibited by ASLA members' persistent claims that they practiced a fine art. One thinks of the opulent, artful gardens of the 1890s or the 1920s, geometrically ordered, built of stone, ornamented with fragments of the Old World, and planted with exotics, all conceived simply for the delight of the eye—or so it would seem. After only a few years in the 1920s, as noted earlier, the ASLA lost Jens Jensen, an intuitive naturalist who advocated simplicity and the use of native plants in design. Yet Jensen, too, was recognized as an artist. And, as Ervin Zube noted in a recent essay on ecology and landscape architecture, Jensen was not the first in the

Midwest to favor native plants in his designs: In 1880 O. C. Simonds had used native plants in adapting some spatial and compositional qualities of the English landscape garden to the design of Graceland Cemetery near Chicago.[7] (Simonds was not a marginal figure in the profession, either; a founding member of the ASLA, he was also the society's president in 1913.) In those remote eras, then, with Simonds, Jensen, Arthur Shurcliff and others, artistic aspirations could mingle with an intuitive feeling for what was later known as ecology.

It could be that an aesthetic appreciation of whole plant communities actually gave some landscape architects a predilection for appreciating wholeness in ecological science. As the biologist Barry Commoner points out, an understanding of ecology has come slowly, with difficulty, for it involves exceedingly complex processes. "We have been trained by modern science to think about events that are vastly more simple—how one particle bounces off another, or how molecule A reacts with molecule B," he explains.[8] Thus, customary thinking in terms of "separate, single events" and studies of phenomena in isolation had to give way before scientists could begin to understand the greater whole—an ecosphere.

Rather than assume that a fascination for art kept landscape architects from appreciating the science of ecology, it seems more useful to look for ways in which artistic and scientific understandings overlapped, or coexisted, at a time before science and technology had attained their current preeminence. In the 1920s and 1930s both *House Beautiful* and *Landscape Architecture* featured articles on ecology in relation to planting and landscape design.[9] And later, perhaps the eloquent reflections of Aldo Leopold in *A Sand County Almanac* (1949) and Rachel Carson in *Silent Spring* (1962) invited landscape architects to seek answers to environmental problems in a wide frame of reference, ethical and humanistic as well as scientific. Still, given the magnitude of the problems brought on by technological development—pesticides that kill birds as well as insects, pollution of air and water, erosion, and flooding—as well as the growing prestige of technical specialists during the Cold War, it is understandable that landscape architects would turn increasingly toward science and technology for answers to their problems. As the physicist Jacob Bronowski put it in 1956, "The world today is made, it is powered by science; and for any man to abdicate an interest in science is to walk with open eyes towards slavery. . . . This is a time when communication and control have in effect become forms of power."[10]

But there is one development that complicated this transition from the arts to science and technology. In the 1950s and 1960s there was a tremendous surge of interest in, and support of, the arts. In government, in corporations and their charitable foundations, on academic campuses, in small towns and in rehabilitated inner cities there were signs of a "cultural renaissance" or "cultural explosion." Some derided the statistics on attendance at museums, concerts, and "culture festivals" as a fad, but others hailed them as part of a rising tide.

While President Eisenhower was in office the future Lincoln Center for the Performing Arts was incorporated as a nonprofit organization. President Kennedy appointed a council of leading designers and consultants to rehabilitate Pennsylvania Avenue, appointed a "Special Consultant on the Arts," and later set up an Advisory Council on the Arts. In 1965 President Johnson called the White House Conference on Natural Beauty, at which distinguished panelists explored the relations among aesthetics, natural resource conservation, urban renewal, and environmental health. That year Johnson also signed the bill that established the National Endowment for the Arts and the National Endowment for the Humanities.[11] And two years later, in 1967, he signed the bill that established the Corporation for Public Broadcasting.

At that time, Richard Eells, an adjunct professor at Columbia's Graduate School of Business, was speaking of the rise of transnational corporations, the need for greater cultural understanding, and a redefinition of the terms "freedom" and "enterprise." "More broadly conceived," he wrote, "these words embrace the aspirations of scholars, scientists, and artists, as well as businessmen." And therein lay the cause of the "tide of cultural interests that now sweeps into the corporate ramparts." Later, Eells paraphrased the words of John D. Rockefeller III, whose recent Panel Report on the Performing Arts indicated that the arts were essential to the human mind and spirit.[12] It was an expansive, optimistic time for many. As the upbeat futurist

Alvin Toffler put it, speaking of the cultural explosion in 1964, "Nothing short of war or economic collapse can halt this progression."[13]

During these years of cultural flowering landscape architects seem to have been relatively untroubled by divisions within their profession—yet some cracks were beginning to show. As early as 1957, when garden designers on the West Coast, particularly in the San Francisco Bay Area, were achieving national prominence for their highly photogenic, small-scale residential work, Sidney Shurcliff of Boston emphasized the less photogenic, larger-scaled work to be done. Campbell Miller of Louisville, Kentucky, gently chided his colleagues for a preoccupation with cosmetics. The social mission of the field, the larger environment, and the historic material of the earth itself should also be considered, he believed.[14] Then, in 1960, Stanley White, retired as professor of landscape architecture at the University of Illinois, reminded his colleagues of the large-scale regional planning work of Charles Eliot, who had worked out "all our current problems. . . under the tutelage of his master, the senior Olmsted." Despite great changes in conditions, institutions, habits, and modes of thought, White asserted, landscape architects were still adapting Eliot's original prescripts without sufficiently conveying the essence of that work to the general public.[16]

This familiar refrain—that colleagues were not forcefully communicating the larger scope and social and environmental significance of landscape architecture—was echoed in comments from a survey of landscape architects published in 1961. Urging that landscape architects be educated more broadly in the social sciences and the humanities, that they become better writers and public speakers, that they use the latest in modern media, the respondents implied not so much a division in the field as a spectrum of attitudes, from somewhat aloof intellectual or aesthetic preoccupations to community activism and aggressive cultivation of public relations.[16]

The following year, in 1962, "aggressive" was the key word in a series of comments. "We must become as aggressively concerned with aesthetics as those around us are aggressively concerned with economics, or with military power," exhorted Clinton Gamble, the national secretary of the ASLA. "It is important for us to seek aggressively larger commissions," noted Campbell Miller, who was soon to be named chairman of the ASLA's Publication Board. "Landscape architects should acquire an aggressive approach, should formulate a modern, dynamic dimension for landscape architecture, based no longer on a generic, naturalistic philosophy but on a courageous plan of action," asserted Bruno Zevi, then editor of *L'Archittetura* and professor of architecture at the University of Venice.[17] These comments allude to growing differences between the old guard and a more progressive group of landscape architects. Meanwhile, a similar gap had already become apparent on the editorial board of the ASLA's official organ, *Landscape Architecture*.

Beginning with the January 1958 issue of that magazine, editor Bradford Williams would be assisted by the new associate editor, Grady Clay. Between the elder statesman, Williams, and the younger journalist and activist, Clay, there were many sharp differences but also bases for cooperation and trust. Clay, then a staff writer for the *Louisville Courier-Journal* and an outsider vis-à-vis the profession of landscape architecture, had already begun to build an informal network of like-minded writers, urban planners, designers, conservationists, and others concerned about the quality of the built environment. In 1948–1949 he had been a Nieman Fellow at Harvard, where he had listened to the lectures and critiques of Dean Joseph Hudnut, Walter Gropius, and Holmes Perkins of the Graduate School of Design and met some of the students, including Ian McHarg and David A. Wallace. He had also contributed to a book put out by Fortune magazine, *The Exploding Metropolis* (1958), with William H. Whyte, Jr., and Jane Jacobs among others. Clay came to the offices of *Landscape Architecture*, then, conscious of the larger social, economic, and environmental issues of landscape architecture, architecture, and planning. From the late 1950s through the early 1980s, when he stepped down as editor, Clay maintained his original stance as an outsider, an independent "interpreter" of the landscape rather than a spokesman for the profession of landscape architecture. Clay recalled, "Brad Williams needed any help he could get. He welcomed me and treated me very professionally, with great care and support. Then, when he died rather suddenly, and there was really nobody to take on the magazine, I moved into the gap and gradually began to set new directions."[18]

Bradford Williams, born March 30, 1897, died at his home on March 23, 1960. His obituary appeared shortly thereafter in the magazine that had become the focus of his professional life. And Norman T. Newton's account of that life records the passing of an era. A graduate of Harvard College, Williams had taken his M. L. A. degree at Harvard in 1924 and worked for the Olmsted Brothers and Fletcher Steele before setting himself up in practice. His work was mainly residential, apparently a source of great joy to him; yet Williams gave it up early on for the increasing demands of service to the ASLA—as corresponding secretary and, from 1926 onward, as assistant to Henry Vincent Hubbard (editor of *Landscape Architecture* from 1910 to 1947). Promoted to contributing editor and, later, managing editor, Williams was editor in chief of the magazine from 1947 to 1960. A perfectionist, a stylist, uncommonly devoted to his work on the magazine, he was twitted for "making everything sound like something by Dickens." He was, after all, an Anglophile and an honorary fellow of the Royal Society of Arts, with a fondness for "whatever reflected the charming life of a country gentleman in eighteenth-century England." And how was he able to function in the world of mid-twentieth-century design? Newton explained that his conservative, good-natured friend Brad "leaned over backwards and strove faithfully to keep so anachronistic a view from coloring what he published and from unduly influencing others. It was a characteristically straightforward effort . . . and a poignant one."[19]

If few landscape architects could see in such a figure a role model for the 1960s, it would be a mistake to assume that an entire set of values and beliefs was set aside with the passing of Bradford Williams. Even the iconoclast Garrett Eckbo had expressed, and would later reiterate, his interest in conserving the best of past achievements. "The serious and intelligent modern artist does not reject tradition," Eckbo wrote in an essay published in a Canadian journal in 1950. "He only rejects imitation of past segments in the stream. The true stream we are describing as having escaped the traps of the academies and the formula collectors includes many elements beyond those most obviously 'modern': all sorts of flexible and developing work, however conservative in appearance, in which serious effort is made to understand the nature and problems of our times."[20] Thus spoke the forty-year-old Eckbo, who, as an impatient graduate student at Harvard in the 1930s, had scribbled defiantly in the margins of his textbook—the classic by Hubbard and Kimball.[21] Currents of thought in the early postwar years sometimes moved in spirals if not in circles, or so it seems, as rebellion, exploration, and reflection brought Eckbo and others around to reconsidering the past in a new light.

In the 1950s the pages of *Landscape Architecture* did feature the occasional calls for changes in the profession. Turning over the editor's page to the outspoken Clay, Williams found space for such figures as Lewis Mumford; Sylvia Crowe, president of the Institute of Landscape Architects in London; and Walter H. Blucher, president of the American Institute of Planners. He also published the thoughts of such younger landscape architects as Francis H. Dean, of Eckbo, Royston and Williams/Los Angeles, who charted new areas for research in 1956, and Lewis Clarke, who, as a visiting associate professor at North Carolina State College in 1959, offered an unusually broad vision that encompassed slum dwellers and factory workers, ecologically balanced environments, and the joyous appreciation of landscape through the five senses.

One of the most prescient articles Williams ever published was written by a young instructor at the University of Illinois, Hideo Sasaki, who had been an outstanding student there under Stanley White and planner/landscape architect Karl B. Lohmann. "Thoughts on Education in Landscape Architecture" appeared in July 1950 just as Sasaki was moving on to teach at Harvard, from which he had received his M. L. A. degree in 1948. Later he would serve as chairman of Harvard's Department of Landscape Architecture from 1958 to 1968, while maintaining his own growing practice. Meanwhile, this essay laid out the framework for changes that would eventually permeate the profession through Sasaki's many students and colleagues—who would themselves become heads of departments and practices of landscape architecture in the United States and abroad.

Shunning what he called "superficial embellishment," Sasaki focused on the needs of site planning and regional planning. And untroubled by debates over traditional and modern design, he emphasized "functional expression consistent with structure and materials used." He also shifted attention away from objects toward relationships among things; away from the solution to any given problem toward the thought processes that led to a solution through research, analysis, and the elusive, creative act of synthesis. Techniques and traditional skills were necessary, he believed, but not sufficient for addressing the needs of the present day. Elsewhere Sasaki noted the importance of ecological surveys in planning efforts, and he persuaded others, including Stanley White, now retired from the University of Illinois, to introduce an ecological perspective to his students at Harvard. But Sasaki never made ecology or the natural sciences the focus of his teaching or practice. In this article it was the questioning and exploration of new ideas—and the process of thinking—that Sasaki emphasized: Students needed new conceptual tools "to forge new knowledge to meet existing and new situations and to contribute toward social progress in their professional life."[22]

Although Williams acquired another significant essay by the young Sasaki, he was not the editor to get writers such as Eckbo, McHarg, and Lawrence Halprin to write for *Landscape Architecture*. In the 1950s these and other leading figures of landscape architecture found outlets for their ideas in the architectural and planning journals of England, Scotland, Canada, and the United States. It was Grady Clay, with his kindred views and his ambition to open more channels of contact among the allied professions, who engaged these and other activists, thinkers, and creators. As associate editor of the magazine from 1958 to 1960 and as editor from 1960 through 1983, Clay would bring together a stimulating blend of work and thought that challenged conventional boundaries among the different disciplines of art and science.

Beginning in 1954 *Landscape Architecture* began to publicize the results of occasional exhibitions of ASLA members' work. These were the exhibitions set up at the society's annual meetings, sometimes adjacent to the tradesmen's and suppliers' exhibits. Often some distinction would be made between an award, a citation, a mention, or a "special mention" for the various projects: parks, playgrounds, multifamily housing, residential subdivisions, campus plans, highway landscape designs, private gardens, and the grounds of automobile showrooms, shopping centers, and sports centers. On the back pages of the magazine Clay would duly record the results of these professional-awards programs. But images of the award-winning projects were infrequent, descriptions were rare, and critical analysis was nonexistent. "There was an awful lot of rather small-scale stuff," he recalled recently.[23] And so he gave major coverage to the ASLA awards program only when, in his view, the totality of award-winning projects was of sufficient sophistication and interest for the larger reading public that he was determined to cultivate.

Clay's first appearance on the masthead in January 1958 was accompanied by the first appearance in *Landscape Architecture* of his old friend, Ian McHarg. "The Humane City: Must the Man of Distinction Always Move to the Suburbs?" was a substantial piece that might be over-looked in some future anthology of McHarg's shorter works—for it is not about ecology, nor does it enumerate many of the environmental values for which McHarg would later become the preeminent spokes-man. The essay is a reflection on art, on civilization, and—briefly—on transcendence. As if in homage to one of McHarg's heroes, Lewis Mumford, it is also a rumination on the roles that artists and designers must assume if the city is to remain truly urbane, humane. While the suburban exodus of jobs, housing, and all but the poorest urban dwellers was under way, McHarg urged that the city must once again represent "the best in our epoch" with a place for elegant buildings, plazas, outdoor restaurants, river walks, greenswards, trees, fountains, and other amenities. Of the city he wrote, "No other artifact is so persistent a testament to our culture."[24]

Thus far in the article McHarg was proving himself a competent student of Mumford and of urban culture generally. But then he went further. In wondering what might constitute a salubrious and humane environment, McHarg saw the need to search for some "objective bases" for the actions of a designer (whose role he compared to that of a medical doctor). He imagined that some answers to the most challenging tasks facing any physical designer would lie in biology, in medicine, in art. Architecture, planning, and landscape architecture would have to develop "within the twin lines of science and objectivity, art and intuition." Here, McHarg, chairman of the Department of Landscape Architecture at the University of Pennsylvania, outlined what a landscape architect should know and be: "Conscious of the importance of open space, its evocative quality, and its possibilities for a philosophical expression, and capable of producing designs which are meaningful, the landscape architect must know the disciplines of his materials, the techniques which are his tools; but overwhelmingly he must be an artist capable of expressing the essence of nature in art and, in so doing, of making the city humane."

Without shaking the foundations of an essentially conservative interpretation of landscape architecture—that is, as an art and a craft in the service of human needs and aspirations—McHarg was now beginning to lay out his own theoretical grounds for a combination of teaching and practice that would profoundly influence the course of his profession's development. All the components of his future contribution to the field were not yet identified, but in the next few years in *Landscape Architecture* and elsewhere he would make many of them explicit: the importance of ecological studies in regional land planning, the modeling of the patterns of uncontrolled growth, "physiographic determinism," and other hallmarks of his teaching and practice.

In 1964 McHarg outlined a new curriculum in his department, "regional land planning," for which students would be recruited from such natural sciences as ecology, biology, geology, and forestry as well as from civil engineering and landscape architecture (and from architecture, he could have added). In time, the Department of Landscape Architecture would itself be renamed the Department of Landscape Architecture and Regional Planning. Here, McHarg was attempting to move his profession from its present obscurity to a role of "influence and consequence." The roles he envisioned for at least some landscape architects were "spokesman for the natural science parameter in the planning process" and "the professional conscience of society" for interventions in the landscape. In retrospect this article represented a passing moment of balance, during which McHarg could calmly observe, "It should be maintained as a matter of principle that a landscape architect is as good a horticulturist as he is an ecologist and an artist." Such balance would be rare in the polarized academic halls and public arenas of the near future. But for the moment—in 1964—McHarg could confidently predict that "regional land planning offers the possibility of assuming professional leadership for the conservation movement."[25] This would be a role of consequence.

And yet this prediction did not exceed the goals set by an ASLA committee that had been appointed in 1961 to make a report on the profession of landscape architecture. In 1963 this committee, consisting of Douglas Baylis, William G. Carnes, William J. Johnson, Campbell E. Miller, Theodore Osmundson, Jr., Hideo Sasaki, and Sidney N. Shurcliff with John O. Simonds serving as chair, proposed that the landscape architect should rightfully assume the "stewardship of the landscape." Given the nature of the large, complex problems that were emerging, environmental study on even a modest scale would require a team approach. The realities of the times now demanded economic analyses, feasibility studies, and compliance with new government guidelines, standards, and regulations. In what the committee viewed as the "socialized democracy" of the United States, or "the era of big government," the historic trend toward a public, rather than a private, clientele continued. The City Beautiful movement had returned, "with a more sound approach," under the name of urban design. And there were other changes, technological and social. Still, this committee did not propose any radical shifts in the field: "We believe that landscape architecture should continue as the art and science of creating out-of-doors spaces and places for the use and enjoyment of man."[26] Except for the explicit linking of art and science this statement could have been crafted by Charles Eliot.

In the mid-1950s through the early 1960s, *Landscape Architecture* continued to feature forward-looking articles. Sasaki's important essay on urban renewal and landscape architecture—in which social and economic concerns are intimately related to aesthetic and cultural values—appeared in January 1955. The July 1957 issue included an article by Benjamin W. Gary, Jr., a student of Sasaki's at Harvard, on "Life Processes and Aesthetic Appearance: Ecology a Factor in Creating an Environment for Man." Karl Linn's article, "Ecology of Cities: Are We Making Space for Consumers Only?" appeared in the Fall 1960 issue. In "The Shape of Erosion," published in January 1962, Halprin suggested a merging of scientific understanding and artistic vision; he

encouraged the landscape architect to study the processes of nature in order to "tap the true source of form."

Two highly influential projects were featured in 1964. William J. Johnson, a former student of Sasaki's, explained a series of plans, diagrams, and drawings with which Johnson, Johnson and Roy had established the framework for "continuous growth" on the Ann Arbor campus of the University of Michigan. And in "Quality Corridors for Wisconsin" Philip H. Lewis, Jr., underscored the importance of the team—the soil scientists, wildlife experts, architectural historians, botanists, ecologists, and landscape architects who contributed to the statewide planning process for recreational resources. As landscape architectural consultant to Wisconsin's Department of Resource Development, Lewis was reporting on work in progress—a multiphase planning effort that involved creating inventories, mapping, identifying both natural and cultural values, and understanding the political process on different levels, from grassroots activism to state legislation.[27]

These articles and projects, together with reviews of important books, piquant editorials by Grady Clay, and letters to the editor from William H. Whyte, Jr., Louis Kahn, Bruno Zevi, and others outside the field of landscape architecture, indicate that both the profession and its official magazine were trying to establish wider connections and sounder foundations on which to make important decisions about the use of land and other resources. While there were some notes of discord and dismay, overall there was a remarkable harmony among the distinctive voices that Clay was gathering together in the late 1950s and early 1960s. These were hopeful years. The profession was expanding its boundaries while its members were engaged in research into new areas of social and natural sciences. People had high hopes for the collaborative process at a time when no leading landscape architect was questioning the artistic aspirations of the profession.

In 1964–1965 the ASLA observed the centennial year of landscape architecture. With assistance from the ASLA and its Boston chapter, from the historian Albert Fein (then a professor at Long Island University), and from the office of Sasaki, Dawson, DeMay Associates in Watertown, Massachusetts, a group of landscape architecture students and faculty at Harvard's Graduate School of Design assembled a seventy-panel exhibition on the legacy of Frederick Law Olmsted, Sr. Sponsored by the ASLA as a permanent traveling exhibition, it was featured at two ASLA annual meetings: in 1964 in Dallas and in 1965 in Hartford, Connecticut—Olmsted's birthplace—then traveled for four years throughout North America.

Professor Fein's centennial address on Olmsted, first presented in Dallas at the 1964 meeting, was published in an eight-page spread in *Landscape Architecture* along with images from the Harvard students' exhibition. And whereas the students had emphasized the broad areas of Olmsted's extensive practice—urban parks, urban design, community planning, country residences, and campus design—Fein stressed Olmsted's belief in democratic processes, his social conscience, his efforts to reconcile public and private interests, and the links between democratic purposes and physical design. In what must have been thundering tones (unforgettable for anyone who ever heard the late Albert Fein speak in public), Fein ended with the reminder that Olmsted did not complete his work in his lifetime; the challenges he had faced were still compelling for professionals of the present day.[28]

And so the 1964 annual meeting of the ASLA was energized by the works of Olmsted, the words of Professor Fein, and other uplifting exhortations. But there was one speaker who raised some of the gravest challenges then facing landscape architects. Speculation, standardization, and segregation were still pervasive, even in the face of sporadic and growing opposition. Rather than segregating people and land uses into "neat compartments," Garrett Eckbo called for more interaction and integration, fewer codes, and more fresh, creative solutions to unique problems. Acknowledging as well the challenges from architects and sculptors, he urged his colleagues to stop diverting their energies into "little arguments" on in-group affairs and to "revive the profession's interest in the larger society."[29] Deemed the most articulate of the "Western revolutionaries," Eckbo, then in his early fifties, spoke from a wide experience of practice, teaching, and writing. Immediately excerpts of his speech were published in *Landscape Architecture*. Soon afterward appeared his revealing essay, "Creative Design of the Landscape" (1965).

This essay forms a good counterpart to the exhibition of Olmsted's pioneering career, for Eckbo was looking critically at the present and the future. As if he were taking stock of his own successful career, he mulled over the idea that the quality of landscape design might be shortchanged, or rendered less creative and effective, by the very success of a large office, its growth, its diversification, its division of tasks, and its emphasis on the big picture. "How does the modest, patient, open-minded search for form relate to the pressures and demands of competition, promotion, and survival in our status-ridden economic jungle?" he wondered. Could one express the imaginative order of man without destroying the wild, free beauty of nature? Would continuously beautiful landscapes be able to provide a comfortable home for the "great game of speculation in land and building, other-wise known as the pursuit of the honest buck?"[30]

Eckbo was fond of philosophical musing mingled with quick jabs of reality—brutally honest, defying complacency. "Design can be efficient. . . . But nothing could be more inefficient than our standard efficient haste which bypasses the design process and is creating the ugliest man-made environment in world history," he wrote in an essay that had begun by methodically cataloging the major roles and con-cerns of landscape architects. Then, as if thinking on his feet during a lecture, the future chairman of the landscape architecture department at the University of California in Berkeley paused to elaborate on the seductions and pitfalls of allowing an office practice to grow, taking on more work, more partners, more associates, more bureaucracy. "When does such expansion divorce [the professional] more or less completely from the design process and leave him as primarily organizer, promoter, administrator, director, critic, and contact man?" Eckbo asked. "It is not enough to think big and make large gestures. We must also remain human and think small," he wrote, thinking of ordinary citizens and the significant patterns of their lives.[31]

This elaboration finally reached a climax—a crossroads. Eckbo saw two basic directions in a landscape architect's career: either toward focusing personally on a limited number of carefully selected projects or toward unlimited expansion of an office. In fact, if they had not already faced this crossroads, many of his colleagues would soon do so as opportunities arose in the late 1960s and then subsided in the mid-1970s. Meanwhile, Eckbo identified several factors in the design process—artistic, social, economic, and environmental—that would be less confidently balanced during the stressful years that followed. His final words were not so much a call to action as a plea for deeper reflection: "The crying need in our urbanizing environ-ment is precisely for more careful and balanced relations between elements which retain the quality of nature and those which are wholly changed by human processing; between geometry and biology, organization and free growth; moving toward human living patterns which are as well adjusted and easily balanced as those in the nature from which they came long ago."

"In time, no doubt, we too shall evolve a new way of gardening to suit our new way

of building, and if any of our creations survive into the twenty-first century, then

our descendants can amuse themselves too in interpreting the character of our age."

Nan Fairbrother (1963)

ALCOA FORECAST GARDEN

Wonderland Park Development, Laurel Canyon, Los Angeles, California

Eckbo, Royston and Williams

Landscape Architects

For The Aluminum Company of America

from 1957

Photograph by Julius Shulman, 1959

"The owner who is to use and pay for the garden must be heard. Any tendency to design for design's sake, to create a pattern within which the owner must live according to rules set by the designer, is headed for frustration, if not disaster."

THOMAS CHURCH (1955)

DEWEY DONNELL GARDEN

SONOMA COUNTY, CALIFORNIA

THOMAS D. CHURCH AND ASSOCIATES

LANDSCAPE ARCHITECTS, FROM 1948

PHOTOGRAPH BY SAXON HOLT, 1992

1992 ASLA CLASSIC AWARD

"Who loves a garden still his Eden keeps,

Perennial pleasures plants, and wholesome harvest reaps."

AMOS BRONSON ALCOTT (1868)

KAISER CENTER ROOF GARDEN

OAKLAND, CALIFORNIA

OSMUNDSON & STALEY

LANDSCAPE ARCHITECTS, EARLY 1960S

THEODORE OSMUNDSON, JR.

PARTNER IN CHARGE

PHOTOGRAPH BY THEODORE OSMUNDSON

148

"This hilltop with its boldly massed, broadly roofed buildings is in the true sense an Acropolis: a high place consecrated to the highest values of its young community. . . . The land has been treated with tact and restraint. Not only have the natural outlines of the hill and outcroppings of rock been conserved, but the hill itself has been made a pedestrian's world inviolate to the automobile."

ALLAN TEMKO (1962)

FOOTHILL COLLEGE

LOS ALTOS HILLS, CALIFORNIA

SASAKI WALKER ASSOCIATES

LANDSCAPE ARCHITECTS

FROM THE LATE 1950S

PHOTOGRAPH BY GERRY CAMPBELL. COURTESY OF THE SWA GROUP

1972 ASLA MERIT AWARD, 1993 ASLA CLASSIC AWARD

"The total environment is the real problem and, in a sense, the new frontier of architecture. . . . Any architecture must hold its head high. But a way must be found for uniting the whole, because the total environment is more important than the single building."

EERO SAARINEN (1959)

DEERE & COMPANY ADMINISTRATIVE CENTER

MOLINE, ILLINOIS, FROM 1961

SASAKI ASSOCIATES

LANDSCAPE ARCHITECTS

EERO SAARINEN & ASSOCIATES, ARCHITECTS

PHOTOGRAPH COURTESY OF SASAKI ASSOCIATES

1981 ASLA HONOR AWARD, 1991 ASLA CLASSIC AWARD

"With the need for information, direction, and action so pressing in the rapid expansion which institutions are experiencing . . . many colleges and universities are turning to the planning process as a device for effectively reaching all members of the academic community and bringing their dreams, ideas, thoughts, ambitions—even complaints—to bear on the problems of design."

RICHARD P. DOBER (1960)

UNIVERSITY OF MICHIGAN

ANN ARBOR CAMPUS PLANNING STUDIES

JOHNSON, JOHNSON AND ROY

LANDSCAPE ARCHITECTS, EARLY 1960S

DRAWINGS BY AND COURTESY OF WILLIAM J. JOHNSON

154

"It might have been possible in 1960 to initiate a visionary departure from the existing pattern—a single-structure campus or a plug-in system that might have accommodated 20,000 students more efficiently. Instead, the design consultants saw and grasped a greater opportunity, to create a harmonious environment and a visible continuity with the past."

JOHN MORRIS DIXON (1963)

THE UNIVERSITY OF COLORADO

BOULDER

SASAKI ASSOCIATES

LANDSCAPE ARCHITECTS

MASTER PLAN, 1960–1970

COURTESY OF SASAKI ASSOCIATES

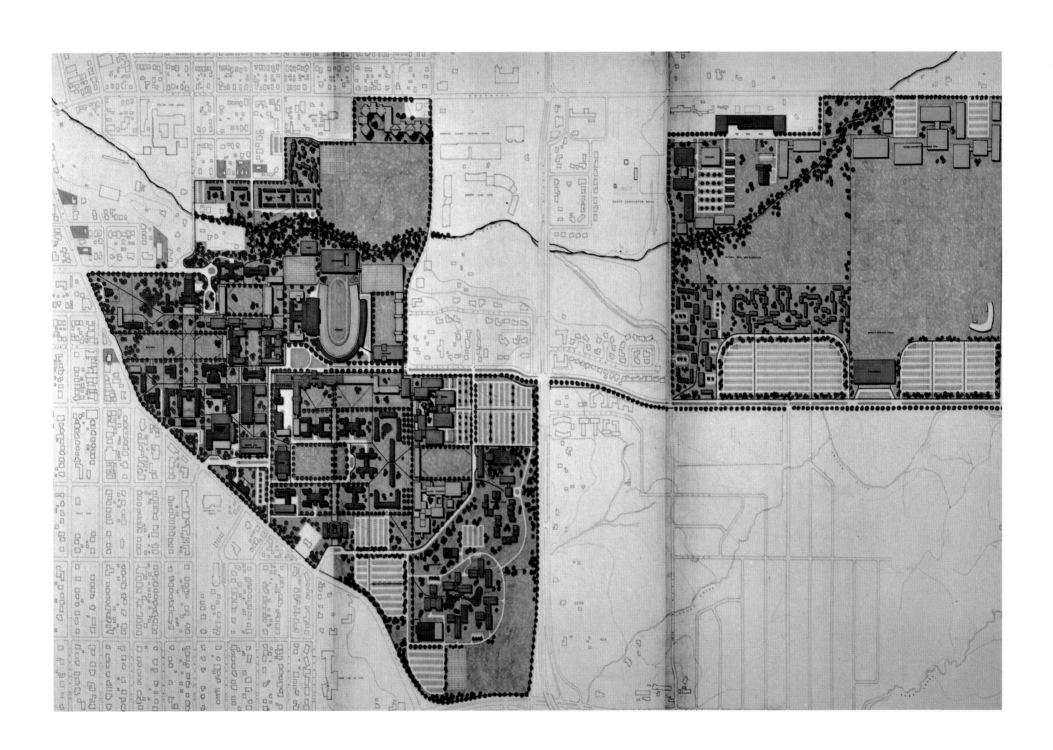

157

"Passersby are users of Paley [Park], too. About half will turn and look in. Of these, about half will smile.

I haven't calculated a smile index, but this vicarious, secondary enjoyment is extremely important—

the sight of the park, the knowledge that it is there, becomes part of the image we have of a much wider area."

WILLIAM H. WHYTE (1980)

PALEY PARK

NEW YORK, NEW YORK

ZION & BREEN, LANDSCAPE ARCHITECTS

ABOUT 1965

PHOTOGRAPH BY ALAN WARD

158

CHAPTER 4

DIVISIONS AND DEBATES WITHIN AN EXPANDING PROFESSION

1966 – 1974

Just a casual mention of those years, the late 1960s and early 1970s, may recall a tangle of feelings, alternating from yearning to despair, from elation to disgust, from anger to delight and hard-earned satisfaction. It was a time of imbalance, extremes. While the United States was engaged in an undeclared war in Southeast Asia, there was also an openly declared war on the polluters and despoilers of the planet's natural resources—a war more commonly known as the "environmental movement." Some landscape architects, thinking of "adventure playgrounds" for children and benches with proper backs for all human beings, proposed new criteria for design and grew wary of "elitism," whatever its manifestations. There was a growing consciousness that women and people from racial and ethnic minorities should be brought into the processes of planning and design. Dividing lines were drawn, and some confrontations on campuses and in public hearings passed beyond the limits of polite, urbane exchanges of opinion. To recapture the sense of this turbulent period and its impact on the profession of landscape architecture, we cannot simply skim over the photographs of much-admired plazas and playgrounds, shopping centers and subdivisions, corporate villas and college campuses, all designed with great care and later acknowledged by a framed award on an office wall. Not for a while would the ASLA's professional awards begin to reflect landscape architects' finest (and sometimes controversial) work in design and their new areas of research, analysis, and planning. Rather, there was a time-lag of several years during which the passions and "cutting edge" explorations of students, their professors, and their elders in practice were expressed in venues other than the professional awards program. The story of these years will be told, then, as two overlapping stories: one, official, formal, and collective,

HAWK'S NEST STATE PARK, WEST VIRGINIA

THE ARCHITECTS COLLABORATIVE, LAURENCE W. ZUELKE WITH V. MICHAEL WEINMAYR LANDSCAPE ARCHITECTS

PHOTOGRAPH COURTESY OF LAURENCE ZUELKE

largely shaped by the internal affairs of the ASLA; and the other, idiosyncratic and personal, responding more to external events and pressures and often running against the grain of an established profession or of the larger society.

Grady Clay preferred the second kind of story. Looking for good, unflinching critical evaluations from both the experts and well-informed laymen, he filled the pages of *Landscape Architecture* with articles that might stir his readers to action. The environment needed tough, critical review, he explained. "Our capacity permanently to alter its form and quality," he wrote in 1968, "from napalming Viet Nam to watering California, from damning [sic] Grand Canyon to cloud-seeding New England, is staggering. To look back at what we did is essential; to review is vital; and to do so with accuracy and mature judgment is the obligation of us all."[1]

This and other editorials, along with articles on site-specific sculpture, ecology, land reclamation, playgrounds, and pending legislation in Congress drew responses in the late 1960s and early 1970s, not only from landscape architects but also from architects, historians, the director of Legal Services at the Rocky Mountain Center on Environment in Denver, the director of the Massachusetts Horticultural Society in Boston, two senior associates at the Conservation Foundation in Washington, D.C., an industrial designer in New York, and even a gentleman from the Eastern Pennsylvania Psychiatric Institute (whose standing at the institute remained unclear). The letters to the editor of *Landscape Architecture* were not uniformly congratulatory; many were motivated by some strong feelings about the larger world, something to be fought or changed. Given the times, we expect occasional outbursts, especially from the younger members of the professions. But even more striking were the outbursts from the elder statesmen.

The distinguished landscape architect from Beverly Hills, Edward Huntsman-Trout (known for his fine early-twentieth-century campus design at Scripps College in Claremont, California) was put off by the proliferation of federal bureaus, the domination by "Big Business," and the massive control held by the "Fast Buck." The year was 1968, and he was acutely aware of contrasting environments. "I have just returned from a visit with a son of old friends who is planting grape vines and building a winery on a mountainside in Napa County, the California wine country," he reported. "Nearby is Saint Helena, a village where people are still people. Their air is like wine. The oaks are bursting into leaf, the fields and orchards are abloom, the red-tailed hawk soars overhead, and the skylarks sing from the fence posts. And I return to unbridled suburbanization which is dominated by an architecture of inhumanism, a decaying city that really never was, the murderous bustle of all highways, free or not, and the dirty poisonous pall that blankets the entire basin. It is no relief to know that the San Francisco Bay area and the Eastern Corridor are almost as bad or worse. Perhaps we shall all be marching down to the open sea with the lemmings."[2]

It was not a time for complacency. Now, backing up a few years, we retrace the steps taken to ensure that the ASLA professional awards would reflect the best of the profession. For before the end of this period—by 1974—the most stimulating work and thought emerging in landscape architecture *were* fairly well represented in the awards, even as new quests and debates continued to surface.

When the ASLA held its annual meeting at Yosemite National Park in May 1966 its theme was the upbeat "New Missions for '66." The director of the National Park Service gave a speech, and panels were held on open space, urban landscapes, and regional land use and landscape preservation—past, present, and future. A century had passed since 1864, when President Lincoln signed a bill withdrawing the magnificent Yosemite Valley from the public lands and ceding it to California expressly for public use and recreation. (Yosemite became a national park only in 1905.) In the afterglow of the recent Olmsted exhibition, someone may have mentioned the report written in 1865 by Yosemite Park Commissioner Frederick Law Olmsted. There, for the first time, Olmsted articulated the philosophical basis for establishing state and national parks.[3] However inspiring the backward glances may have been, surely the landscape architects who gathered together that summer of 1966 could gaze upon some of the most sublime landscapes the country had to offer—from gaunt Half Dome to the misty green meadows below—while they spoke of planning and design at the large scale.[4] At that 1966 ASLA meeting, the program

included exhibits and an "awards luncheon." But no professional awards were reported in *Landscape Architecture* that year. Then in 1967 eight professional awards were listed in the magazine—in fine print. Eventually a few of the award-winning projects were published, including Michael Hough's campus planning for Scarborough College in Toronto and the development of Hawks Nest State Park in West Virginia, by TAC (with landscape architect Laurence Zuelke).[5] But as a body of work the 1967 award-winning projects could not command much attention. Individually they varied in scale from a private garden to the transportation corridors of Minneapolis.

Without denying the individual merits of these projects, the ASLA awards jury was disappointed by the totality of entries in 1967. Joseph Perrin, dean of the school of art at Georgia State College in Atlanta, wondered if the competition had been poorly promoted—or was there some apathy among the firms and the schools? "In most cases," he observed, "the entries are not imaginatively presented, articulately explained, or esthetically or compellingly cast, visually and/or verbally." Atlanta landscape architect John A. Patton felt the entries did not represent what was being done, generally, in North America. And Atlanta architect Joseph Amisano pointed out that important work of landscape architects in the fields of high-density housing and civic design was not represented. Both the selection and the presentation of the work, he felt, were not of "real professional quality."[6]

This situation would soon change. From 1970 through 1974 the ASLA published the annual award-winning projects in separate brochures, then gathered the material together in an illustrated book to show "the scope and direction of the best landscape architectural projects during the last five years."[7] In 1971 Grady Clay began to feature the annual professional awards prominently in *Landscape Architecture*. And in 1976, when the magazine was expanded to a bimonthly, the annual awards began to absorb one issue a year. What prompted these changes? Apparently landscape architects were beginning to look upon the awards program with more interest, perhaps as something useful for their own purposes. Younger, less established landscape architects in particular could hope for some valuable exposure from an award-winning project. In fact, younger professionals did become a force in the late 1970s and early 1980s, by virtue of their numbers, their energies and passions, and their award-winning contributions to the field. But in the late 1960s younger landscape architects were less visible, in part because there were only a few accredited schools that could have trained them. (In the United States, there were only eighteen such schools in 1968, but that number rose to twenty-eight schools by 1972.)[8]

Stepping down as ASLA president in 1969, Theodore Osmundson still yearned to make his profession a force in the larger society. From 1967 through 1969, he noted in his final report, the ASLA had not grown appreciably, and the society's finances were limited. Neverthe-

less, he and his colleagues had spent the past two years reorganizing the ASLA, upgrading its publications, and making other changes that were urgently needed. "In a country racked by protest and riot, racial inequality, inflation, burdensome taxes for military rather than needed domestic programs, a debilitating and futile foreign war, urban congestion, and an economic system characterized by almost unlimited privilege to use privately owned land and resources for profit regardless of its degradation and ultimate waste, this profession has been silent, irrelevant, and unnoticed," he declared. Following the White House Conference on Natural Beauty in May 1965, environmental degradation had become a more potent political issue on both national and local levels. But where were the leaders? "We are even unable to fill the overwhelming demand for trained people, to say nothing of providing leadership and answers to these problems," he wrote. Much later in his report Osmundson credited the exceptional contributions of a few landscape architects: urban studies and reports by Lawrence Halprin, Ian McHarg, Philip Lewis, Michael Rapuano, John Simonds, and Marvin Springer; books by McHarg and Garrett Eckbo; and projects in urban ghettos by M. Paul Friedberg. Osmundson's ending was also optimistic, yet the sting of his words—"silent, irrelevant, and unnoticed"—may have disconcerted some in the profession.[9]

A later ASLA president, Raymond L. Freeman, could report in 1972 that the society's membership was growing larger and on average becoming younger. In 1968 sixty-one percent of the ASLA's "constituency" was under forty years of age. In 1972 seventy percent of the ASLA membership was under forty. Urging these younger members to become involved in the society's various committees and programs, Freeman noted new grants for research, funneled through the ASLA's Landscape Architecture Foundation. (Established in 1966, this nonprofit foundation received grants from the Ford Foundation, the National Endowment for the Arts, and the U.S. Department of Housing and Urban Development, as well as other sources.) "We are no longer small and we are no longer weak," Freeman insisted in 1972. "We have the resources and the manpower and the intelligence within our membership to lead this nation to a better understanding and improvement of the environment."[10]

Part of the ASLA's recently augmented resources were to be used for improved public relations—including a revitalized professional awards program. Thirty-five-millimeter slides would soon become the standard format of submissions for awards, in lieu of the more expensively produced panels. Meanwhile, beginning in 1963 but more frequently from 1970 onward, *Landscape Architecture* would contain tipped-in pages from professional brochures, often with large fold-outs printed in at least two colors. In April 1971 an article about the Wissahickon Valley Watershed study by Rahenkamp Sachs Wells featured the first four-color graphics printed as an integral part of the magazine. These innovations helped to disseminate ideas about both the substance and the graphic presentation of technically complex large-scale projects.[11] And as the technical means of communication were refined, so some of the more intriguing projects came to light, both in the professional awards competitions and in the magazine that publicized them.

Economics was also a factor in the revitalized and better publicized awards program. Grady Clay still recalls the lean years of the late 1950s, when *Landscape Architecture* was a drain on the ASLA's finances. Then, in 1960–1961, the ASLA Publication Board determined that the magazine should report, enlighten, lead opinion, and elevate the quality of public discussion; it should therefore focus on broad issues and "present to the widest possible audience the subject of landscape architecture from the professional point of view."[12] Thereafter, the magazine began to expand its scope—and its readership—far beyond the membership of the ASLA. Revenues from subscribers and advertisers expanded, the magazine became profitable, and the graphic quality of the magazine was improved.

Since the mid-1960s, Clay notes, the majority of his subscriptions came from outside the ASLA—that is, from architects, planners, urban designers, conservationists, lawyers, natural scientists, and public officials. Following the 1965 White House Conference on Natural Beauty, at which Clay was chairman of one of the panel discussions, interest in both conservation and the magazine *Landscape Architecture* surged.[13] Even the First Lady, Mrs. Lyndon B. Johnson, wrote to commend Clay for the magazine and thank him "for all you do to inform and alert all of us to our conservation opportunities."[14] By reaching a larger, more diverse and influential audience—most of whom would not be attending ASLA annual meetings—the magazine further enhanced the value of any award it covered. In 1974, when ASLA membership had reached 4,360, it represented only about a third of the magazine's readership—which reached 12,000 by the end of 1974.[15]

The human factor was also critical to the awards program. Grady Clay credits the late Campbell Miller, president of the ASLA from 1969 to 1971, for his determination to make both the profession of landscape architecture and its official magazine "count for something." "We believe the professional awards exhibit is a most valuable part of our public relations program in bringing executed works of landscape architecture before the attention of the general public," Miller declared in 1971.[16] Accordingly, the 1970 awards exhibit was displayed at the U.S. Department of the Interior and at several universities throughout the country. At the same time, Miller fully supported the enhanced coverage of these awards in *Landscape Architecture* magazine.

And so a symbiosis of economic, political, technological, and human factors—the ASLA's new sources of funding, the expanding scope and "relevance" of the profession, the enlarged coverage of topics considered vital to an expanding readership, the more sophisticated techniques of publication, and the personal commitment of a few individuals—all tended to heighten interest in the revitalized awards program. But these factors fall short of explaining exactly why an awards program that could not attract many of the finest talents in 1967 began to do so in the early 1970s. There were other reasons for a change in the attitudes of a somewhat heterogeneous group of professionals—who were becoming increasingly differentiated, with agendas and aspirations of their own. By the end of the 1960s it had became apparent that some small cracks in the ideal harmony of interests among landscape architects were becoming wider and more troubling. A great deal was suddenly at stake, including the potential of a small profession to rise out of obscurity and take the lead.

The late 1960s saw the last of the "low-profile" awards programs—as well as a surge of interest in expanding the range of issues debated at the annual meetings. There was still a discrepancy between the most hotly debated issues and the award-winning projects, but if this indicated a time-lag between cutting-edge ideas and workable projects, that lag was diminishing.

Both in 1968 and in 1969, the lists of awards—unillustrated—occupied less than a quarter of a page each in *Landscape Architecture*. As in the past a few award-winning projects were published as separate articles: in 1968, for example, a park, some urban renewal greenways, and a townhouse project by Collins, Dutot and Associates of Philadelphia; a portion of a campus by the San Francisco firm of John Carl Warnecke and Associates with Michael Painter as landscape architect; a rural park for preschool children by Richard Haag Associates of Seattle; and street furniture and urban playgrounds by M. Paul Friedberg and Associates of New York.[17]

These awards were handed out in June 1968 at Niagara Falls, Ontario, during a three-day annual meeting focused on changes in the environment. There, leading members of the ASLA sat on panels with sociologists and urban planners, discussing such topics as "Space, Time, and Population" (Garrett Eckbo, presiding) and interdisciplinary environmental research programs (Philip H. Lewis, Jr., presiding). What attracted the most coverage in *Landscape Architecture*, however, was Karl Linn's account of his own work in inner-city neighborhoods. This work, he believed, outlined a "totally new direction" for landscape architecture in the United States.[18]

At that 1968 meeting Linn laid out the framework for much of the progressive, socially-focused work of landscape architects that followed. He was among the first to use (if not to introduce) the notions of "advocacy planning" and "advocacy design" along with the intertwined concepts of an "ecological esthetic," a "participatory esthetic," and "open-ended design." These were distillations of his many years of working in the inner cities of Philadelphia, New York, Washington, D.C., Baltimore, and elsewhere, joining his professional skills with the energies and talents of teenagers from the African-

American community, Peace Corps candidates, school drop-outs, and others who were usually left out of the planning and design process. Linn faulted the traditional "school" of architecture and landscape architecture for its "isolated and segregated esthetic, which is separated from the living community and forces of the environment." He challenged landscape architects to conduct "armies of builders" and to orchestrate many energies and talents, thus reviving an old practice—barn-raising—to set up the framework of community.[19] But this sort of grassroots effort would not be submitted for an ASLA award for many years to come.

"Land, People and Plants" was the theme of the 1969 ASLA annual meeting. Billed as a conference, it attracted such prominent figures as Barry Commoner, (whose *Science and Survival* had recently appeared in paperback); David Brower, then director of the Sierra Club; Gaylord Nelson, a U. S. Senator from Wisconsin who was interested in environmental issues; and Charles O. Eames, the brilliant designer.[20] Apparently no public record of the speeches and debates has survived. Given the theme and the range of speakers, we assume that someone was hoping to sustain the delicate balance of humanities, social sciences, and natural sciences on which landscape architecture had long been based. By then this balance was precarious.

Ian McHarg's highly personal and passionate, yet also methodical and rational book, *Design with Nature*, appeared in 1969, a year of milestones and turning points when some students were shutting down universities over a tangle of grievances related to the war in Southeast Asia. Those students who took the time to read this book carefully (and many soon did) found lengthy case studies detailing selected regional planning projects by McHarg's firm interspersed with fragments of McHarg's own life story. They also found attacks on conventional wisdom, such as the notion that buildings, books, institutions, and laws are among the most enduring things on earth. As a naturalist McHarg found this notion "incredible" and fairly myopic. "Save for the atoms themselves, it is life that has longest endured—while continents rise and fall and towering mountain ranges emerge only to erode into inconsequence. . . . It is life that endures, not artifacts. . . . Certainly we can dispose of the old canard, 'form follows function.' Form follows nothing—it is integral with all processes." These were among the thoughts that McHarg later admitted were pieced together like a quilt, with a few imperfect seams, and yet they constituted "one piece of cloth."[21] An enigma? Or perhaps the poetic license of a landscape architect who was committed to turning out superbly trained "spokesmen for the natural science parameter in the planning process."

Also in 1969 Congress passed the National Environmental Policy Act, which President Nixon signed into law on January 1, 1970, initiating a whole new area of environmental planning with mandated environmental impact reports. Initially understood to apply only to projects undertaken by the federal government, this act even-

tually covered a great range of planning and development work, while it stimulated some states, including California, to enact even stricter environmental legislation for projects within their own borders.

Within the profession, 1969 saw the beginning of one of those prickly controversies that developed over articles in *Landscape Architecture*. In "Ecological Basis for Planning a New Campus" Neil Porterfield set out to explain how the new 600-acre campus for the University of Wisconsin in Kenosha would become an ecological laboratory. Although the site was not virgin land and much of the vegetation was not native, a series of ecological factors had been analyzed, overlays were drawn up, the ratios of distribution of native plants in the area had been determined, and a plan had been developed, all in the interest of simulating nature's own processes. Thus, maintenance would be reduced, and the designers would build on existing conditions, "rather than imposing a predetermined 'design' upon the landscape."[22] In response, Garrett Eckbo wondered if the design process was being "rationalized out" in favor of "ecological determinism." Was there any hope left for man to experience landscapes directly, naively, visually, like a child? Eckbo wondered. Then he made his case for maintaining a designer's range of choice against "analysis paralysis" and for seeking a happy marriage between reality and fantasy.[23]

Porterfield's countering response in 1970 contained his personalized history of landscape architecture since World War II along with arguments for an ecological approach to design. A graduate of Pennsylvania State University in 1958, then a student of McHarg's and Linn's at the University of Pennsylvania, Porterfield had absorbed their environmental and social views along with a rational, matter-of-fact approach to solving problems. "I did not come to love ecology or consider it religion or poetry," he explained. "Ecology was, and still is, a branch of science dealing with the interrelationships of organisms and their environments. That is all it is."

Porterfield went on to summarize a personal view that, in retrospect, seems representative of an era and a generation: "Ecological determinism does limit the designers' choices: It tends to eliminate the less rational choices; it tends to minimize fantasy and maximize reality; it adds credibility in the historic sense. There remains now, and there always should be, some room for a designer to introduce a bit of fantasy in his work. However, I have grown up in a world in which many of the fantasies of the past have contributed to the environmental nightmares of today. The cities of today are basically a collection of designers' fantasies. If the ecological realities had been known and understood seventy-five or one hundred years ago, we landscape architects might still be privileged today to limit our concern to backyard design, gardens, shopping malls, etc. This is not the case, however." In the end, Porterfield preferred to risk "analysis paralysis" rather than succumb to "fantasy fatigue."[24]

In one more round, published in October 1970, Eckbo complimented Porterfield and acknowledged the contributions of McHarg and Linn before presenting arguments for a concept he had been mulling over for several years—the designer as "anonymous transformer." The prospects for such a designer, he admitted, were still not very good. "In a competitive commercial society," Eckbo noted, "anonymity is suicide. Hence the need for stylized things which are identifiable and photogenic." But in an ideal world, perhaps less competitive and profit-driven, Eckbo could conceive of a designer who would connect the "general cultural resources" with specific problems and bring together environmental understanding, imagination, and creativity. Ideally the designer could afford to be anonymous and perhaps unite ecology with fantasy. "If that be heresy," he concluded, "make the most of it."[25]

By 1970, then, in different venues and moods three major concerns of the landscape architect—imaginative design, social responsibility, and ecological relationships—had been identified and championed. The links among them were obvious to some educators and professionals, yet one concern was often played against another to the extent that some felt the need to take sides—often polarizing different views in the process. Some components of a generalist's practice—planning and design, science and art, art and social purpose, research, analysis, and design synthesis—were pursued along paths that would eventually diverge. But there remained another component in the shadowy, futuristic realm where sociology, psychology, and politics meet ecology and technology.

Donald Appleyard, the architect/planner who succeeded Eckbo as chairman of the Department of Landscape Architecture at the University of California, Berkeley, in 1969, consciously looked beyond polarized interests toward some common ground. Formerly a colleague of Kevin Lynch's at MIT, he came to Berkeley with wide interests in engineering, psychology, signs, symbolism, and the vernacular landscape. One of his quests was to evaluate projects systematically on ecological, social, and economic grounds. In the vein of such educators as Carl Steinitz at Harvard (a former student of Lynch's), Appleyard was intrigued by new technological means of aiding the evaluation process. While Steinitz was engaged in pioneering work on computer modeling programs to devise "defensible processes of design," Appleyard became involved in similar efforts at Berkeley's "environmental simulation" laboratory, where he could simulate the visual experiences of walking or driving through a present or future environment.[26]

In time, the technologically sophisticated devices used by Appleyard, Steinitz, McHarg, Philip Lewis in Wisconsin, and Donald Belcher at Cornell would become familiar in many schools and departments of landscape architecture and planning. The computer would supersede the old handcrafted acetate overlays used to map the natural resources of a site or a region. Meanwhile, Appleyard appraised the future of environmental design: Three revolutions, "the social, the natural and the methodological will transform the profession over the coming years. They will be the focus of a great deal of emotional discussion, since the established professionals who have mastered the traditional array of skills will find it difficult to see the importance of a whole new set, while the young will eagerly master the new competencies as part of their rebellion against the older generation. Tolerance on both sides will be needed for a creative evolution of the profession" (1970). And, later: "We do not really need to waste our energies . . . debating whether landscape planning or landscape design is more important. . . . They are different professional paths, but both can be equally creative, both should involve design in the broadest sense of the word, and both should be equally concerned with the quality of the environment" (1971).[27]

Appleyard was clearly looking for reconciliation among professionals, even as the larger society was troubled by division, polarization, and fragmentation. The two exceedingly trying years between the spring of 1968 and the spring of 1970, for example, were marked by hostilities in Vietnam, campus unrest, and the assassination of the Reverend Dr. Martin Luther King, Jr., at the one end and at the other, by Earth Day celebrations and the deaths on the campuses of Kent State University and Jackson State College. These were among the defining moments for the nation as a whole.

And what was happening in landscape architecture? In May 1968 a group of students at California State Polytechnic College in Pomona were frustrated when the members of the ASLA's local chapter showed little interest in their presentation, "A Systems Approach to Environmental Analysis and Evaluation." (It was said that the members either lived too far away or didn't have time.)[28] In March 1969 when the ASLA held a Washington Workshop on Urban Open Space with support from the U.S. Department of Housing and Urban Development (HUD), grassroots activists sat down with bureaucrats and professionals. The upshot was a call for more workshops nationwide; demands of academic credit for community service in order to help bring African-Americans into the profession; and demands that the ASLA offer membership to grassroots activists—with or without professional credentials.[29] In April 1970 Denis R. Wilkinson, associate professor at the University of Wisconsin, Madison, urged his colleagues to communicate better with students. Wilkinson saw three dangerous rifts forming: between the "Old Guard pros" and the "New-blood upstarts," between traditional professional education and "what the schools feel the profession should be getting," and between schools and the students—who wanted learning to be "meaningful."[30]

These isolated instances of tensions that landscape architects were experiencing at the end of the 1960s were part of the "profession in confusion" that Norman Newton would later describe in 1974.[31] In this uncertain, often polemical atmosphere the ASLA's professional-awards program could offer a validation of methodologies or strategies, a measure of achievement and significance, or some exposure for more experimental, untested ideas. It might also attract those professionals who had long ago looked elsewhere for recognition. Through-

out this century garden designers could turn to a wide range of publications and competitions to showcase their work. Fletcher Steele remained one of the most articulate and prolific, writing for both *Landscape Architecture* and the popular garden and shelter magazines. Beginning with Thomas Church, however, leading American garden designers and landscape architects of the mid-century gained greater coverage and perhaps even more useful recognition outside their own professional venues. In the late 1920s Church began writing for *California Arts and Architecture* and soon joined its editorial staff. Later he would find good coverage for his work in *Sunset* magazine, and in the late 1930s his garden designs would be exhibited at the San Francisco Museum of Art and the Architectural League of New York. From the late 1930s Garrett Eckbo, Dan Kiley, and James Rose began to be known through publications—first in *Architectural Record* and later in many other publications and exhibitions focused on art, architecture, planning, and environmental design. After the war Hideo Sasaki, A.E. Bye, and Ian McHarg became prominent in architectural and planning circles, often collaborating with award-winning colleagues, and their work was featured in *Progressive Architecture*, *Architectural Forum*, the *AIA Journal*, and elsewhere. Still, it may have been the gregarious loner Lawrence Halprin who commanded the widest recognition in his own right. He was sometimes identified as an architect, but he was also known as an urban designer or "eco-architect." The term "eco-architect" suggests why landscape architects began to take their own professional competitions more seriously in the early 1970s. Gaining momentum, the environmental movement attracted many young people who might otherwise have turned to medicine, or social work, or architecture toward the promising, potentially healing field of landscape architecture. In June 1974 *Progressive Architecture* even devoted a whole issue to landscape and environmental planning, featuring long articles on environmental-impact reports, A. E. Bye's landscape design, and the "strategies and tactics" of Wallace McHarg Roberts & Todd (WMRT).

Today, when we look back on the ASLA awards program in the context of the environmental movement of the early 1970s, it seems as if a dam had burst. Or as if a long silence had been broken. Suddenly firms that had never appeared in the program were winning awards for several projects at a time, for both recent work and older, maturing landscapes. In 1970 a total of thirty-three awards were given, including four honor awards: to Lawrence Halprin & Associates for Ghirardelli Square in San Francisco; to John Carl Warnecke and Associates with Michael Painter as landscape architect for the John F. Kennedy gravesite in Arlington, Virginia; to A. E.Bye & Associates for the Soros residence in Southampton, New York; and to M. Paul Friedberg & Associates for a Bedford Stuyvesant superblock in Brooklyn, New York. In 1971 somewhat fewer awards were given, but the number and variety of entries were reported to be "at an all-time high." Apparently the revitalization of the awards program proposed in 1970 was a success. It attracted a wide range of work that represented "more landscape analysis, more multidisciplinary teamwork, and new interest in inner-city and degraded-environment renewal."[32]

What can be said of the ASLA awards made during the years 1970 through 1974? First, notwithstanding the growing polarization within the field, the jurors acknowledged a wide spectrum of project types, from small single-family residences and tiny urban or suburban sites to planning and analysis projects on a regional scale. Rather than label a project as a "planning" or "design" effort the jurors seem to have agreed with Appleyard—that both planning and design should involve design in the broadest sense of the word. The juries sometimes included an artist (William Tarr, Charles E. Parks, and Tony Smith) and a student (Richard Halsey) as well as architects, arts administrators, educators, and practitioners. A few awards were given to public agencies; most went to firms. Finally, the award-winning firms included individuals, small firms, partnerships, and larger incorporated entities—some multidisciplinary, some based on architecture or planning, some based on landscape architecture.

In the midst of this diversity some trends suggest the influence of a few individuals, schools, and philosophies. First, two of the most prominent firms that had not received an ASLA professional award before 1970 were Sasaki, Dawson, DeMay Associates, Inc. (SDDA) and McHarg's firm, WMRT. Then, from 1970 through 1974, these firms and others that employed students of either Hideo Sasaki or

Ian McHarg became frequent award winners. At Sasaki, Walker Associates, Inc. (SWA) Peter Walker and several of his colleagues were former students of Sasaki's. At Anthony M. Guzzardo & Associates Guzzardo was formerly a student of Sasaki's and a colleague of both Sasaki's and Walker's. At Johnson, Johnson & Roy, Inc. (JJR) William J. Johnson had studied under Sasaki as had Peter Rolland of Peter G. Rolland & Associates, Benjamin Gary of Moriece and Gary, John Frey of Mason and Frey, and Grant Jones of Jones & Jones, who had also studied under Richard Haag, a former student of Sasaki's. Meanwhile, when McHarg's students did not go directly to San Francisco to work for Lawrence Halprin (and some of the best of them did, McHarg recalls), they stayed in Philadelphia to work in McHarg's firm.[33] One student of McHarg's, Neil Porterfield, went to HOK Associates, Inc. Another student, Roger Wells, became a partner in Rahenkamp Sachs Wells. The list could continue, but these firms alone accounted for 43 of the 139 awards given in 1970 through 1974.

It should go without saying that the quantity of awards is ultimately less important than the quality of work done and its impact in cultural, social, and environmental terms. Still, there is significance in the strands of influence on the part of individuals whose teaching and practice established certain standards and imbued in younger people a set of values that many would maintain throughout their professional lives. Apart from Sasaki and McHarg, both of whom taught at renowned graduate schools on the East Coast, we might also consider the influence of such practitioners as Garrett Eckbo and Robert Royston on the undergraduates they taught at the University of California, Berkeley, and at the University of Southern California. The paths of Eckbo and Royston, formerly partners in a three-person firm, diverged in the late 1950s, but their larger firms of Eckbo, Dean, Austin and Williams (later EDAW, Inc.) and Royston, Hanamoto, Beck & Abey won many ASLA professional awards in the early 1970s. We could trace the backgrounds of their younger colleagues as well.

Indeed, what prized qualities did the award-winning projects possess? Some were celebrated for fine design: SDDA's Place Bonaventure in Montreal; SWA's Foothill College in Los Altos, California; Lawrence Halprin & Associates' Auditorium Forecourt in Portland, Oregon. Other projects were better known for their innovative planning processes: WMRT's study of Amelia Island in Florida, Rahenkamp Sachs Wells' study of the Wissahickon Valley Watershed, Jones & Jones' study of the Nooksack River in Washington State. Tentative conclusions about the cultural artifacts produced and the processes employed occasionally appeared in *Landscape Architecture* in the late 1960s and early 1970s. Franklin D. Becker studied the Sacramento Mall. Roger Martin looked at a group of built landscapes in and around Minneapolis. And Clare C. Cooper (later, Cooper Marcus) evaluated playgrounds.[34] But some educators and practitioners were looking for ways to measure qualitative phenomena more precisely.

Striving for standards set by scientific research, they tended to quantify as much as possible. Others remained wary of any attempt to quantify elusive qualities and experiences.

The tendency to quantify may have been unavoidable in one expensive study, undertaken for the ASLA and NCILA (CELA) in 1969 through 1971, to assess the goals and directions of the profession. Professor Albert Fein was director of the study, supported in part by the Ford Foundation and aided by a group of Gallup pollsters and such individual consultants as the planner Edmund Bacon, the ecologist Rene Dubos, the historian James Marston Fitch, and the urbanist William H. Whyte, Jr. Also advising Professor Fein was an ASLA and NCILA (CELA) committee consisting of Theodore Osmundson and Charles W. Harris (cochairmen), Garrett Eckbo, William J. Johnson, Philip Lewis, Ian McHarg, and Edward D. Stone, Jr. First presented in 1971 and later published as a fifteen-page condensation, Fein's report provided a fairly durable baseline for further discussion.[35] Responses were, however, sharply divided.

In this report Fein warned of a growing schism between planners and landscape designers and, in the end, sided with those environmental planners who were working on "massive urban problems" on a "truly comprehensive scale." Newton asserted the traditional and broad aims and scope of landscape architecture and cautioned against a narrow and one-sided (that is, a large-scale and planning-oriented) view of the profession. Eckbo was disturbed by the landscape architect's new wealth of operations research, systems analysis, and computer technology—which allowed the masters of these tools to speak in a language that few could understand. "What they have gained in technology they have lost in vision," he wrote. Ralph Griswold had an "intuitive horror of polls and questionnaires," while Osmundson asserted the long-term value of Fein's report, noting that it was meant to encourage ASLA members to assess their own purposes and directions.[36] These were among the voices that could be heard fairly often in the lively pages of *Landscape Architecture*. But some voices were barely audible—women's voices, for instance. On one occasion in 1968 two women wrote letters to the editor protesting the use of false "towers" to camouflage some oil rigs in the Pacific Ocean near Long Beach, California. Writing independently, both Diane McGuire, ASLA, and Ann Satterthwaite of the Conservation Foundation thought the towers shocking and annoying. (They had been contrived to look like high-rise buildings set among palms.) Let the oil rig stand for what it is, "a reality of industrial society," argued McGuire. But such voices were rarely heard. There were few women in the ASLA. As late as 1973, when the ASLA membership hovered about 4,000, fewer than five percent were women. Nor was there much racial or ethnic diversity in the ASLA. In 1973 ASLA President Raymond Freeman knew of only nine African-American members of the society—of whom he spoke admiringly.[37]

Finally, there was another minority whose numbers may have been declining in academia—the broadly cultivated generalist among landscape architects who was conversant with a wide range of human knowledge lodged in the humanities and the social and natural sciences. One of these generalists, the articulate and unconventional Stanley White, had long been retired from his teaching (and occasional practice) at the University of Illinois. Living in Denver, he would pass away from this earth in 1979, his memory cherished by those whom he had once stirred to action or new thoughts. Equally prepared to explain a mystery of ecology or to point out a good "fit" in site design, White relished the diversity of his profession. Back in the early 1950s he could even put in a good word for tension and debate. "Originally our profession arose as a protest against what the architects, the engineers, and the gardeners were doing to the land," he wrote. "It is very likely that these tensions will not disappear. It is probable that these tensions are a good thing." Rather than deny any of the professions its own point of view, White called for a coming together of all concerned—in order to "save for posterity the most valid approach to the most fundamental resource of creation, the landscape."[38]

"A boundless vision grows upon us; an untamed

continent; vast wastes of forest verdure;

mountains silent in primeval sleep; river, lake,

and glimmering pool; wilderness oceans

mingling with the sky."

FRANCIS PARKMAN (1865)

CHRISTIAN SCIENCE CENTER

BOSTON, MASSACHUSETTS

SASAKI ASSOCIATES LANDSCAPE ARCHITECTS

PHOTOGRAPH BY DAVID ALEIBA, COURTESY OF SASAKI ASSOCIATES

1973 ASLA HONOR AWARD DESIGN, 1987 CLASSIC AWARD

"Play is the child's work. The world is his laboratory, and he is its scientist. Play is the

research by which he explores himself and his relationship to the world."

M. PAUL FRIEDBERG (1970)

BEDFORD STUYVESANT SUPERBLOCK

BROOKLYN, NEW YORK

M. PAUL FRIEDBERG & ASSOCIATES

LANDSCAPE ARCHITECTS

DRAWING COURTESY OF M. PAUL FRIEDBERG & ASSOCIATES

1970 ASLA HONOR AWARD URBAN PLANNING

179

"The art of Cities is an art of creative assemblage and change requiring the

constant and energetic input of all its citizens. It is, in the grandest sense, a

participatory environmental art without boundaries."

LAWRENCE HALPRIN (1972)

FREEWAY PARK

SEATTLE, WASHINGTON

LAWRENCE HALPRIN, LANDSCAPE ARCHITECT

1960S

PHOTOGRAPH BY DAI WILLIAMS

COURTESY OF THE OFFICE OF LAWRENCE HALPRIN, INC.

"Our ability to perceive quality in nature begins, as in art, with the pretty. It expands through successive stages of the beautiful to values as yet uncaptured by language."

ALDO LEOPOLD (1948)

RESIDENCE OF

MR. AND MRS. GEORGE SOROS

SOUTHAMPTON, LONG ISLAND, NEW YORK

A.E. BYE & ASSOCIATES

LANDSCAPE ARCHITECTS

PHOTOGRAPH BY A.E. BYE

1970 ASLA HONOR AWARD

"Above all [Kennedy] gave the world for an imperishable moment the vision of a leader who greatly understood the terror and the hope, the diversity and the possibility, of life on this planet and who made people look beyond nation and race to the future of humanity."

ARTHUR M. SCHLESINGER, JR. (1965)

JOHN F. KENNEDY GRAVESITE

WASHINGTON, DC

MICHAEL PAINTER, LANDSCAPE ARCHITECT

JOHN CARL WARNECKE & ASSOCIATES

ARCHITECT

PHOTOGRAPH COURTESY OF FREDERIC P. WARNECKE

1970 ASLA HONOR AWARD

"It is the best of mankind, the noblest, not destroying the

natural world but completing it."

Vincent Scully commenting on the Villa Almerico Capra (La Rotonda)

(1986)

WEYERHAEUSER HEADQUARTERS

TACOMA, WASHINGTON

SASAKI WALKER ASSOCIATES

LANDSCAPE ARCHITECTS

Photograph by Dixi Carrillo, Courtesy of Peter Walker and Partners

1972 ASLA Merit Award Commercial & Industrial, 1998 ASLA Classic Award

"Our eyes do not divide us from the world, but unite us with it. Let this be known to be true. Let us then abandon the simplicity of separation and give unity its due. Let us abandon the self-mutilation which has been our way and give expression to the potential harmony of man-nature."

Ian McHarg (1969)

Amelia Island Plantation

Florida

Wallace, McHarg, Roberts and Todd, Inc.

Landscape Architects and Planners

Photograph courtesy of the ASLA

1973 ASLA Honor Award Community Planning

"It is only in contemplative moments that life is truly vital, when routine gives place to intuition, and experience is synthesized and brought before the spirit in its sweep and truth."

GEORGE SANTAYANA (1930)

PEPSICO HEADQUARTERS

PURCHASE, NEW YORK

EDWARD D. STONE, JR. & ASSOCIATES

LANDSCAPE ARCHITECTS

PHOTOGRAPH BY ALAN WARD

1973 ASLA MERIT AWARD COMMERCIAL & INDUSTRIAL, 1986 ASLA CLASSIC AWARD

CHAPTER 5

PROCESS AND PRODUCT, METHOD AND MEANING

1974 – 1981

Sometime in the late 1970s a gap was closed between the most advanced practice and research on the one hand and the ASLA awards program on the other. *Landscape Architecture* gave expanded coverage of the award-winning projects, and readers followed the results closely, demanding better images and sharper, more illuminating criticism—something beyond "nice" or "fine." The time lag between cutting-edge experiments and built work was no longer an issue, since work in progress was now being considered for major professional awards. The very idea of commending someone's process—rather than focusing on a tangible product—was no longer a novelty. From 1971 onward award-winning projects were commended for such achievements as a thorough, clear inventory based on ecological determinants; the documentation of methodology; and the use of "good methodology to arrive at important conclusions." One jury noted of an award-winning firm, "The way they use the computer made it possible to succinctly analyze their process."[1]

These comments by jurors in 1971 and 1972 represent a point of view that became dominant by the end of the decade. Process and method counted for a great deal among many prominent landscape architects. At stake were the leadership of the environmental movement and the "stewardship of the landscape." And hanging in the balance was the stature of landscape architects vis-à-vis other environmental-design professionals. To some it appeared that the surest route toward widespread recognition of the profession of landscape architecture would be via the explanation, validation, and publication of politically defensible processes and scientifically proven methods. These notions were implicit in many articles at the time, including some highly regarded pieces by Carl Steinitz and Ian

McHarg. As Lawrence Halprin had mentioned in his *RSVP Cycles* of 1969, it was a "process-oriented society," and even the creative process of environmental design—aspiring to artistic quality and much more—needed to be explained, made visible, and publicized.[2]

Quick to publicize his work and thought, more often in architectural journals and popular magazines than in *Landscape Architecture,* Halprin would come under fire from landscape architects for many reasons. He did not always identify himself as a landscape architect. He avoided prescriptions and precise goals. He shunned "teamwork," preferring the less hierarchically structured, more open-ended phenomenon of "group creativity." Approaching middle age, he became fascinated by the counterculture commonly associated with youth and defiance of the status quo. He also publicized the notion of "scores," which laid out but did not precisely define the kinds of activities that he believed would lead, ultimately, to an ecologically sound, socially vibrant, and aesthetically satisfying physical product. Here, Halprin was merely charting his own personal and yet collective course toward professional fulfillment, something other landscape architects would seek in their own fashion, on their own terms. What they would share with Halprin, whether they cared to admit it or not, was a fascination for process (or something more orderly and predictable—method) and a desire for some kind of recognition, including publicity (or "visibility," as the chair of the 1980 awards jury, Theodore J. Wirth, put it).[3]

What was often missing in the expanding literature on process and method, however, was something that transcended scientific accuracy, political defensibility, social and economic requirements, and sensitivity to ecological relations in the natural world—of which human beings were a part. The landscape-preservation activists recognized this missing ingredient early on—in the late 1960s. This was something that geographers, philosophers, psychologists, historians, garden designers, and artists also cared about. Some may have been intrigued by the more abstract concepts of Carl Jung, Christian Norberg-Schultz, and Gaston Bachelard; others, by the more accessible ideas of J. B. Jackson, Leo Marx, Jay Appleton, Yi-Fu Tuan, and Christopher Alexander. The earthwork artist Robert Smithson looked for it in the work of Frederick Law Olmsted, Sr. The missing ingredient was meaning, which can only be understood in some cultural context, high or low, elite or vernacular—and in the ascendancy or on the decline, contemporary or remote in time.

In a process-oriented technological society that seemed here to stay some forays into the wilderness of meaning were slow to command the larger world's respect. Fewer grants were forthcoming for these studies than for quantitative, verifiable, more scientific research. And although some foundations and institutions encouraged this sort of cultural inquiry, such as Dumbarton Oaks, the American Academy in Rome, and the National Endowment for the Arts, their impact can hardly be compared with that of the National Science Foundation, the U.S. Army Corps of Engineers, NASA, and the defense-related industries as well as the research-and-development interests of giant transnational corporations. Still, it was encouraging for some, in the midst of tentative, doubt-ridden investigations into the realms of meaning, to find one of the Old Guard, Sir Geoffrey Jellicoe, publishing books and articles (including one piece in *Landscape Architecture* in 1980) about meaning, the fine arts, landscape architecture, and the future of civilization.[4]

To appreciate landscape architects' struggles to determine the relative importance of process and product, method and meaning, as reflected in the ASLA professional awards, we must step back in time as well as look ahead to the 1980s and 1990s—when the struggles, although not entirely resolved, became less visible and controversial. In principle, we can assume a continuity between process and product. But in the 1970s professionals often focused on one or the other. Some were stimulated by the increasing integration of the computer and related technological tools into planning and design processes. Yet in retrospect it will help to note a few scattered instances of resistance to the computer's extraordinary capabilities and "user-friendly" attributes. Although scattered, these clues will be important, for they indicate some of the creative tensions that may be essential for the vitality of landscape architecture in years to come.

In one of his first editorials in 1958 Grady Clay noted that *Landscape Architecture* was trying to keep alive "the almost forgotten art of landscape criticism." He was referring not to an appreciation of the subtle nuances of artistic form and content, but to a concern with the overall quality of the built environment, the widespread ugliness of which went all but unnoticed in the popular media. In the real estate and building sections of major newspapers, for example, Clay noted the tendency to report on how a project came to be (or might come to be), noting the costs of land, who got the commissions, who would be displaced, and how many people would be affected—while ignoring the final impact in the neighborhood and on the larger environment.[5] Pursuing this idea two years later, he identified one reason for the persistence of ugliness in the built environment: "our obsession—yours and mine—with the process of planning, rather than with its end results, with its products."[6]

Two readers of the magazine strongly agreed. C. McKim Norton, executive vice-president of the Regional Plan Association in New York, and Robert L. Parson of the Department of Earth Science, Northern Illinois University in DeKalb, both felt that too much emphasis was being given to planning as a process. "No specialist, technician, or engineer has the social vision to develop a suitable plan," Parson argued. "The generalist concerned with both physical elements and cultural factors should monitor the project development."[7]

In the years that followed, the increase in collaborative planning and design projects, involving both specialists and generalists, would take some of the edge off this criticism. Meanwhile, among students, educators, and practitioners there was increasing interest in process—but not the kind of "process" Clay had in mind. In 1960 Clay was referring to the interaction of political, economic, and social forces in altering the physical environment. The process that fascinated landscape architects in the 1960s and 1970s was a complicated and not always predictable set of interactions, in part political, economic, and social, in part biological and technological. At times the landscape architect's process was intuitive, but increasingly it would be shaped by the needs of scientific accuracy, verifiability, and predictability. Then, too, many landscape architects consciously focused on the creative process, which could be more intellectually and emotionally engaging than a layman might guess from reading about the process of urban development in the real estate section of the Sunday papers. To many professionals, in short, the excitement in their field was inseparable from process.

To appreciate this growing interest in process we must step back even further in time. It will be recalled that in 1950 Hideo Sasaki had drawn attention to the "process of critical thinking," a fluid, dynamic process that defied preconceptions and dogmas—the "arch enemies of design." In his article on education in landscape architecture this young instructor at the University of Illinois was directing students to something beyond "mere techniques of earning their bread

and butter." Sasaki encouraged them to experience the "questioning and exploration of new ideas," to "forge new knowledge to meet existing and new situations," and to "contribute toward social progress in their professional life."[8] In other words, inquiring into the process of thinking could be a route toward personal intellectual freedom and stimulation as well as toward some socially significant collective goal.

At that time, these experiences were not common on college and university campuses. A Cold War mentality had set in. And in the wake of the first explosion of a Soviet atomic bomb and the fall of China's Nationalist government to the Communists in 1949 the un-American committee of the U.S. House of Representatives ferreted out suspected Communists and Communist sympathizers within the United States. Liberal causes and liberal thinking became suspect. Educators at many state-supported institutions were required to take the loyalty oath. Some educators were fired; some quit in disgust. And the influential figure behind these measures, Senator Joseph McCarthy from Wisconsin became a force to be feared.

In 1950, then, Sasaki was leaving the exceedingly unpleasant McCarthyism on the campus of the University of Illinois (a state-supported public institution) for the opportunity to think and speak somewhat more freely at Harvard.[9] This politically charged situation would naturally add another layer of meaning to Sasaki's focus on the process of critical thinking. And his concern was widely shared. In 1951 *The New York Times* surveyed the state of intellectual freedom on seventy-two major campuses around the country and found "a subtle, creeping paralysis of freedom of thought and speech" that limited the "free exploration of knowledge and truth." At the University of Wisconsin the student board had been tagged as "subversive" for issuing a statement opposing the views of Senator McCarthy. At Yale there was an ominous "thought-conformity" closing in. "We see college men growing more and more docile, more and more accepting the status quo, paralyzed by the fear of their futures," reported the *Yale Daily News*.[10]

By the 1960s the mood on college and university campuses had changed. In landscape architecture, as in other environmental design fields, people were opening up to new ideas, new areas of research, and more connections among the disciplines. Specialists in the social and natural sciences as well as practicing landscape architects came to teach in landscape departments. Shortly after his article on art and natural processes, "The Shape of Erosion," appeared in *Landscape Architecture* in January 1962 Halprin began teaching part time at the University of California, Berkeley. And, living in Vermont, Dan Kiley occasionally served as a visiting critic at Berkeley and elsewhere.

In a rare essay, published in January 1963, Kiley dismissed the designer's preoccupation with form. "We are not searching for form," he wrote. "Forms are results of the nature of process. Are we not rather searching for our relationship to the universe as we grow in all our faculties, a continuing process of development? . . . In landscape design, one does not copy nature but tries to understand underlying processes or workings of nature—it is all there. Man as a part of nature, not man and nature." This short, pithy piece was highly quotable, but Kiley would never become a spokesman for the kind of process that many landscape architects would write about, struggle over, refine, and defend. He was too intuitive, too elusive. And he delighted in simplicity. Here, he ended with the notion that "the living of this life is the all-important end. Not Design."[11]

It is a long leap from January 1963 to the end of the decade. In the intervening years the profession of landscape architecture could hardly remain aloof from the shocks of assassinations, the war in Vietnam, and changes in the political, economic, social, and technological spheres. While educators were trying to make sense of these developments—John Kenneth Galbraith's *New Industrial State* (1967) and Theodore Roszak's *Making of a Counter Culture* (1969) come immediately to mind—professors of landscape architecture were observing significant changes in the interests and abilities of their students. "Today's students are inured to objects, but interested in processes," observed Richard A. Moore, head of the department of landscape architecture at North Carolina State University in Raleigh. "Talk to them about objects and you won't reach them. Talk to them about problem-solving on an environmental scale and they will pursue you to the limit of your knowledge."[12]

Having made this point in 1966, Moore pursued it a year later. He noted that freshmen were more informed, more aware, and more intellectually involved in society than any previous generation of students. The reasons were intertwined with technological change, current events, and countercultural sensibilities; there was the "fantastically accelerated accumulation of knowledge and technological capabilities," the ease and sheer volume of communication, and the generation gap. "The teacher's background no longer approximates the students' and is probably poorer in areas outside the teacher's discipline," he noted. Students and teachers now lived in different worlds. Students were appalled by the regular, graphic depiction of environmental degradation and war on television and in the print media, he explained. Students were also rejecting a value system in society that had led to a preoccupation with imagery and objects (advertised as the key to happiness, security, and comfort). Their rejection of materialism was, in turn, leading them to reject traditional, solution-oriented design education. Rather than focus on the end product, Moore explained, students were interested in asking the right questions. What mattered to students was process: "ideas, information, explanations, and processes which will help them understand the environmental dilemma." In the end Moore advised that "obsolete opinions and antiquated traditionalism" be cleared away in order to allow students to progress "beyond the limits of the teacher."[13]

Judging by a contemporary report, Moore's views seemed to be in line with the progressive views expressed by educators at four major institutions: William Tishler at the University of Wisconsin; Roger Martin at the University of Minnesota; Michael Laurie at the University of California, Berkeley; and Julius Fabos at the University of Massachusetts. Among these four Tishler gave relatively more attention to landscape architecture as an art, but favored a kind of design process that would discourage "arbitrary indulgence." Martin and Fabos tended to focus on problems of the larger scale and sensitivity to natural processes. All four educators were interested in processes, but they differed in their ways of structuring the continuum from process to designed product. Laurie preferred a tutorial system that might supplant the design studio, allowing freely ranging discussions of philosophical, psychological, and scientific aspects of a problem. Fabos's planning and design process would be more tightly structured with a sequence of steps that would give students "graduated and specific background knowledge" at each step and allow them to make "wise and informed choices."[14]

As processes of planning and design were developed and defended, so landscape architects' interests in highly structured processes and precise methods intensified. At Harvard in 1968-1969, working with a grant from the Corps of Engineers, Carl Steinitz and several of his colleagues studied fifteen methods of resource analysis, then "abstracted the logic of each approach" and applied it to "the common base of a computer data bank" that described a particular region of Boston. In one report Steinitz explained how the various methods were slotted into five categories in the order of increasing complexity. Apparently aiming for objectivity and fairness throughout, he welcomed the "revolution in data handling" that would lead to new ideas and methods. But there were at least two implied preferences underlying this study: one, toward the higher levels of precision and predictability that were expected from engineering and the natural sciences; the other, toward higher levels of technical sophistication, which were in part dependent on the financial resources available.[15]

By the end of the 1960s, then, a focus on process had offered landscape architects intellectual stimulation and freedom; a link between art and science; a way to relate to the universe; a means to develop an alternative set of values (less materialistic and more environmentally sensitive than the marketplace allowed); a way to avoid arbitrariness and make informed choices; and a basis for gaining the professional respect (and the financial resources) enjoyed by engineers and scientists. There remain two other very attractive aspects of this focus on process. One, described in minute detail in the April 1974 cover article of *Landscape Architecture*, was the personal satisfaction that Lawrence Halprin was seeking and trying to share with others—not only in his office, but also out in the community in "take part" design workshops, in the streets, and on the beach. For Halprin and those he gathered around him, the creative process was a difficult, emotional, sometimes frustrating, but also exhilarating journey across previously unquestioned boundaries of the self and of society. It

was a venture into unknown regions where countercultural values and environmental concerns might be sustained among the disparate values and aims of scientists, poets, psychologists, and designers.

The other attraction of a focus on process was power. Although this was not always clear in Ian McHarg's writing and lecturing, the power to determine the main characteristics of a physical product through a strictly regulated planning process was, for him, a desirable and worthy goal. Not only could landscape architects gain the stature needed to lead the environmental movement; they might also control, in broad concept and general environmental quality, the physical outcome of a large, complex planning project or a multidisciplinary team of strong-willed people. As McHarg and coauthor Jonathan Sutton wrote of their work at The Woodlands, a new town in Texas, "Any engineer, architect, landscape architect, developer, and the client himself were bound by the data and the method," and "anyone who employed the data and the method would reach the same conclusions."[16] In theory, then, whoever directed the gathering of the data and the development of the method should have the power to shape and protect the environment. But what actually happened in practice? This question will return in the next chapter.

When we look through the ground-glass viewing screen of a single-lens reflex camera while adjusting the focus, there comes a moment when all the particles of seemingly incoherent matter coalesce into a sharp image. If the depth of field is limited, most of what lies within the frame is out of focus—while something emerges in perfect clarity. Looking back in time, we hope to find a few such precious moments of clarity. But such clarity has its cost. Was there ever a time, we have wondered, when the most advanced work in landscape architecture was clearly reflected in the ASLA professional-awards program? If so, then presumably the less forward-looking or less compelling kinds of projects were allowed to slip out of focus. Now it appears that one of these moments occurred in the late 1970s. And one thing that was allowed to slip out of focus—shunned as irrelevant—was the single-family house and garden.

Private gardens did not often win ASLA awards in the 1970s. As private possessions of relatively small scale they did not usually offer the environmentalist, the social activist, or the designer in a large corporate firm the scope, the milieu, or the budget to make them attractive as projects. And as reminders of the more elegant old traditions of landscape architecture private gardens were not the forward-looking types of projects that ASLA awards juries tended to encourage in the 1970s. Of more than 200 award-winning projects that decade, there were apparently only five single-family residences.

No records have surfaced of any ASLA professional awards made in 1975. This may be a reflection of two key factors. First, there was a severe recession in the housing and building industry following the Arab oil embargo in October 1973. Economists and others later looked back on the 1974–1975 recession as a watershed, the beginning of a sharp decline in the rate of U. S. economic growth.[17] In the midst of the recession, forced to make deep cuts in staff, some of the largest landscape architecture firms may have been too deeply preoccupied with survival measures to submit projects for awards.[18] Second, those firms and educators with a high percentage of research-oriented and grant-supported work may have been insulated from the worst blows of recession—but there was no category of awards for "research and analysis" projects until 1978. That year, when these awards began to be made, Grady Clay genially observed, "As it turns out these days, a good planning-and-design office may survive erratic building cycles only by mastering research as well as the art and technique of design."[19]

"What the hell does that have to do with Landscape Architecture?" replied an outraged Will Hooker, landscape architect from Durham, North Carolina. His full response, perhaps written in the heat of indignation, remains emblematic of the environmental fervor of the late 1970s—just as Neil Porterfield's response to Garrett Eckbo in 1970 seemed emblematic of that time. In Hooker's view the idea of mastering research to survive erratic building cycles "has about as much to do with the recognition of the new category as the estate planning of the 1920s has to do with the heart of the practice of landscape architecture today. If competence in research and analysis is primarily to insure an even cash flow in today's offices, Solzhenitsyn's

comment about the climate of a spiritual desert in this country certainly rings true." The search for a higher quality of life was what moved the framers of the Constitution in the 1770s, Hooker believed; and to insure that quality of life "we must not only thoroughly understand the elements we manipulate, but we must also be able to foresee the long range effects of such manipulations. With the present unbridled growth and the subsequent intense pressures on the environment, we must master increasingly sensitive and sophisticated methods of understanding that which we are manipulating. That, not capital gain, is the reason behind the importance of research and analysis."[20]

He was right, of course. Porterfield was right. But so were Eckbo and Clay. Here were some of the most articulate and passionate spokesmen for environmental quality of their time. They viewed the environment from somewhat different angles, but their broad goals were compatible. Their reservations about some emerging aspects of their profession were not nearly so strong as those of the elderly Ralph E. Griswold, ASLA fellow emeritus. On his return from the American Academy in Rome in 1923 Griswold had built a successful practice of landscape architecture. But fifty years later he found that the field had changed utterly. "Only the nursery advertisements seem familiar," he confessed in 1974, and he wondered who bought the plants.[21] For Hooker—and Clay, Porterfield, and Eckbo—the profession was still comprehensible and deeply engaging. And yet the critical forces of change—the advancing technology, the shifting, globalizing economy

with the dollar no longer tied to the gold standard, and the sheer mass of information to be read, processed, "saved," and somehow used—such forces seemed overwhelming at times.

Whatever the degree of turmoil (or "confusion," Norman Newton's preferred term) in the face of developments both within and beyond the profession, the annual ASLA awards program became one potential means of clarification. In trying to select the most forward-looking projects and the most useful exemplars of research and communications, the jurors were indicating what they thought the profession of landscape architecture was all about. They were also setting standards and, in some small way, shaping the future.

In the bicentennial year of 1976, when an entire issue of *Landscape Architecture* was devoted to the preservation and restoration of historic gardens and landscapes, a "special recognition award" went to Duryea and Wilhelmi of New York for the historical reconstruction of Fort Stanwix, a Revolutionary War-era British garrison in Rome, New York. "Explores new horizons," noted the jury, which included former ASLA president Raymond L. Freeman, architect Aram Mardirosian, Renwick Gallery director Lloyd E. Herman, planner Charles H. Conrad, and Ervin H. Zube, head of landscape architecture and regional planning at the University of Massachusetts, Amherst, and director of the Institute for Man and His Environment. That year the awards recognized projects in housing, urban design, and commercial, industrial, institutional, and recreational work. Some large-scale planning projects were praised for their planning process—the 29,700-acre Cuyahoga Valley National Recreation Area study by Land Design/Research of Columbia, Maryland, and the 5,000-acre Shelby Farms, a conversion from penal farm to park by Royston, Hanamoto, Beck and Abey and Garrett Eckbo & Associates. (Eckbo had left EDAW, Inc., at the end of 1973.) At the same time the jury admired the small, "beautifully developed" Wilshire Pocket Park in Los Angeles by Fong/Jung/La Rocca of San Francisco. "More work of this nature should be encouraged," they said.[22]

A year of turning points, 1977 was the last time that a single jury gave awards in what was still termed a professional design competition. Although there were many specific categories for submission, the competition was both judged and graphically presented in the magazine as a whole. This treatment implied a continuum of planning and design in all projects. Appropriately, the jury represented several disciplines: landscape architects Meade M. Palmer (chair) and Darwina Neal; engineer John McNair; planner Joseph K. Schofield; architect J. Norwood Bosserman; and Nash Castro, general manager of the Palisades Interstate Park Commission in New York.[23]

In the pivotal year of 1977 the awards recognized both process and product, but the balance was tipped slightly in favor of product. Of two honor-award-winning projects, one entailed built work—site planning, landscape design, and construction at the College of Charleston in South Carolina by Edward Pinckney/Associates, Ltd., while the other

was a set of design guidelines by HOK for the mixed-use redevelopment of "Laclede's Landing" in St. Louis. Of Jones & Jones' long-range plan for the Woodland Park Zoo, which won a merit award, the jury noted, "If it had been executed, it would have merited an honor award."

In 1978 to accommodate the new category of research and analysis, two juries were formed to judge the ASLA awards, each with its own chairperson. From 1979 onward there would usually be three juries for three different, evolving categories: one for "design"; one for "planning, analysis and communication" (which later became "planning and analysis"); and one for "research" (which later became "research and communications"). These reflections of growing specialization within the profession of landscape architecture might be applauded for finer degrees of discrimination among projects within narrower frames of reference. Specialists ought, arguably, to be the best judges of the kinds of work in which they themselves are immersed. Then, too, some degree of continuity and general overview could be expected from 1979 through the early 1990s, when one individual would chair each of the several juries.

But these several juries, reminders of the divisions within the profession, may also have reinforced those divisions. While champions of one special concern or another were competing for financial resources and students' loyalties in academia, there was increasingly less incentive—in academia, in practice, and even in the awards program—for landscape architects to maintain the old, traditional balance among the many aspects of this hybrid "generalist's" profession. Meanwhile, the economic, political, and technological forces that had served landscape architects well for decades were inexorably transforming the conditions of private practice. Increasingly critical to the success of many firms would be speed, visibility, and imageability—as foreshadowed by the controversial debut of Philip Johnson's AT&T building in New York City in 1978. As a design on paper, in March 1978 it first struck *New York Times* critic Paul Goldberger as perhaps a joke or a game—a skyscraper masquerading as a piece of eighteenth-century furniture—but a few years later he would praise the building's nobility, sumptuousness, and drama.[24] The postmodern era had arrived.

In 1978 landscape architecture's controversial postmodern icons had not yet appeared, and perhaps few observers could have predicted the imminent loss of momentum among the social and environmental movements, which still appeared to thrive. Years later Ian McHarg looked back on his years as chairman of the Department of Landscape Architecture and Regional Planning at the University of Pennsylvania and recalled that "1977 was, for me, an apex, mainly in terms of the intensity of the students. They were really concerned with the problems of the world. At that time, it was very difficult to get people engaged in design at all! There was a real resistance. If you had offered a garden [problem] to the students at Penn, you'd have been mightily abused! Because they wanted to deal with larger-scale problems."[25] This attitude was shared by Warren Burgess of Charlotte, North Carolina, who thought the May 1976 issue of *Landscape Architecture* devoted to pompous kings, Le Nôtre, and the preservation of lavish gardens was a joke.[26]

But to a few landscape architects in the late 1970s, including Diane McGuire, who taught garden and landscape history at the Radcliffe Seminars, and Peter Walker, an adjunct professor at Harvard's Graduate School of Design, Le Nôtre was not a joke and the gardens of seventeenth-century France were worth looking into. Walker's large corporate firm on the West Coast had barely survived the 1974–1975 recession to emerge as The SWA Group, and he was painfully aware of economic and environmental constraints and the pressures of deadlines and bottom lines. But he also collected pieces of minimal art and shared, with his artist friends, a fascination for the old gardens, churches, town centers, and rural landscapes of France and Italy. Taking on the chairmanship of Harvard's Department of Landscape Architecture in 1978, he tried to maintain a balanced curriculum of technical, environmental, and economic studies along with reinvigorated design studios and explorations of art and history. Meanwhile, in 1978 Garrett Eckbo was writing from San Francisco about the balance of ethics and business, idealism and pragmatism. "The professional approach . . . is motivated by an inner vision of more beautiful and livable continuities of landscape than most of those which surround us today," he wrote. "Money and power are incidental to these satisfactions insofar as they are necessary for achievement. The professional approach tends not to hesitate to lose money on the job in order to do it better. Only the threat of economic trouble may force compromise."[27]

Some of the attitudes recollected here were clearly evident in the 1978 ASLA awards program, which attracted the largest number of entries in its history. More than forty projects were submitted in the new category of "research and analysis," including one merit-award-winning study of energy conservation by the Center for Landscape Architectural Education and Research. This study, for a consortium of federal agencies, was completed with assistance from a long list of consultants: Rahenkamp Sachs Wells; Land Design/Research; Sasaki Associates; Sasaki, Walker, Roberts; Edward D. Stone, Jr.; and Johnson, Johnson and Roy. Overall, the jury for research and analysis applauded the attention to social and environmental concerns but looked for more rigor in research and testing. And Grady Clay noted a turning point. "Many student and faculty radicals of the 1960s," he wrote, "are now part of the establishment in schools, offices, and agencies, using their expertise to bring about changes seen as impossible a decade ago."[28]

In 1979 Clay offered an awards summary that was upbeat, noting the great number of important surveys, analyses, and studies, and the "continuing strength of the environmental movement." He also mentioned the growing interest in historical landscape studies that

was reflected in such merit-award-winning projects as Heritage Square in Wichita, Kansas, by Oblinger Smith Corporation; Pioneer Square in Seattle by Jones & Jones; and the general development plan for Franklin Village near Detroit by Johnson, Johnson & Roy. That year a new award, the President's Award of Excellence, went to Robert L. Zinser for his contributions to Robson Square in Vancouver, designed by Arthur Erickson Architects (with Cornelia Oberlander and Raoul Robillard, landscape consultants). And for the first time a slide presentation of the awards, accompanied by a written narrative, would be made available for sale or rental after the 1979 annual meeting. (The ASLA hoped this "slide-show format" would prove to be more marketable and versatile than the former panel exhibits.)[29]

Between the lines something else had developed. Among the design jury's comments it was often difficult to detect enthusiasm for the quality of physical design—although the jury did praise many specific features of site design and urban design at Robson Square. This was a jury of accomplished, knowledgeable designers: landscape architects Carol R. Johnson and James H. Bassett, architect Edward Sonnenshein of Carl Warnecke's office, and Michael Pittas of the National Endowment for the Arts. Yet many of their published comments amounted to little more than encouragement for more such projects: "hopefully it is a forerunner," "a very sound approach," "a unified natural solution." Or "the most significant

aspect of this project is the community process." From comments like these it was difficult for the reader to appreciate what the designer had actually achieved in built form. Some points along the continuum of planning and design remained clear and compelling—at least to this jury of four—while, for the reader, the end product remained somewhat out of focus.

Attempting to extract from an annual awards competition some meaningful conclusions about the state of the profession, individual achievements, collective goals, and new opportunities cannot be easy—not for the jurors or observers at the time nor for those who come along years later. Some promising works are inevitably passed by, and—as is evident in hindsight—some fine achievements are never even submitted for awards. Still, each year the ASLA hopes to elicit a large, diverse body of work and to honor the best.

In 1980 the President's Award of Excellence went to Jones & Jones for the Woodland Park Zoological Gardens in Seattle, Washington. Beginning with a preexisting "sterile" monkey island and bear grotto, Grant Jones and his colleagues treated the animals as the client, and the jury praised the firm's creation of seemingly natural environments, from concept and research to final execution.[30]

Underlying the Woodland Park Zoo and many other award-winning works of landscape architecture were undoubtedly layers of meaning that the awards program could never convey in photographs and a few lines of text. Each project might be examined in much greater detail than was possible in a few pages of a magazine. And yet by 1980 the ASLA awards program—together with its jurors, the magazine *Landscape Architecture*, and its editors—was beginning to move out of the realm of snapshots and captions and into a larger arena of critical debate. Soon the jury's discussions would be sifted and published. No doubt this reflected a growing interest in meaning nurtured by the controversial postmodern movement in the arts. One early sign of this interest was a deeper engagement with issues of place and time.

In 1980 and 1981 some awards went to projects that could be realized only over long periods of time. Some dealt with the reclamation of degraded landscapes, others with historic reconstructions or revitalizations of decayed urban and rural environments. In 1980 honor awards went to Point State Park, an urban revitalization project in Pittsburgh by GWSM and Clarke & Rapuano, and to "Old World Wisconsin," an outdoor collection of historic structures and artifacts assembled as a multicultural "living" museum for which William H. Tishler served as landscape architect. In all but one of the honor awards for design in 1981 history, reclamation, or long periods of time were critical to the project's success. At Harborplace Wallace, Roberts and Todd revitalized a portion of Baltimore's old harbor. The Cashio, Cochran, Torre Design Consortium focused more intently on historic preservation and restoration along the railroad-lined riverfront of the Vieux Carre in New Orleans. Long-term maintenance and evolving design were critical to both the Deere and Company Administrative Center in Moline, Illinois, where Sasaki Associates had been shaping the landscape since the late 1950s, and to Cuesta Park, a neighborhood park in Mountain View, California, designed in the late 1960s by Royston, Hanamoto, Alley & Abey.[31]

This interest in historic or degraded landscapes had been faintly evident since the awards of the mid-1970s, but it grew more striking after 1980. What accounts for it? The awareness of limited financial and natural resources, the scarcity of unaltered or "greenfield" sites in urban and suburban areas, a growing curiosity about layers of meaning embodied in the traces of human habitation, the writings of geographers and cultural historians, and the enthusiasm of sculptors and other artists to find scope for their work beyond the conventional walls of galleries and frames of a canvas? All may help to explain this phenomenon. Another reason probably lies with the spread of a new technology—the computer and other devices indebted to the silicon chip. In 1964 Marshall McLuhan observed of various "world views" since Plato's time, "Each new technology creates an environment that is itself regarded as corrupt and degrading. Yet the new one turns its predecessor into an art form."[32] Now, three decades later, this observation remains valid. In our so-called information age of clean, fluorescent-lit, climate-controlled workplaces rusting rails and blackened industrial artifacts have gained a new aura. Meanwhile, the brave new high-tech worlds of work, commerce, and entertainment at the intersections of interstate highways—the "edge cities"—appear soulless and placeless, even though the occasional writer comes to their defense.[33]

In 1981 the design jury gave the President's Award of Excellence to Richard Haag Associates for their extraordinary efforts in the early 1970s to save an obsolete gas plant from demolition and incorporate it into a park. Haag had seen a kind of strange, fearful beauty in the enormous rusting hulk of a structure that had once produced gas from coal. Looming several stories over the edge of a lake in Seattle, the conglomeration of towers, pipes, stacks, and sheds was comparable to a vast work of modern sculpture. It also embodied other layers of meaning for a postindustrial society and an information age. Rising up from the notoriously polluted soil, the gas plant was a powerful reminder of a disappearing way of life and kind of work—arduous, dangerous, more rooted in a physical place than is common in America today. By 1981 Gas Works Park was also proof of a landscape architect's ability to garner public support, to alter public perceptions, to reclaim polluted soils (via the slow, natural process of bioremediation), and to invite contemplation. The park was a place for simply gazing out over an urban skyline from the water's edge or flying a kite from the summit of the Great Earth Mound (made of excavated matter from a con-

struction site). In the end this award made a connection between landscape architecture and industrial archaeology, a field with prospects as potent as the revitalization of decayed inner cities and the transformation of capped landfills.

With the selection of Gas Works Park for the highest honor in 1981 the ASLA design awards jury reached a plateau of sorts, a high place from which to look back on a reclaimed past as well as forward to "evolutionary design," in the words of the awards-program chairman, Grant Jones. Responding to a charge from ASLA president William Behnke, the jury looked for two things above all: excellence in the project itself and public appreciation of the profession of landscape architecture. For the first time in the history of the published ASLA awards the jury included a writer and historian: J. B. Jackson, who had been made an honorary member of the ASLA for his writings on landscape. And serving on the design jury with Jackson were Grant Jones; Theodore W. Brickman, Jr., president of a large Midwestern design/build company; Donald F. Hilderbrandt of Land Design/Research; and architect and landscape architect Sir Peter Shepheard.

The 1981 awards program represented a turning point in several respects, all related to a quest for meaning. For the first time an award-winning landscape architect, Richard Haag, was singled out for a profile that gave a glimpse into the mind and sensibilities of one human being behind the work. Also for the first time each of the three juries wrote a lengthy statement about what they had seen and failed to see. "We were consistently repelled by overdesign," the design jury confessed. "We were also disappointed that there were not more exemplary cutting-edge projects." Grant Jones had asked this jury to apply Aldo Leopold's environmental ethic to "our true habitat, the city." He also stated for the first time the underlying justification for the awards. They were given not so much for landscape architects as for the profession of landscape architecture. In addition, the awards recognized the efforts of municipalities, clients, and community activists. Such were the "new meanings" of the ASLA awards. But they would not remain the only ones. The quest for meaning would continue—with even more candid discussion in the years to come.

"Make it a wonderful people place with parks."

ROBSON SQUARE

VANCOUVER, BRITISH COLUMBIA, CANADA

ARTHUR ERICKSON ARCHITECTS

LANDSCAPE CONSULTANTS:

ARTHUR ERICKSON ARCHITECTS

CORNELIA HAHN OBERLANDER

AND RAOUL ROBILLARD

1979 ASLA PRESIDENTIAL AWARD OF EXCELLENCE URBAN DESIGN

"You must remember that when we began hardly anyone had thought about a zoo this way. Everything was based on the needs of the keepers and the requirement that the public always must be able to see every animal at every visit. It took effort to see things, so to speak, from the animal's side of the fence; and it took serving the needs of the staff and the public."

DAVID HANCOCKS (1980)

WOODLAND PARK ZOOLOGICAL GARDENS

SEATTLE, WASHINGTON

DAVID HANCOCKS, DIRECTOR

JONES & JONES, LANDSCAPE ARCHITECTS

PHOTOGRAPH BY EDUARDO CALDERON, COURTESY OF JONES AND JONES

1980 ASLA PRESIDENTIAL AWARD OF EXCELLENCE PARK AND RECREATIONAL PLANNING

"To downplay cultural antecedents, while it may promote the notion of a new

order and bolster the ideology of American exceptionalism, does little to clarify

the means by which the old ways were superseded."

MICHAEL P. CONZEN (1990)

OLD WORLD WISCONSIN

EAGLE, WISCONSIN

WILLIAM H. TISHLER

LANDSCAPE ARCHITECT

PHOTOGRAPH BY WILLIAM H. TISHLER, COURTESY OF THE ASLA

1980 ASLA HONOR AWARD HISTORIC PRESERVATION AND DESIGN

"All alongshore, thoughtful observers ponder the growing numbers of individuals, couples, and families afloat in the tiny muscle- or sail-powered vessels that poke around hazards, gunkhole along salt creeks, probe sandbanks and surf. In some inchoate way, the thoughtful observers half know, half sense that the vigorous few rightfully know the coastal realm, the hazards, the marginal zone, for the realm rejects the structures so beloved by the flabby, the inactive, the visitors unfit for the marge almost as quickly as it rejects the flabby, the inactive, the lazy themselves. Only those who exert themselves, who accept the risks, reach the secret beach and enjoy the realm through which Conrad hoped only to pass on his way inland, or to the safe, open sea."

JOHN R. STILGOE (1994)

JUNEAU MARINE PARK AND

TOURIST FACILITY

JUNEAU, ALASKA

KRAMER, CHIN & MAYO, INC.

LANDSCAPE ARCHITECTS AND PLANNERS

PHOTOGRAPH BY MARK KELLEY

1980 ASLA HONOR AWARD PARK & RECREATIONAL PLANNING AND DESIGN

"It is not too much to say that classical civilization has always defined itself

against the primeval woods."

PONDEROSA LODGE

MOUNT HERMAN, CALIFORNIA

JOHNSON, JOHNSON & ROY, INC.

LANDSCAPE ARCHITECTS AND PLANNERS

PHOTOGRAPH COURTESY OF THE ASLA

1980 ASLA HONOR AWARD PARK & RECREATIONAL PLANNING AND DESIGN

216

"The positioning of stone in the landscape is an ancient and sacred tradition and has always interested me—from the stone walls and megaliths in Europe to stone gardens in Japan. What attracts me to Japanese gardens lies in the essence of quietness which they express; their meditative emptiness, the illusion of nature, the effects of shadow and filtered light, and their stark simplicity. These gardens provide a sense of 'wabi,' the absence of any ostentatious element, and a sense of humility and melancholy. There is a dark, mysterious quality about them, an undiscoverable unknown which goes beyond our individual small self, which could be described as 'yugen' in Japanese."

ROBERT MURASE (1997)

MYODO KYO KAI

SHIGA PREFECTURE, JAPAN

ROBERT MURASE ASSOCIATES

LANDSCAPE ARCHITECTS

PHOTOGRAPH BY ROBERT MURASE

COURTESY OF THE ASLA

1980 ASLA HONOR AWARD INSTITUTIONAL DESIGN

"Baltimore illustrates the way a retail center links into a chain of projects. . . . Its new downtown became an instant success with the opening of Harborplace in 1980, but that success was thirty years in the making. Shoreline improvements around the Inner Harbor—a new bulkhead, landfill, marina, piers, public parks, and promenades—date from a bond issue voted in 1948."

BERNARD J. FRIEDEN AND LYNNE B. SAGALYN (1989)

BALTIMORE INNER HARBOR

HARBORPLACE

BALTIMORE, MARYLAND

ROUSE COMPANY, DEVELOPERS

WALLACE, ROBERTS AND TODD, INC.

LANDSCAPE ARCHITECTS AND PLANNERS

PHOTOGRAPH BY WILLIAM A. ROBERTS, COURTESY OF THE ASLA

1981 ASLA HONOR AWARD URBAN DESIGN

"In its random clutter and its rich variety of forms, Lake Union's [gas works] structure belongs to a time when Orwellian visions of depersonalized efficiency were still remote. Curiously, for something that represents an age not especially noted for its humanism, its dominant feeling is one of innocence. . . . History sits on this little wasteland, not only the parochial history of a given city but also a fragment of the chronicle of world culture."

KENNETH E. READ (1969)

GAS WORKS PARK

SEATTLE, WASHINGTON

RICHARD HAAG ASSOCIATES

LANDSCAPE ARCHITECTS AND PLANNERS

FROM 1970

PHOTOGRAPH BY ALAN WARD

1981 ASLA PRESIDENTIAL AWARD OF EXCELLENCE

CHAPTER 6

SURVIVAL OF THE FIT

1982 – 1989

Landscape architects in the United States will remember the 1980s as a period of expanding opportunities to plan, design, and build—especially to design and build. Although there were occasional periods of recession in some parts of the country, particularly in the oil-producing regions centered around Denver and Houston, the nation as a whole experienced surges in commercial and residential development that were most noticeable in and around the new "edge cities." On the previously undeveloped and sparsely built fringes of large metropolitan areas—at such places as Tysons Corner near Washington, D.C.; Irvine on the southern fringe of Los Angeles; at Las Colinas, west of Dallas; at Perimeter Center, north of Atlanta; and Princeton Forrestal in New Jersey—landscape architects joined architects, engineers, and planners to create new office parks, plazas, hotels, and residential and mixed-use complexes. These developments were sometimes criticized for a lack of community or sense of place. Still, edge cities appeared to fit the clients'.purposes. They responded to powerful forces in the marketplace, they reflected Americans' fondness for private transportation and ample parking, and—so the argument went—they might someday evolve into layered, more complex, and broadly satisfying environments.[1]

A small portion of this work garnered high praise and visibility through the ASLA awards program. In 1985 an honor award went to The SWA Group for Williams Square in Las Colinas, and a few merit awards for other edge-city projects followed. These awards no doubt reflect an evolution of collective views among a continually changing group of jurors. In the 1980s there was also a gradual assimilation of different generations among ASLA officers and jurors. Early in the decade ASLA jurors—mature landscape architects and their colleagues in allied professions—tended to show more enthusiasm for work in center cities, small

A MEMORIAL TO THE 56 SIGNERS OF THE DECLARATION OF INDEPENDENCE, WASHINGTON, DC

EDAW, INC. LANDSCAPE ARCHITECTS AND PLANNERS

PHOTO BY DIXI CARILLO. COURTESY OF EDAW, INC.

towns, and rural areas, particularly work for civic and institutional clients. But increasingly as somewhat younger landscape architects began to serve as jurors—even as chairpersons—juries more diverse in age and inclinations found much to admire in corporate and commercial work as well.

Meanwhile, still younger landscape architects, who had grown up in the waning of New Frontier and Great Society idealism, were gaining a voice. They had come of age during the turbulent years of the mid-1970s and early 1980s—with Watergate scandals, oil crises, environmental activism, recession, high unemployment, double-digit inflation, the hostage crisis in Iran, and recession again in 1981–1982. The apparent prosperity during most of the 1980s allowed many recent graduates in landscape architecture to be selective in accepting their first jobs. And the ASLA awards published in *Landscape Architecture*, which was also profiling honor-award-winning firms, could help graduates sort out their own winning prospects. Once hired, these landscape architects could develop skills quickly, as the pace of work accelerated and projects went from planning and design to construction in record time. In this period of rapid economic and environmental change, the fit had ample opportunity to survive, and many of them prospered.

But there was a down side to these years of promise. The prosperity that was conspicuous in so many edge cities and even in center cities, along the revitalized waterfronts and in the restored historic districts, was not apparent in small towns and rural communities in many parts of the country. Observers from different ends of the political spectrum, from John Kenneth Galbraith to Kevin Phillips, have mulled over the ever-widening gaps among income levels that became conspicuous in the decade of widespread deregulation, large federal tax cuts, and other "supply-side" economic measures, mergers, acquisitions, leveraged buyouts, and "golden parachutes" for departing executives of major corporations.[2]

Without detailing the growth in the number of millionaires and billionaires, the declines in percentages of home-ownership and in federal housing assistance, or the rise in numbers of farms foreclosed and factory towns shut down, we can still appreciate why the phrases "Social Darwinism" and "survival of the fittest" turned up in more than one retrospective study of the 1980s in America. Those most able to adapt to new technologies and to an economy and an environment increasingly less regulated appeared most likely to survive. Beyond personal survival, the rewards could be considerable—even excessive. As Phillips observed, "disproportionate rewards" went to society's economic, legal, and cultural manipulators: to lawyers, investment advisers, advertising executives, fashion designers, and leaders in finance, entertainment, and communications.[3]

Landscape architects and other environmental planners and designers did not fall into this group of disproportionately rewarded people—although some of these people became clients of landscape architects. The profession's clientele came from so many sources that it is difficult to generalize, but it seems that in the 1980s a complex of interacting economic and technological forces made landscape architects more conscious of the need for speed, efficiency, cost-effectiveness, and bottom-line profit. Of course pragmatic concerns were a part, but not always the focus, of the larger picture for landscape architects. Traditionally they had been drawn to their profession for a number of highly idealistic and altruistic reasons. In the 1980s, as in the 1880s, there was still a healthy strain of what the late Stanley White had considered essential to the profession's existence—a critical point of view. "Landscape architecture is criticism," White asserted in 1953. And he reiterated a link between the profession and opposition to the status quo. "Landscape architecture as theory emerged (1850 - 1899) as a protest against what gardeners, engineers, and architects were doing to the American scene."[4]

If the tone of landscape architects' protest was muted in the 1980s, they could still sustain the historic effort as they tried to enlighten clients and reorient projects toward worthier goals—outcomes more sound in environmental, social, or aesthetic terms than originally conceived. Admittedly, a grasp of changing financial, legal, and technological tools, the ability to communicate effectively, and insights into evolving cultural norms all became increasingly important for professional survival. In the absence of strong commitments from the federal government to support housing, urban development, alternative-energy research, and environmental regulations, new alliances would have to be formed (and new clients found) in the private sector. Generalizations are hazardous, but one challenge for ambitious, inner-directed landscape architects was

to adapt to rapid and profound changes in the environment and yet resist complete and uncritical adaptation.

In the 1980s the ASLA professional awards program reflected these evolving conditions, both in the nature of award-winning work and in the extended discussions among jurors. The phrase "evolutionary design" echoed in several commentaries. Jurors began to emphasize linkages, connections, and interactions within increasingly diverse environments. To a certain extent Charles Darwin's theory of evolution, initially applied in the nineteenth century to the biological development of life on earth, offered a useful metaphor for the development of the profession. For example, the evolution of life forms by means of adaptation to new conditions helps to explain the rise to prominence of one type of project or activity and the decline of another—largely in response to external conditions such as clients, grants, legislation, and regulation. Then, too, the profession itself was evolving. As landscape architects had to adapt to a changing environment, there was more talk about "positioning" oneself and one's profession for success. And as the process of adaptation continued, landscape architects became increasingly differentiated—not as different "species" exactly, but as professionals with some distinctly different interests and agendas.

The story of the 1980s, then, breaks down into several stories, the threads of which can best be brought together after each story has been told. We begin with an account of environmental planning, along with the basic research that some believed essential to the advancement of

227

both environmental planning and the profession as a whole. The next story involves design and art. The third story, about technology and the media, will appear in the final chapter. There, threads of all three are brought together in a synthesis that continually threatens to break apart.

In 1982 submissions for professional awards in research rose to twelve—up from only five in 1981. The research jury was pleased not only by the quantity of submissions, but also by their quality and diversity, with topics ranging from water conservation and visual perception to low-income housing and agricultural land management. What the jury could not have known was that 1982 would represent a high point for ASLA award-winning research projects. Never again would research projects garner so many ASLA awards (eight), nor would the quality of the research be so highly esteemed.

In retrospect, an observation by a team of landscape architects and educators gives a clue to the rise—and eventual decline—in the number of research projects submitted for ASLA awards. In 1982 Ervin H. Zube, James L. Sell, and Jonathan G. Taylor noted in the summary of their honor-award-winning research project, "Landscape perception research in the past two decades has developed in a climate encouraged by increased governmental concern for environmental quality."[5] This was presumably written during the second year of the new Reagan administration. At that time even a journalist suspicious of the "aristocratic" roots of American environmentalism had to admit that, according to many

polls, "the overwhelming majority of the public wants clean air, clean water, an improved quality of life, and an end to environmental degradation."[6] By 1982, however, Secretary of the Interior James G. Watt had already declared national stewardship an obsolete ideal and announced his intention to "reverse twenty-five years of bad resource management."[7] At the Environmental Protection Agency (EPA), which President Nixon had created by executive order a decade earlier, enforcement proceedings dropped nearly seventy percent in one year.[8] And after four years of this new administration, the EPA's permanent staff would be cut by twenty-one percent and its budget reduced by thirty-five percent.[9]

These changes in governmental policy at the federal level represent only one clue to the decline in research submissions and awards. Another clue lies in an ASLA merit-award-winning study that examined attitudes toward research within the profession itself. Attempting to measure productivity in academic research, landscape architect Mark Chidister and social psychologist Richard Chenoweth undertook an extensive survey, sending out lengthy questionnaires to educators in landscape architecture. In the end they found several obstacles to research, including the lack of a shared definition of research, insufficient time for research, and a perceived apathy toward research on the part of some colleagues in landscape architecture.[10]

A third clue brings together the interests of academic research and environmental planning practice. Sometime in the mid-1980s the driving forces of the outside world became assimilated within the smaller world of landscape architecture and the ASLA awards. Pragmatic concerns were increasingly prominent in the juror's comments, even as the projects they chose to honor radiated a quality of idealism, inspired activism, or poetic vision that transcended the imperatives of the times. In hindsight, the implied struggle between competing values and goals seems poignant, disturbing. In 1983 juror Vincent Bellafiore, chairman of the landscape architecture program at Virginia Polytechnic Institute in Blacksburg, spoke of the need for shortcuts, for ways "to compress our thought processes without sacrificing quality" at a time, he noted, when endowments for landscape architecture lagged far behind those for, say, physics. "We used to think that they were hiring us for our process, but they aren't," juror Neil Porterfield admitted. "Clients want an answer, and it had better be a good one; they don't particularly care how we got there."[11]

By 1984 landscape architects were moving away from the exhaustive analytical studies that had once been so highly regarded—particularly after Congress passed the National Environmental Policy Act in 1969. In 1984 juror John J. Reynolds, assistant superintendent for land use and resource management at the Santa Monica Mountains National Recreation Center, alluded to these studies as he noted the absence of awards for "paralysis by analysis." In his view, the profession had retained the positive features of that phase and "come back to our strengths." That year awards chairman Thomas Zarfoss raised many questions about Reaganomics, communications, a high-tech society, stewardship, aca-

demic research, and elitism. Not presuming to offer definitive answers, he did cull a few ideas from the best-selling 1982 book about successful businesses, *In Search of Excellence*, by Thomas J. Peters and Robert H. Waterman, Jr. Zarfoss also noted, "We need to do a better job of documenting, teaching, and marketing our history."[12] In 1985 the ASLA awards chairman John J. Reynolds regretted that both the art and the environmental base of landscape architecture had suffered in recent years. He viewed the present as an era of "regaining our energy, putting our financial house in order."[13]

These comments help to sketch in a collective view of the profession, as represented by Zarfoss (who was in private practice with William A. Behnke and Associates), Reynolds (in the federal government), Porterfield (with the multidisciplinary firm HOK), and Bellafiore (in academia). Like snapshots, the comments quickly capture a few moments in time. In contrast, John W. Simpson offered a somewhat unflattering formal group portrait in his "Environmental Planning in the Backwash" (1985). In this *Landscape Architecture* article Simpson, a doctoral candidate in environmental planning at Ohio State University, cited data that revealed a dramatic decline in the numbers of environmental impact statements submitted to the EPA between 1970 and 1983. Given these and other statistics, Simpson argued that "the wave of environmental planning typically conducted by landscape architects during the past twenty years is receding."[14] In previous years, Simpson noted, this wave had been generated by two sources: the private sector and, for the most part, the federal and state government. In the future, he predicted, environmental planning would involve increasingly more quantitative analysis and more highly technical risk/benefit analyses than in the past. Data mapping and overlay techniques would, he believed, become less relevant to the new kinds of work, which would most likely be secured by the large engineering/environmental planning firms that could afford to maintain "the full range of in-house Ph.D.s." Meanwhile, he warned, competition from engineers, city planners, geographers, and others would crowd out many landscape architects from their "once-safe job niche in the environmental planning habitat."

Simpson had hoped to provoke a dialogue on these issues, and he did. *Landscape Architecture* published thoughtful replies from William G. Swain of GWSM in Pittsburgh; Robert W. Ross, Jr., chief landscape architect at the U. S. Forest Service; and John T. Lyle, chairman of the landscape architecture department at California State Polytechnic University in Pomona. Among their insights, two need to be recalled here. First, Ross emphasized a point of historical continuity. He asserted that, regardless of "waves" that might rise or fall, landscape architects had been deeply engaged in environmental planning since Olmsted and Vaux first worked on Central Park and that the landscape architect's unique skills, combined with those of management, communication, and mediation, should continue to serve them well as they become "more effectively outspoken," critical, and politically active in environmental issues at all levels. Second, Lyle emphasized an evolutionary change in environmental plan-

ning. In the 1970s, he believed, the field had been more narrowly defined and rather negatively oriented. By 1985 emerging perceptions of nature as an "infinitely complex web of largely indeterminate interactions that includes humans" suggested a more positive concept of environmental planning—that is, "the movement toward mutually life-enhancing relationships between humans and the biosphere."[15]

By 1985, then, a combination of historical perspective and awareness of contemporary developments in philosophy and the natural sciences would help landcape architects recognize their diverse and potentially wider roles in environmental planning—even while they witnessed their own declining participation in more narrowly defined quantitative studies that were meant to be controlled by technically skilled experts. These kinds of studies, it will be recalled, were the basis for the power that Ian McHarg had hoped to maintain in his quest for environmental well-being. That was the theory. But what happened in practice? The historical development, as traced in ASLA award-winning planning projects since 1985, seems to suggest a gradual, collective, but not always unified effort to reclaim the whole of something.

By the mid-1980s, in many fields, people were expressing some regret that wholeness had been lost in the Cartesian mode of thinking in dichotomies (body/mind, man/nature, science/art). Now, rather than reduce a problem to its small, constituent, and objectively verifiable parts (thereby eliminating the messy, unpredictable, or ambiguous factors), landscape architects were increasingly including these unpredictable factors in their planning, analysis, and research. Thus local people—their grassroots organizations and their local governments—became more intimately engaged in the landscape architect's larger vision of "environmental planning." This vision was to some extent anticipated in the pioneering work of Kevin Lynch, Philip Lewis, and a few others in the late 1950s and 1960s. And yet now it was different, perhaps more comprehensive, because of the tremendous growth in knowledge, understanding, and personal commitment to environmental values during the late 1960s and 1970s.[16]

Given this broader concept of the term, "environmental planning" is now recognizable in a wide range of ASLA award-winning planning projects since 1985. In 1986 one honor-award-winning project, the New Orleans Historic Warehouse District Study by the Caplinger Group, Ltd., integrated the concerns of historic preservationists with those of developers, civic agencies, and others. In the process, the landscape architects found the existing qualities of space, light, and the ambience of the whole neighborhood to be as important as the architecture. The other honor-award winner in planning that year, the Chester County (Pennsylvania) Open Space and Recreation Study by Roger Wells Inc., involved not only large-scale resource inventory and analysis but also a "model for diplomatic persuasion." The landscape architect developed a questionnaire that brought local county employees and interns into the process of gathering and classifying data, evaluating needs, shaping goals, and guiding future plans for land acquisition, easements, preservation, and new

landscape amenities. "A wonderful model for looking at the whole picture," noted the diversified jury, which included Adele Chatfield-Taylor, director of the Design Arts Program of the National Endowment for the Arts; David Dillon, architecture critic for the Dallas Morning News; and landscape architects Edward Pinckney and Philip Lewis.[17]

In the late 1980s ASLA award-winning projects in the planning and analysis category ranged from highly quantitative scientific studies, aided by innovative technologies, to qualitative studies with or without a strong design component as the ultimate product. At points along this spectrum were projects that engaged the local communities and governmental agencies—in gathering data and opinions, assessing needs, communicating landscape values, and implementing strategies of planning and management. As the composition of the juries varied, so did their selections. But in bestowing honor awards, juries tended to single out those projects in which public participation or the communication of landscape values to the public were key factors.

By the end of the decade the ASLA awards program had looked favorably on work that revealed the connections, perhaps even a symbiosis, between environmental and social values. Meanwhile, a new term, "sustainability," had entered the common language. Conferences, committees, and such books as Sim Van der Ryn and Peter Calthorpe's *Sustainable Communities* (Sierra Club Books, 1986) all envisioned a new synthesis of environmental planning with the traditional concerns of architects, landscape architects, engineers, traffic planners, sociologists, and urban designers. This enlarged concept of environmental planning brought even more players—and potential competitors—onto the field that was once, in the words of Harvard Professor Emeritus Charles W. Harris, the "lonely turf" of landscape architects.[18]

How many students of landscape architecture have skimmed the opening lines of Norman Newton's classic text, *Design on the Land: The Development of Landscape Architecture* (1971), without giving them a second thought? "Landscape architecture. . . will be taken here to mean the art—or the science, if preferred—of arranging land, together with the spaces and objects upon it, for safe, efficient, healthful, pleasant human use."[19] In the decades following the textbook's first appearance whether the profession was an art or a science was a compelling issue for those in the field. And the profession still suffers from this difference of opinion. Newton, along with colleagues of his generation, who came of age during the First World War, simply assumed that landscape architecture was made up of components from both science and art. He also assumed something else, detectable in his choice of adjectives. Safe. Efficient. Healthful. Pleasant. His older colleagues had had no difficulty in placing this kind of work within the realm of the fine arts. But in Newton's mature view landscape architecture was an art of design.

The differences are not merely semantic. Yet few members of this hybrid, not easily defined profession have paused to clarify these terms while other matters were more pressing, such as keeping a practice alive or fighting battles against the most egregious polluters of the planet. But the 1980s were a time when some felt obligated to take a stand. Already familiar were notions about happenings, earth art, site-specific sculpture, and entropy in the design of Central Park in New York. Then the Bagel Garden by Martha Schwartz appeared on the cover of *Landscape Architecture* in January 1980. In the opinion of the editor, Grady Clay, Schwartz's accompanying article was the latest in a series of thought-provoking "new ideas," a series he had begun with writings by Ian McHarg and Karl Linn, along with the poetry of Grant Jones.[20] While focusing on a single experimental garden in Boston's Back Bay, Schwartz went on to discuss new materials, her workplace in the small experimental office of The SWA Group East, their ties to academia and the art world, and the possibilities for transforming vacant city lots into gardens made of found or discarded objects. As it turned out, the Bagel Garden drew many responses, both appreciative and derogatory.

In 1981 to invite further dialogue Clay sent proofs of an article by young Steven R. Krog to several prominent figures, asking for comment. Krog had begun "Is It Art?" by asking "Is landscape architecture an art? Can it be a fine art?" "No," Newton replied to the second question. In his view creators of fine art solve their own problems; landcape architects try to solve other people's problems. But Krog had persisted with ruminations on the lack of interest in history, critical theory, and critical review among landscape architects. Citing views of Plato, John

Dewey, and Susan Sontag among others and tossing out dour remarks about the primacy of function and the number of cars in porous-paved parking lots, Krog was looking for some kind of response. He got it. Kenneth C. Caldwell of Jones & Jones in Seattle, Garrett Eckbo, Norman Newton, J. B. Jackson, William A. Behnke (president of the ASLA), and educators Richard Williams and Walter Cudnohufsky (Conway School of Landscape Design in Massachusetts), Peter Jacobs (University of Montreal), Marc Treib (University of California, Berkeley), Carl Steinitz (Harvard), and Catherine M. Howett (University of Georgia) all replied. Most applauded the call for further enquiry, debate, and criticism, but two types of reservations recurred.[21]

Resisting the either/or choices that Krog posed, Behnke and Eckbo emphasized the diversity of approaches and emphases in the field. And resisting Krog's dichotomies between form and function, art and function, art and science, others emphasized the potential for synthesis or continuity among these things. Jackson recalled European ornamental gardens in the Late Middle Ages that could be seen as miniaturized, formalized portions of a larger agricultural landscape. The design of these gardens, he believed, was not so much an "artistic creation" as a domestic-scaled evocation of the surrounding productive landscape, subject to the same environmental constraints. Cudnohufsky, who was then running a school of landscape design on a farm in Western Massachusetts, had a similar response. To him the separation of artful landscape from functional landscape was as disturbing as the separation of

intuition from scientific thought— for these things were interdependent. In parting words, Cudnohufsky wrote, "Living well is one form of art, especially in these troubled times."[22]

The articles by Schwartz and Krog and the varied responses they received were overtures to more discussions of art and postmodern design in *Landscape Architecture*. The magazine's January 1982 issue was devoted to postmodernism, featuring articles on the gardens of Luis Barragan by Mario Schjetnan and on "art into landscape" by Peter Walker along with a journalistic account of postmodernism by Norman K. Johnson and a somewhat more theoretical piece on the subject by Susan Rausch Eastman. It was not an entirely new topic in landscape architecture, and it would not soon disappear, nor would letters of protest—calling for more attention to pressing environmental and social issues—cease to appear in *Landscape Architecture*. While postmodern design continued to provoke discussion, even as the term itself eluded precise definition, the ASLA awards juries had to confront it in some way, openly or tacitly.

In 1983 jury chair landscape architect Cheryl Barton revelled in the luxury of sitting back for all of two days and discussing design, the profession, philosophical approaches, and more. That year three honor awards were given for design—the Mystic River Reservation Park near Boston by Carol R. Johnson and Associates and the downtown Salem (Massachusetts) Central Business District Plan and Chestnut Park in Philadelphia, both by the Delta Group of Philadelphia. Two planning projects also won honor awards—a preservation study of the Sautee and Nacoochee valleys in Georgia by Allen Stovall with EI Design Associates and the First Historic Landscape Report for the Ravine in Prospect Park, Brooklyn, by Friedman Walmsley & Company. Drawing "tremendous confidence and optimism" from the scope of these and other award-winning projects, Barton touched on many of the profession's concerns: thinking globally and acting locally, "high touch with high tech," the stewardship ethic, poetry and humor, aesthetic perceptions, scientific principles, and advocacy in educating and even creating the client.[24]

Barton remained sanguine about one issue that troubled design juror William J. Johnson, who had by then left his large multidisciplinary firm, Johnson, Johnson and Roy—or JJR, Inc.—to form a smaller office. Not that the two jurors disagreed: The glass was either half empty or half full. Barton sensed that in some cases the "artificial boundary" between planning and design was beginning to dissolve. The Mystic River Reservation, for example, involved a continuum from planning policies, engineering, and soil reclamation through design and construction. Johnson noted, however, that the ASLA award categories still divided the world into "designers and non-designers." In academia, too, designers were forced to choose between a research or design career. Johnson, a former academic dean at the University of Michigan, still felt the need to stress continuity and the superior work that would result when designers engaged in planning—thereby transcending the unhealthy divisions that still existed in the profession.[24]

In 1984 Garrett Eckbo, the elder statesmen among the jurors, found it heartening that many award-winning landscape architects—and very young ones—were approaching the wide scope that the elder Olmsted had initiated. Anne Whiston Spirn, a professor of landscape architecture at Harvard and a former student of Ian McHarg's, received the Presidential Award of Excellence for her book, *The Granite Garden: Urban Nature and Human Design*. An honor award went to landscape architects Michael Van Valkenburgh and Alan Ward for their photographic exhibition and catalog, *Built Landscapes: Gardens in the Northeast*, featuring work by Beatrix Farrand, Fletcher Steele, James Rose, Dan Kiley, and A.E. Bye with essays by John R. Stilgoe and Jean E. Feinberg. Meanwhile, honor awards went to Randolph T. Hester for the Manteo, North Carolina, Community Design Plan; to the fledgling firm Hargreaves Allen Sinkosky & Loomis for Fiddler's Green Amphitheatre in Englewood, Colorado; and to Joseph E. Brown, Cales Givens, and their colleagues at EDAW's Alexandria, Virginia, office for the memorial to the fifty-six signers of the Declaration of Independence in Washington, D.C. These and other professionals in their thirties and forties won awards for a wide range of work, from planning and communications to garden design and a new subcategory, "landscape art and earth sculpture."

Responding to all this, Cheryl Barton asserted, "Our diversity is a strength—as in the basic ecological principle—and is very exciting, although some people have trouble with that concept." In her view a single "school" or image of the profession did not exist, and the multiple directions indicated growth.[25] Still, the environmental passions of the 1970s were evident in much of the work submitted for awards. There were traces of a lingering focus on the planning process and the ethic of stewardship that often informed it. Carl D. Johnson of Johnson, Johnson and Roy observed that some good candidates for design awards were entered in the planning and analysis category instead. "Clearly there is a planning process in every design solution," he remarked, "but the product is more important."[26]

This statement, a reversal of priorities held by many landscape architects in the 1970s, reflected a growing tendency in the 1980s to recognize achievement in small- to middle-scale design for both private and public or institutional clients. By the mid-1980s even private gardens were once again winning honor awards.

In 1985 ASLA awards chairman John J. Reynolds, superintendent of the North Cascades National Park Complex, assembled a design jury that included landscape architects Diana Balmori, Meade Palmer, and Stewart O. Dawson along with architects Bronson Binger and Peter Jacobs. This was the jury that gave an honor award to The SWA Group for Williams Square. Two other honor awards went to gardens: Longfellow Garden, a public urban oasis in the South Bronx, New York, by Lee Weintraub and the New York City Department of Housing, Preservation, and Development; and Toad Hall in East Hampton, New York, a contemporary villa that owed its integrity to a witty and informed dialogue among the site, the client (François deMenil), the landscape

architects (Daniel D. Stewart and Associates), and the architects (Gwathmey Siegel & Associates) and others.[27]

The new element in these awards lies in the fact that qualities of delight, humor, attention to fine detail, and sheer beauty were now not merely mentioned in award-winning project descriptions and jurors' comments. These qualities seemed to be able to hold their own against the obvious merits of many competing projects of civic, social, cultural, and environmental significance. Now the spiritual value of beauty, magic, wonder, and many other qualities that had gone unremarked in awards programs before the 1980s was formally recognized.

In 1986 awards went to three gardens, all originally in private hands. The design jury, made up entirely of landscape architects—Tito Patri, Peter Rolland, Peter Walker, Anne Whiston Spirn, and Stuart O. Dawson (chair)—gave merit awards to two gardens. One was a six-acre seaside residence on Long Island, New York, by Daniel D. Stewart and Associates at which beach grass was restored and a secondary dune built as a base for the house. The other was John T. Lyle's own residence in Sierra Madre, California. There, the jury sensed the hand of a designer deeply involved with the work, particularly in the loving, personalized attention to detail and the inventiveness with humble materials. In a third garden, these qualities were again apparent, along with something more.[28]

In 1986 Richard Haag's work at the Bloedel Reserve, formerly a private estate on Bainbridge Island in Puget Sound near Seattle, brought him the Presidential Award of Excellence for the second time. This was a breakthrough—not so much because it was the first time anyone had won the award twice, but because this highest of ASLA awards did not call attention to many commonly stated criteria for awards: making the profession better known to the public, for example; or taking the leading role and directing the process of change; orchestrating a diverse group of players; eliciting citizens' participation; restoring a degraded landscape; or revitalizing a central city or small town. *Landscape Architecture* editor Susan R. Frey *did* feel that Haag had demonstrated an ethic of steward-ship—a familiar criterion for awards. But if Haag did so, it was in a gentle, "non-striving" way. In fact, he ruefully admitted that had he been more aggressive and completed projects quickly, while the elderly owner was still around to savor them, more of his work might have remained intact. As it happened, some portions of the series of gardens did not survive the transition from private ownership to control by a board of directors. In the short time between the ASLA jury's decision in May and publication of the award in September, the Garden of Planes was utterly transformed—or "vandalized," in Haag's view.[29]

In the series of four gardens at Bloedel Haag, who had once studied in Japan on a Fulbright grant, tried to remain free of Western cultural con-ditioning. He was intrigued by the notion of an "inexorable cosmic will" whereby matter pulsates, coalesces, dissolves, nourishes, and somehow manages to "flow through life with a life of its own." He later wrote of being at Bloedel, alone or with a loved one, and submerging the senses, becoming "selfless to the subliminal nuances."[30] But in 1986 what moved

the jurors was something beyond these particular philosophical notions, beyond the physical movement through space and the alternation from abstraction to organic processes and back again. "It's about emotion, but it's so damned intelligent," one juror said. "He didn't separate knowledge of the ecological from knowledge of art," said another. "The one quality you see very, very rarely is the quality of soul or magical response. This project is made of that," said a third.[31]

And so a kind of threshold was crossed. The tangled, contradictory, often frustrating realm of the emotions was now accessible to the formal pro-cess of bestowing ASLA awards. And across this threshold more works of landcape architecture imbued with eloquent artistic expression began to enter the ASLA awards program. There, depending on the predilections of the jury, these works were warmly welcomed or coolly scrutinized for other redeeming qualities. Not that an intense concern for artistic expression was new; from Olmsted to Steele to James Rose and his con-temporaries, the thread was strong. Rather, the ASLA awards program, which gained momentum and genuine respect only since the early 1970s, had for years operated with a tacit preference for work that stood up to the tests of rational, objective, pragmatic criteria. Now, from 1986 onward, subjective, emotionally moving, and even ephemeral qualities could constitute admissable evidence of merit. This change did not happen quietly. When the Office of Peter Walker and Martha Schwartz won an ASLA merit award for their roof garden in Boston in 1988, Bud

Parker from Mercer Island, Washington, expressed indignation that the jury had been "seduced" by this project. He felt it lacked qualities that should have been criteria for judgment.[33] Similar protests would surface in the letters column of *Landscape Architecture* from time to time. But no action by a juror drew as much criticism—virtually a flood of long, thoughtful letters—as the selection of an all-male jury in 1989. Jury chair Joseph E. Brown explained that he had tried to win commitments from several women—who later declined to serve on the jury for lack of time. Brown also observed that women were now winning awards "in disproportionately greater percentages than their representation in the profession—or in the ASLA."[34]

Toward the end of the 1980s a few patterns in the ASLA awards program became clear. Each year, one or two jurors from the previous year's competition would serve again, sometimes stepping up to, or down from, the chairperson's role. Award-winners from previous years were invited to serve on juries. Editors from *Landscape Architecture* or other publications participated as jurors, as commentators, or as journalists who transformed the raw material of edited transcripts into coherent essays. All of this provided a measure of continuity, while it justified jurors' observations that the profession was "evolving," not simply changing. Yet the shifts and changes could be dramatic. In 1988 guest editor and chairman George Hargreaves declared that a veil had been lifted from the critical debate during that year's deliberations. He had assembled an outstanding group of jurors in all areas: landscape architects and educators

Richard Haag, Reuben M. Rainey, Richard S. Hawks, Carol R. Johnson, Grant R. Jones, Robert Thayer, Catherine Howett, and Sue Weidemann; architect Peter Eisenman; artist Robert W. Irwin; *Architectural Record* editor Mildred F. Schmertz; and consulting editors Grady Clay and Susan R. Frey. (James G. Trulove had just become editor and publisher of *Landscape Architecture*.) This "tough" jury, which made no honor awards, was stimulated by a great deal of what they saw. And a series of probing discussions followed, focused on both projects and issues.

The issue of meaning surfaced often. Hargreaves was searching for environments that not only provoked thought but also revealed a genuine fusion between environmental planning and design. The effort would be rigorous, laborious, demanding a strong heart, but it might yield work that elicited many levels of perception. Haag, too, looked for a closing of the gap between planning and design. Wary of a Newtonian view of the landscape—mechanistic, quantitative—he feared for the poetics that became lost in Newtonian processes and regretted the resulting lack of enthusiasm, elegance, even boldness in the final product. In planning projects Eisenman searched beyond the "generic" design solutions that they implied for some design integrity, some hint of the specific site, its history, its uses, its buildings. He envisioned, but did not yet find, a truly integrated view of land and buildings. This stirred Jones, trained in both architecture and landscape architecture, to admit a longing for an architecture of the landscape that might be nearly indistinguishable from the landscape of the architecture. The site was also critical for Johnson and Irwin. Johnson noted that ecological principles were not being used in truly broad, "form-giving" ways. And Irwin, wary of metaphors, warned that meaning—the game of meaning—could deflect one from the physical reality of a place.[35]

Talking about meaning, history, poetics, and integration, these jurors were ultimately concerned about connections and interactions. Hargreaves looked for more interactions between design projects and research. "The truths that are uncovered in the analysis of environmental phenomena should be the fodder and the subject of design work," he suggested. "And design research can be the precursor for how that connection is remade." These efforts take time, of course. And nearing the end of a decade notorious for speeding up the process of planning, design, and construction, jurors craved more time to think through certain relationships to the site, the people, the culture, the traditions of landscape architecture. Rainey hoped that out of profound explorations of what is possible in landscape architecture there might emerge "more meaningful places that say something about our culture and who we are." "The key is evolving landscape architecture," Hargreaves insisted, "not isolating art ideas and building them as landscapes." He closed that discussion by noting, "The issue for landscape architecture is staying alive, continuing to evolve."[36]

After a year of restraint in bestowing awards, the 1989 jury gave three Presidential Awards of Excellence. Two went to design projects: the Parque Tezozomoc in Mexico City by Grupo De Diseño Urbano and the Codex World Headquarters, in Canton, Massachusetts, with landscape architecture by Hanna/Olin. The third went to landscape architect and educator Linda Jewell for nine years of columns in *Landscape Architecture* that examined the art and craft of construction. But these achievements were not the subject of the jury's published dialogues. What disturbed the jury was the work not submitted. The chairman, Joseph E. Brown, a senior vice president at EDAW's Alexandria, Virginia, office, called for submissions in important but missing areas, such as suburban design and planning, inner-city landscape design, moderate-income housing, and the integration of new technologies. Sam W. Brown, Jr., a general partner of Centennial Partners, looked for some linkages to the history of design, something evolutionary. Reflecting on the exemplary planning of John Nolen and Elbert Peets in the early twentieth century, Alan Ward, a principal at Sasaki Associates who was trained in both architecture and landscape architecture, sensed that landscape architects were ignoring opportunities to be "shapers of built environments" at the large scale. This was a design problem, he added—not simply a question of planning.[37]

That year two jurors returned to a major concern of the previous jury—a yearning for connections that might transcend the divisions in the field. Michael Van Valkenburgh envisioned the sort of project that would cross the boundaries within, and between, categories, "a kind of design/research/planning." And in an accompanying article John T. Lyle urged that diversity alone was not sufficient. Most of the 1989 award-winning entries, in his view, had the free-standing quality of virtuoso pieces. Looking for greater connections among them and a greater flow of information among landscape architects, he posed the model of biologists or physicists, who must build upon past achievements before they can transcend them. One might have wished that Lyle had clarified some differences between creativity in science and creativity in art. But his call for more connections, greater eloquence, and more flow of ideas was unassailable.[38]

Given landscape architects' fascination for diversity, interconnections, and their own evolving profession in the 1980s, Darwin's concept of evolution has hovered over these pages, darkening them like a long shadow. But the conventional phrase "survival of the fittest" (Herbert Spencer's phrase, not Darwin's) has been absent; it has not seemed quite appropriate for thinking about landscape architecture, particularly in light of recent developments in biology.[39] Pondering the continual "outward expansion of life on earth," some scientists prefer the ramifications of the Gaia hypothesis, in which life forms appear to be intimately connected within communities of interactions that constitute a whole, living system.[40] In this context, the notion of "survival of the fittest" has given way to the idea of "survival of the fit"; for the old preoccupation with bloody, fight-to-the-death competition for survival—itself a survival of a nineteenth-century Western world view—conflicts with instances of a kind of altruism, or symbiosis, in nature.[41]

Looking for some affirmation of their own values and beliefs, landscape architects can turn not only to contemporary biological theory but also to one of the profession's heroes, Loren Eiseley. In *The Unexpected Universe* (1969), Eiseley, the late distinguished archaeologist and anthropologist at the University of Pennsylvania, explored themes that had haunted and fascinated him over a lifetime—particularly natural selection and its relation to the finer qualities of human beings that had been ignored by evolutionists who were obsessed by struggle. Turning instead to qualities such as altruism, cooperation, a sense of beauty, and language, Eiseley cited instances of "mutual aid" among much earlier forms of life as well as among human beings. But he also remained fond of the misfits of prehistory: the wet fish gasping as he crawled up on shore, the lizard-bird struggling upward into the air, and other creatures that somehow escaped the "living screen" between one environment and another. "It was the failures who had always won," he wrote, "but by the time they won they had come to be called successes. This is the final paradox, which men call evolution."[42]

"To a large extent, landscape architects have become design facilitators—assuming the broadest roles in bringing about quality change in the global landscape. We are now choreographers of major interdisciplinary planning and design efforts. And, in some instances, the artificial boundary between planning and design is beginning to dissolve, with very positive results."

CHERYL BARTON (1983)

OCEAN SPRAY CRANBERRIES, INC.

LAKEVILLE/MIDDLEBORO, MASSACHUSETTS

CAROL R. JOHNSON ASSOCIATES, INC.

LANDSCAPE ARCHITECTS AND PLANNERS

PHOTOGRAPH BY ALEX MacLEAN, LANDSLIDES

COURTESY OF CAROL R. JOHNSON ASSOCIATES, INC.

"I do not know much about gods; but I think that the river

Is a strong brown god—sullen, untamed and intractable."

T.S. Eliot (1941)

AKRON RIVERWAY

GOODYEAR TECHNICAL CENTER

AKRON, OHIO

JOHNSON, JOHNSON & ROY

LANDSCAPE ARCHITECTS

PHOTOGRAPH COURTESY OF THE ASLA

1984 ASLA MERIT AWARD URBAN DESIGN

"An incredible piece of wildness within the urban fabric, with access planned

for all people that heightens everyone's sensitivity to nature; not at all conde-

scending to handicapped. The name says it all."

ASLA JURY (1984)

ALL PEOPLE'S TRAIL

SHAKER HEIGHTS, OHIO

SCHMIDT COPELAND AND ASSOCIATES

LANDSCAPE ARCHITECTS

PHOTOGRAPH BY GREGORY A. COPELAND, COURTESY OF THE ASLA

1984 ASLA MERIT AWARD PARK AND RECREATIONAL FACILITIES

"A garden is an experience. . . . If it were possible to distill the essence of a garden, I think it would be the sense of being within something while still being out of doors. That is the substance of it; for until you have that, you do not have a garden at all."

JAMES ROSE (1958)

A GARDEN BY JAMES ROSE

FROM *BUILT LANDSCAPES: GARDENS IN THE NORTHEAST*, CATALOG OF AN EXHIBITION

AT THE BRATTLEBORO MUSEUM & ART CENTER, BRATTLEBORO, VERMONT, 1984-1985,

ESSAYS BY MICHAEL VAN VALKENBURGH,

JOHN R. STILGOE, AND JEAN E. FEINBERG

PHOTOGRAPH BY ALAN WARD

THE CATALOG AND EXHIBITION WON A 1984 ASLA HONOR AWARD.

"The reason to devote attention to this design lies in its attempt to shift the boundary of what is acceptable, to retrieve an artistic strategy that has slipped beyond the grasp of the modernist norm. It is a powerful and evocative work; it has been embraced by the community. . . . It is art regardless of how lasting or great it may turn out to be."

LAURIE OLIN (1988)

WILLIAMS SQUARE

LAS COLINAS, TEXAS

THE SWA GROUP, LANDSCAPE ARCHITECTS

ROBERT GLEN, SCULPTOR

SKIDMORE, OWINGS & MERRILL, ARCHITECTS

PHOTOGRAPH BY TOM FOX, COURTESY OF THE SWA GROUP

1985 ASLA HONOR AWARD COMMERCIAL DESIGN

"Being Alive. The search which we make for this quality, in our own lives, is

the central search of any person and the crux of any individual person's story.

It is the search for those moments and situations when we are most alive."

CHRISTOPHER ALEXANDER (1979)

LONGFELLOW GARDEN

SOUTH BRONX, NEW YORK

LEE WEINTRAUB, LANDSCAPE ARCHITECT

WITH THE CITY OF NEW YORK, DEPARTMENT

OF HOUSING, PRESERVATION AND DEVELOPMENT

PHOTOGRAPH BY LEE WEINTRAUB, COURTESY OF THE ASLA

1985 ASLA HONOR AWARD PARK AND RECREATIONAL FACILITIES

"We are today living in a machine age. What is to follow no one knows, but

there is one thing sure: Nature will survive."

TOAD HALL, RESIDENCE OF FRANÇOIS deMENIL

EAST HAMPTON, NEW YORK

DANIEL D. STEWART & ASSOCIATES

LANDSCAPE ARCHITECTS

GWATHMEY SIEGEL & ASSOCIATES, ARCHITECTS

PHOTOGRAPH BY FELICE FRANKEL

1985 ASLA HONOR AWARD RESIDENTIAL & GARDEN DESIGN

"I am still searching for an approach to garden making, one that transcends culture, one that gets to the root of the matter. Suppose the clues are above culture, above intellect, beyond protohumanism, even beyond the reptilian recesses of our minds?"

RICHARD HAAG (1987)

A SERIES OF GARDENS

BLOEDEL RESERVE, BAINBRIDGE ISLAND, WASHINGTON

RICHARD HAAG, LANDSCAPE ARCHITECT

PHOTOGRAPH BY RICH HAAG

1986 ASLA PRESIDENTIAL AWARD OF EXCELLENCE

"Do we have to surrender the visions of Mies, Le Corbusier, Church, or Eckbo to a

tawdry and asocial public environment and a protected and sentimental but illusory

private one? . . . We should retain the viable aspects of the dream and devise a new

modernism that is more sympathetic to land use, to historic fabric, and the Earth itself.

In short, we should revise and humanize modernism."

PETER WALKER (1990)

TANNER FOUNTAIN

HARVARD UNIVERSITY, CAMBRIDGE, MASSACHUSETTS

PETER WALKER WITH THE SWA GROUP

LANDSCAPE ARCHITECTS

PHOTOGRAPH BY ALAN WARD

1987 ASLA HONOR AWARD LANDSCAPE ART AND EARTH SCULPTURE

"The great campus quadrangle of the University of Virginia was the pinnacle

of Jefferson's achievement as architect—and as landscape architect as well,

in fitting the complex to the site."

NORMAN T. NEWTON (1971)

UNIVERSITY OF VIRGINA

HISTORIC CENTRAL GROUNDS LANDSCAPE STUDY

CHARLOTTESVILLE, VIRGINIA

EDAW INC.

LANDSCAPE ARCHITECTS AND PLANNERS

PHOTOGRAPH BY ALAN WARD

1987 ASLA HONOR AWARD

The master plan aims to re-create a grand vision of the past—a vision which informs us of our cultural

antecedents and inspires us to maintain its high aesthetic standards into our future.

Susan Child (1987)

Stan Hywet Hall

Akron, Ohio

CHILD ASSOCIATES, INC.

LANDSCAPE ARCHITECTS

PHOTOGRAPHS BY ALAN WARD

1987 ASLA HONOR AWARD HISTORIC PRESERVATION & RESTORATION

"Art is irreducible to the land, the people, and the moment that produce it; nonetheless, it is inseparable from them. Art escapes history, but it is marked by it. . . . The work of art allows us to glimpse, for an instant, the there in the here, the always in the now."

OCTAVIO PAZ (1983)

PARQUE TEZOZOMOC

MEXICO CITY, MEXICO

GRUPO DE DISEÑO URBANO, SC

LANDSCAPE ARCHITECTS AND ARCHITECTS

PHOTOGRAPH COURTESY OF THE ASLA

1989 ASLA PRESIDENTIAL AWARD OF EXCELLENCE

"Now the habits and patterns of our civilization impose a staccato and more shallow comprehension. There seems to be time only to look, note, and look away. . . .It is a gardener's pleasure, as it could be the designer's privilege, to break this crazy rhythm, to change and break the rush of time, and make the garden a quiet island in which a moment has a new meaning."

RUSSELL PAGE (1962)

CODEX WORLD HEADQUARTERS

CANTON, MASSACHUSETTS

HANNA/OLIN, LTD., LANDSCAPE ARCHITECTS

KOETTER, KIM AND ASSOCIATES, ARCHITECTS

PHOTOGRAPH BY TIMOTHY HURSLEY, COURTESY OF THE OLIN PARTNERSHIP

1989 ASLA PRESIDENTIAL AWARD OF EXCELLENCE

"The landscape improvements will lead to a more human and used environment and

eventually make a significant contribution to life in the Washington, DC, area.

The park offers an articulated garden environment in an otherwise barren cityscape

where the landscape has typically been a filler for unused space."

ASLA JURY (1989)

CRYSTAL PARK

ARLINGTON, VIRGINIA

HUNTER REYNOLDS JEWELL

LANDSCAPE ARCHITECTS

PHOTOGRAPH COURTESY OF REYNOLDS & JEWELL LANDSCAPE ARCHITECTURE

1989 ASLA HONOR AWARD PARK AND RECREATIONAL DESIGN

"In printing, a margin is that odd space between the edge of the text and the edge of the page, a space that may shrink or expand slightly without troubling the reader, a space the author may fill with gloss, a space the reader may embellish with hand-scrawled notes. Margin in fact derives from marge, an old term for coast or shore, strong and vital in Spenser's time but obsolescent by the nineteenth century."

JOHN R. STILGOE (1994)

GREAT HIGHWAY OCEAN BEACH

SAN FRANCISCO, CALIFORNIA

MPA DESIGN GROUP

MICHAEL PAINTER, PRINCIPAL IN CHARGE

PHOTOGRAPH BY MICHAEL PAINTER, COURTESY OF THE ASLA

1989 ASLA HONOR AWARD LAND AND WATER RECLAMATION AND CONSERVATION

REGIS GARDENS

WALKER ART CENTER, MINNEAPOLIS, MINNESOTA

MICHAEL VAN VALKENBURGH ASSOCIATES, INC.

LANDSCAPE ARCHITECTS AND

BARBARA STAUFFACHER SOLOMON

N E W   T O O L S ,   O L D   W A Y S   O F   C O M M U N I C A T I N G

1 9 9 0   –   1 9 9 8

As the centennial of their profession coincides with the end of this century and the millennium landscape architects have lately scanned their own past with more than momentary curiosity. In 1990 alone special issues of *Landscape Architecture* reviewed the course of modernism and the history of the profession of landscape architecture. Even looking over competing visions of "landscapes for the twenty-first century," jurors and critics could not avoid references to history. Critic M. Paul Friedberg, FASLA, gleaned from the 1990 visionary projects the notion of design as mediator between the past and the future. "While the tools remain the same as those of our antecedents—plants, stone, water, and space," he observed, "what is critical to comprehend is the cultural change. We are no longer a passive, meditative, social, communal people. Our values no longer reflect the village mentality." Hence, landscape architects could no longer

simply record society's relationship to the natural environment. In Friedberg's view they should be taking on new tasks and reflecting the emerging society, even at the risk of some crises of identity and disorientation. In the end they should create places that would expand our visions of ourselves, our social relations, and our relations with the environment.[1]

In his concise article, part criticism and part speculative essay, Friedberg, the landscape architect of many award-winning urban spaces, made no effort to hide his agenda: "I feel like the welcoming committee greeting my profession as it emerges from the woods, leaving behind its love affair with romantic, rustic, naturalistic landscapes." Once focused on the conservation and preservation of the natural environment, the profession of landscape architecture, in Friedberg's view, was now "maturing." It was ready to join a dialogue with art and architec-

CALIFORNIA SCENARIO, COSTA MESA, CALIFORNIA.

ISAMU NOGUCHI, DESIGNER 1980-82

PHOTOGRAPH BY ALAN WARD

ture. And what of the profession's forebears and their dialogues? Friedberg acknowledged the historic contributions of Capability Brown, Frederick Law Olmsted, Sr., and Jens Jensen. Yet in the overthrow of their "antiquated" design vocabularies he recognized a primordial, mythical act—like the defiance of our ancestors, the father, in particular—followed by catharsis, hope, and enthusiasm.

Only two months earlier tributes to these ancestors and their colleagues—from John Muir and Frederick Law Olmsted, Sr. to Aldo Leopold and Lewis Mumford—had reaffirmed some connections with the past that landscape architects of the late twentieth century still cherished. Laurie Olin, a partner in the firm that had received the ASLA's Presidential Award of Excellence in 1989 for the Codex World Headquarters in Canton, Massachusetts, surveyed the eminent nonlandscape architects who had influenced the profession. In addition to Muir, Leopold, and Mumford, Olin wrote about Rachel Carson, Jane Jacobs, Picasso, Einstein, Harold Ickes (secretary of the interior under Franklin D. Roosevelt), and Robert Venturi, the architect whose challenges to modernist conventions from the 1960s onward had prepared the ground for more recent theoretical and formal investigations in landscape architecture. In the same issue Professor William A. Mann of the University of Georgia drew up a timeline of landscape architects' memorable works. And *Landscape Architecture* contributing editor Jory Johnson skimmed the relatively small volume of literature in the field, from Hubbard and Kimball's classic *Introduc-*

tion to Landscape Design (1917) to recent monographs on the work of Lawrence Halprin, Dan Kiley, M. Paul Friedberg, Peter Walker, A.E. Bye, and Sir Geoffrey Jellicoe. "No Real Heroes," was Johnson's tantalizing title, drawn from Walker's comments about the lingering distrust of intuition within the field. The implication was that heroes could be found only in the past—not in the present.[2]

Nevertheless, a genuine respect and affection for heroes surfaced in the October 1990 LA Forum discussion among four leading landscape architects: Ian McHarg, M. Paul Friedberg, Ray Freeman (a thirty-year veteran of the National Park Service and former ASLA president), and William H. Tishler (professor at the University of Wisconsin). As moderator Tishler was unable to stir discussion about Charles W. Eliot's notion, back in 1911, that landscape architecture was a fine art.[3] McHarg preferred to dwell on that gentleman's son, the Charles Eliot who had already begun to expand Olmsted's open-space vision with an ecologically based metropolitan plan for open spaces around Boston. McHarg considered the premature death of Eliot a "terrible tragedy," comparable to the architects' rejection of Lewis Mumford's strong reservations about the commonly accepted technological imperatives of modernism in the early 1960s. Freeman then reminisced about the contributions of Charles Eliot II (Charles Eliot's nephew), the influential twentieth-century landscape architect and planner who had laid out Rock Creek Park in the Washington, D.C. area.

"That's nostalgia," Friedberg countered. The editors of *Landscape Ar-*

chitecture picked up on this discordant note, and for good reason. In fact, nostalgia had nothing to do with the feelings of these leaders for their forebears. McHarg, Freeman, and no doubt many of their colleagues maintained a living connection with their old mentors and heroes. Memory, whether personal or collective, is infinitely more powerful than the sentimental, nostalgic longing for times past—frozen, embalmed, or otherwise preserved from corruption. Memory is more powerful, and potentially more dangerous, because of the living connections or conduits through which influences and alterations travel in both directions—both forward to the future and backward to the past. And in this context a greater tragedy than even the premature death of one Eliot or the rejection of Mumford's ideas would be the severing of memory, the vital connection between their contributions and the consciousness of present and future generations.

And so the need for potent, perhaps even inspiring, connections to the profession's past underlies this account of nearly a century of landscape architecture. History can offer landscape architects some intellectual and cultural connections, some adaptable methods and conceptual tools, some lodes of resources yet to be mined specifically for emerging new problems. And these resources need not be limited to extraordinary built works in history, from Stonehenge to Paley Park. In tracing the historical threads of ecological thinking in landscape architecture, Ervin Zube, FASLA, found no evidence that the pioneers of overlay planning techniques in the 1960s had been aware of the overlay methods used by Warren Manning some forty and fifty years earlier.[4] For lack of awareness of their own

history, then, were landscape architects reinventing the wheel? In this final chapter we shall have to look backward as well as forward as we approach the unassimilated facts and experiences of the present. We are too close to landscape architects' achievements of the 1990s to see them in historical perspective. And yet their recent work needs to be placed into some context. This is the traditional rationale behind the ASLA awards program—to sort out from a mass of work and thought those things that a group of jurors believe to be most important at the time. Thus, the program serves as a barometer of opinion and values, and over time it has become a lens through which to view the past. The program has also been a sieve through which to sift for the finest particles of beauty, responsible stewardship, wisdom, and prescience. When Grady Clay was involved in the ASLA awards program, often as editor and once as a juror, he used to look forward to the process of plucking something out of obscurity and then giving it life, visibility. Always looking for new directions, he reflected recently, "A good selection committee will have the wit and the ability to take out portents of the future. That's when an award is really worth its weight in gold."[5]

But do the awards reflect the most critical issues of our own time? Are landscape architects making places worth paying for and caring for in inner cities? Or are they leaping beyond several rings of city, suburb, and edge city to build yet again on the greenfield sites that were once agricultural land or some kind of wilderness? As reflected in the pages of *Landscape Architecture* over the past ten years, many issues thought to be critical both to society and to the profession hover around the search for a good place to live. The spectrum of opinion is fairly wide, encompassing ASLA fellow John Rahenhamp's defense of suburban sprawl as "the vehicle by which the middle class found a decent place to live" as well as landscape architect Ignacio Bunster-Ossa's insistence on drawing "hard urban limits and sticking to them."[6] Most landscape architects would agree that, for all people—whether in the inner cities, in suburbs, in "pedestrian pockets" with integral transportation systems, or in "traditional neighborhood developments"—the quality of life is a critical issue. They would agree on the importance of environmental quality, energy and natural-resource conservation, and some kind of sustainability. Most would probably agree on the need for some measure of aesthetic quality—although in 1994 ASLA juror Randy Hester, a professor at the University of California, Berkeley, pointed out with regret that "we award the projects that are really beautiful and a little irresponsible, but never those that are environmentally responsible but a little bit ugly."[7]

Added to these critical issues of the larger society, some in the profession are still hoping to encourage more critical review of projects, more theory, more research in the field, and more attention to history. "The history of the profession is our group memory. It is not just the exercise of antiquarian interest," asserted University of Virginia Professor Reuben Rainey not long ago. In his view, a knowledge of history—even of the fairly recent past—is essential to good practice. And Kenneth Helphand, a professor at the University of Oregon, would agree, while noting that the profession has only begun to discover its own history in the last decade—since the 1980s.[8]

One issue that has not yet stirred much concern among landscape architects is the interrelated challenge of technology and the media since the advent of computers, fax and satellite transmissions, plotters, e-mail, virtual reality, and the internet. In a steadily increasing volume of articles about the application of new technologies to practice, there is little mention of the risks and down sides that are not limited to sore wrists, eye-strain, and the disappearance of freehand drawing.[9] This issue will be seen in some historical perspective below. Meanwhile, we can look for tentative conclusions to the stories of environmental planning and research—and of art and design.

It will be recalled that by the end of the 1980s an enlarged concept of environmental planning had brought more players to the field in which landscape architects had once hoped to be undisputed leaders. It was not the first time that landscape architects faced interprofessional competition. This time, however, instead of trying to close ranks and defend the boundaries of the profession, the ASLA made a bold move. In 1990 the society opened its awards program to nonlandscape architects in all categories except design. This allowed the art historian Robin Karson to win an ASLA honor award in 1990 for her book, *Fletcher Steele, Landscape Architect* (1989), the same year that other honor awards for communications went to the U. S. Forest Service Reserved Water Rights

Case (with critical input from EDAW's landscape architects) and to *Saving America's Countryside: A Guide to Rural Conservation* by a group of authors that included landscape architect J. Timothy Keller.[10] As professional boundaries became more permeable, so the awards categories encompassed a broader range of critical factors.

In 1990 the single honor award for planning went to the Grand Main Corridor plan by Howard Needles Tammen & Bergendoff of Kansas City (with landscape architects F. Christopher Dimond and Rick S. Howell). Based on the "rich history of Kansas City's park and boulevard system," this plan was praised for expanding upon that history as well as for garnering a broad-based consensus in the city. In 1991 of the two honor awards for planning, one recognized excellence in urban design and revitalization (Sasaki Associates' Gateway Project in downtown Cleveland, directed by landscape architect and urban designer Alan L. Ward), while the other recognized excellence in "ecological planning" (the Tijuana River Valley Management Plan by a group of landscape architecture graduate students at California Polytechnic University in Pomona and their teachers—John T. Lyle, Francis Dean, Jeffrey K. Olson, and Arthur Jokela).[11]

In 1993 of three honor awards for planning one award recognized grassroots participation (the Loess Hills Scenic Byway in Oakland, Iowa, by Mimi Wagner Askew of the U.S. Soil Conservation Service); another recognized historic landscape preservation (the Mount Auburn Cemetery Master Plan by The Halvorsen Company of Boston); and the third celebrated a "bold juxtaposition between culture and nature" (EDAW's

plan for the Sutro Baths Historic District, overlooking the Pacific at the western edge of San Francisco). Dealing with a portion of the Golden Gate National Recreation Area, the Sutro Baths rehabilitation project entailed research into environmental, economic, historical, and cultural factors. Its end product was a proposal that would provide two things: public access to the magnificent ocean cliffs and a conceptual reconstruction of the old baths to be projected via lasers onto the city's notorious fog as a ghostly reminder of another era. Were Cheryl Barton and her colleagues at EDAW engaged in environmental planning? Or a high-tech art piece? When the 1993 jurors considered this work "planning and urban design" of a high order they in effect encouraged further explorations of planning intertwined with art.[12]

It may be too soon to detect a new direction for environmental planning in the ASLA awards of the 1990s. In 1995 honor awards in planning went to the Forty-Mile Loop Master Plan, a system of parks and parkways to encircle Portland, Oregon, by David Evans & Associates with Mel Stout as landscape architect; and to PLACE3S, a computer-assisted methodology for designing sustainable communities by landscape architects McKeever/Morris. In 1996 the three honor awards for planning shared a common concern for physical connections both within and beyond the project's boundaries. The University of Cincinnati Master Plan by Hargreaves Associates was a study in linkages, connections, and networks of open space and pathways. There, a concept of "force fields" generated by existing buildings, landforms, and vegetation became the framework for design. Another project, the plan for Harima Science Garden City in Hyogo Prefecture, Japan, by Peter Walker William Johnson and Partners involved considerable reforestation—for the magnificent mountainous site had been insensitively regraded before the landscape architects arrived. This plan also introduced new systems of circulation for vehicles, pedestrians, and cyclists along with an open-space system that linked the new town center with housing and trails in the forested periphery. (Thinking of such garden cities as Radburn, New Jersey, juror Robert B. Riley, FASLA, remarked, "It could be Clarence Stein talking.")[15]

Finally, a third honor-award-winning planning project in 1996—the Lincoln Park Framework Plan, directed by landscape architects in the Chicago Park District Office of Research and Planning—entailed four years of public involvement and ultimately considered the open spaces beyond the park's 1,200-acre domain. Juror Kurt Culbertson, FASLA, found a great deal to praise in this project: the level of scientific research, the vegetation and visual assessment, the respect for historic and contemporary urban context, and the lengthy public involvement—for this was a grassroots effort from the start, begun at the instigation of local organizations.

Looking back on these awards of the 1990s we sense that the pipe dream of ASLA awards juror Michael Van Valkenburgh back in 1989 was actually materializing—that projects were crossing the boundaries of planning, design and art, and communications and research. In the process the work became richer, more layered, offering new bases on which

to build and grow. In the late 1970s few of these projects would have been considered "environmental planning," as they are today. In the absence of a commonly shared redefinition of the term, landscape architects' notions of environmental planning seem to have shifted from a focus on scientifically based studies controlled by experts to a diverse array of studies based on scientific, social, economic, and even aesthetic concerns that can be widely understood and shared by the public.

If this is the case, then it may be that landscape architects have quietly moved among the vanguard, the "fourth wave" of American environmentalism that Mark Dowie has identified in *Losing Ground: American Environmentalism at the Close of the Twentieth Century* (1995). Here Dowie traces much of the recent decline in the American environmental movement to a tragic flaw among some of our most prestigious mainstream environmental organizations—their lack of attention to the concerns of their own grassroots or regional chapters. Notwithstanding the title, *Losing Ground* recognizes a glimmer of hope in the current wave of efforts by coalitions of ordinary working people, especially minorities, to secure "environmental justice" for all people.[14] This idea emerged from reaction to such calamities as the contamination of Love Canal in upstate New York, which was recognized in the 1970s, and the toxic leak at Bhopal, India, in 1984. For landscape architects it is a familiar notion—high-minded yet basic. Environmental justice was the first tenet in a "Humanistic Design Manifesto" put out in 1982 by a group in Berkeley, California, that included Donald Appleyard, Randy Hester, and Clare Cooper Marcus.[15] Surely it is also embedded in

John Lyle's concept of a "movement toward mutually life-enhancing relationships between humans and the biosphere."[16]

In April 1990 an entire issue of *Landscape Architecture* was devoted to the landscapes of Isamu Noguchi. Historians, critics, journalists, educators, and practicing designers all reflected on the sculptor's achievements and his influence on landscape architecture worldwide. In a separate article Peter Walker, a partner in The Office of Peter Walker Martha Schwartz, offered a historical overview of the ways in which Noguchi had both interacted with, and remained aloof from, mainstream developments in American landscape architecture. And Walker ended with thoughts of the road not taken: "What if the interest in scientific and technological knowledge and economic and social problem-solving had been tempered with a not-so-rational interest in the beautiful and the subconscious? Perhaps, then, some of us would have followed the lead of this creative and unique landscape architect toward a deeper instinctive understanding of the Earth, its life and psychic forces, and the mysteries of its sacred stones."[17]

A month later John O. Simonds, FASLA, drew a fine line between art and landscape architecture. An early recipient of ASLA professional awards and cofounder of the Pittsburgh-based firm, Simonds and Simonds (now EPD), Simonds is also the author of some widely used textbooks on landscape architecture. In May 1990, responding to *Landscape Architecture's* recent LA Forum on modernism—a discussion with Peter Jacobs, Martha Schwartz, and Elizabeth Meyer, an assistant professor at

Harvard's Graduate School of Design—Simonds wanted to differentiate landscape art from landscape architecture. Whereas the first was a matter of "pictorial design or aesthetic experience," the second was "the art and science of preserving or creating compatible relationships between people and their activities and the natural world about them." While he welcomed new ideas from artists and the art world, Simonds cautioned, "Landscape architecture is not primarily a visual art. Like architecture and engineering, it is basically functional." He believed function could include such things as a sense of well-being, ecological fit, and even philosophical integrity. But one thought remained provocative: "Landscape architecture is not primarily a visual art."[18]

In that year, 1990, the ASLA awards jurors did not bestow any honor awards in the design category. The fact that the number of award-winning built works dropped sharply (to eleven, down from thirty-six in 1989), while the total number of awards in the other categories rose somewhat was not mystifying. Parts of the United States, especially the Northeast, were suffering from a severe recession that would dampen prospects for the building industry through 1993. Then, too, by opening the competition in planning, analysis, communications, and research to nonlandscape architects, the number of entries in those categories rose. In any event, the ASLA awards chair Ervin Zube felt that bestowing fewer awards overall would raise the value of each award.[19]

And so began a decade of awards programs in which some evolutionary changes of the past twenty years—the rekindling interest in garden design, the increasing sophistication of graphic communication, the growing concern for critical review, the dissolving of old boundaries between categories and professions—all had to be reconciled with the collective values of each new jury, year by year. It disturbed Zube that some 1990 merit awards for design enjoyed disproportionate coverage in *Landscape Architecture*—apparently because of bold imagery rather than the jurors' evaluations.[20] Some readers might be put off by an award that seemed unwarranted, but increasingly readers would also protest that the published criticisms of entries that did (or did not) win awards had gone too far. Back in the 1980s the published discussions conducted by jury chairs Cheryl Barton and George Hargreaves had been remarkably frank—mainly about issues but also about projects. In the early 1990s, however, published comments began to seem unduly personal, unnecessarily negative. In recent years attributed comments have been sharply limited, while journalists' nonjudgmental descriptions have expanded.

The 1991 awards juries, chaired by Laurie Olin, were "remarkably harmonious," according to David Dillon, the journalist and 1986 ASLA awards juror who summarized the proceedings. In 1991 Sasaki Associates received the ASLA's first Classic Award for the Deere and Company Administrative Center in Moline, Illinois—a serene corporate landscape dating from the late 1950s with a formidable Cor-ten steel building by Eero Saarinen. Stuart O. Dawson, FASLA, the partner in charge, has freely acknowledged the contributions of his mentor, Hideo Sasaki, on those grounds, while also crediting the client (different CEOs, same company), who retained the firm over three decades to design additions and oversee the maintenance of their landscape.[21]

While President George Bush referred to the 1990–1991 recession as "relatively short," lasting only eight months, landscape architects had to make the best of the slow recovery that stretched into 1993 without a definitive end.[22] Thus cyclical economic concerns may lie behind some of the frustration voiced by ASLA awards jurors in 1992 and 1993. Yet the issues raised seemed to be long-term and deep-seated. In 1992 William J. Johnson urged landscape architects to speak out on major issues, to stand up for what's right, and to "get inside the system that builds America." His fellow design juror, Martha Schwartz, seemed to agree. Landscape architects had little power, she noted. Still, they needed to have the "courage of their convictions" and to imagine the future. Meanwhile, landscape architect Susan Child, also a design juror that year, regretted the abundance of short-term solutions and the absence of independent thought.[23] In 1993 journalist Mac Griswold characterized the current phase of the profession as reflective. It seemed that landscape architects were willing to adopt new methods of research and to contemplate new technologies. Although individual jurors were openly and freely critical of what they saw, the jury as a whole was ultimately hopeful, she sensed. With "dogged realism" they could better appreciate grassroots and neighborhood projects even while they honored the larger, monumental works. In the end she recognized two current approaches to design: monumental and environmental—or what Darrel Morrison viewed as "sequential landscape."[25] Such was the context in 1992 and 1993 when a Classic Award was bestowed on two projects. These were years when the relatively rare President's Award of Excellence was also given—perhaps not by coincidence. For these highest honors were bestowed at a time of searching, uneasiness, and discontent with the status quo, both within and beyond the profession. No doubt they indicate at least a desire to look back into the profession's past and recognize excellence in something enduring, mature, cared for, and widely appreciated.

In 1992 the Classic Award went to the Donnell Garden (1948) in Sonoma County, California—an early postwar landscape where the permanent residence was built long after Thomas Church and his associates laid out the garden, including a pool and its attendant structures. That year the President's Award of Excellence went to the Central Park Conservancy in New York City—not for any single achievement but for a continuum of restoration, maintenance, fund-raising, public education, and the efforts of volunteers. Thus two icons of the profession were honored: one private and distinctly modern; the other public, rooted in a design tradition that can be traced back to Olmsted, Repton, Brown, Sir William Chambers, and the time-hallowed gardens of China.

In 1993 the Classic Award went to Foothill College in Los Altos Hills, California. This project of the late 1950s and early 1960s was the work of a firm—Sasaki, Walker Associates/San Francisco—that shared common roots with the firm that won the President's Award of Excellence that year—the multidisciplinary firm of Sasaki Associates. Back in the late 1950s it was all one firm—Sasaki, Walker Associates, in Watertown, Massachusetts. Hideo Sasaki, Peter Walker, Stuart O. Dawson, and others made early contributions to the Foothill project before Walker moved back to California to complete the work. Thus the 1993 jurors bestowed their highest honors on one highly influential project that had matured for more than thirty years and on a forty-year-old organization of people of diverse backgrounds and talents—not all of them landscape architects.[25]

Lately there have been changes in the way ASLA awards are selected and published. In 1994 *Landscape Architecture* first presented the awards for research—led by Robert L. Thayer's book, *Gray World, Green Heart*, which won the President's Award of Excellence. Jurors have also sensed a need to attract more "unknown" firms and projects to the competition. Meanwhile, juries have become more diverse. Since 1990 they have included more people from different ethnic groups, including African-Americans Juanita Shearer, David Lee, Walter Hood, and Karen Phillips. In 1995 the jury included six women and three men. In 1996 and 1997, however, no jurors' portraits were published. And lately the identity and role of the jury chair have been less apparent to the reader. The few published comments by jurors have remained anonymous. As a result, any sense of authority—in leading a jury, in shaping the framework of debate, in asserting a set of values—is difficult to detect. Instead, we remember the quotable lines.

In 1994 landscape architect Walter Hood, a professor at the University of California, Berkeley, noted, "We think we have to interpret. We are always trying to tell people how to feel, smell, touch, when, in fact, experience only becomes personal through discovery."[26] In 1997 veteran awards juror Alan Ward asked of the awards program, "Is its purpose to recognize excellence or is its purpose to advance the art of critical analysis? Now, one can say 'Both,' but one has to get in front of the other."[27] Before the early 1970s Ward's question would not have made sense. And there would have been no connection between what Hood and Ward were saying. But in our postmodern era—when absolute standards of excellence and all kinds of authority are questioned—personal experience seems as valid a basis of judgment as social and environmental values or theories of semiotics and structuralism.

There is indeed an "art" of critical analysis, which can be as personal as Bernard Berenson's or Sigfried Giedion's or as apparently objective as that of H.W. Janson—whose *History of Art* has introduced countless undergraduates to the world of art since 1962. However different their approaches, these earlier historians and critics looked at works of art and architecture with at least an intuitive understanding of excellence, the criteria for which could be widely shared once they were stated in simple language. But postmodern critics often speak in a language that remains incomprehensible to the literate nonspecialist. In addition, postmodern critics have challenged not only culturally determined standards of excellence but even the concept of authorship. Some literary critics now see themselves as coequals, in a sense coauthors or even "authors" of what they read, for they assume that the "text" no longer has any absolute

authority of its own.[28] The postmodern critic may aspire to be an artist, less humble, and more versatile than critics in the past. In the process, however, the purposes of criticism change. As *New York Times Magazine* editor James Atlas reflected in a recent inquiry into the controversies over postmodern criticism and the Great Books, "The civilizing purpose of literature, its capacity to inculcate values even as it instructs us in the ambiguity of human conduct, is disparaged or ignored. . . . Literary criticism has become an elaborate game of interpretation."[29] How will critics of landscape architecture resist the allure of this game, having found the tools and the specialized languages to play it? Will landscape critics convey their own artful perceptions and articulate their criteria for judgment without resorting to language comprehensible only to a few? The outcome is important, for the civilizing purpose of landscape is at stake.

The honor awards for design from 1994 through 1996 were few, but each recognized a different kind of beauty, derived from different purposes and explorations, sometimes from the use of unusual materials: in 1994 the line of waterproof pipe, at grade, that illuminates and unifies the different gardens at IBM Japan's Makuhari Building by Peter Walker William Johnson and Partners; in 1995 the plastics and recycled materials of the Durfee Gardens at the University of Massachusetts, Amherst, by Dean Cardasis and Associates; and in 1996 the stainless steel at the Plaza Tower and Town Center Park in Costa Mesa, California, by Peter Walker

William Johnson and Partners. The other honor-award-winning design project in 1996, the Neurosciences Institute in La Jolla, California, was viewed as a symbiosis between the architecture by Tod Williams Billie Tsien & Associates and the landscape by Burton Associates.[30]

That year the President's Award of Excellence went to the Village of Yorkville Park in Toronto, Canada, by Martha Schwartz, Ken Smith, David Meyer Landscape Architects (designed by Smith, directed by Meyer). Using new and old materials—stone, brick, concrete, galvanized and stainless steel, cold-cathode lighting, and vegetation—Smith achieved a synthesis of the profession's diverse interests from urban design and artistic expression to biodiversity. The long, narrow urban park presents a microcosm of the diverse Canadian landscape. Each portion is distilled to an essence—a garden—and the series of gardens is geometrically ordered within the geometrically ordered city.

Juror Kurt Culbertson, FASLA, observed of the evaluation process generally, "At some point it really boils down to what is memorable and what moves you . . . ."[31] True. Yet by 1997 ASLA awards jurors were also yearning for a more apparent, clearly articulated basis for making judgments. Alan Ward's call for a fresh look at the purpose of the awards program—which might be to advance the art of critical analysis—was seconded. Landscape architect Mary Margaret Jones felt that a more open critical debate would extend the learning process. And William H. Roberts, FASLA, suggested that display panels of award-winning projects be exhibited at the next annual meeting. Back in the 1950s, it will be

recalled, this was standard practice, and out of it arose the current awards program. Now the ASLA would set up a video program about the awards to run continuously through the 1997 annual meeting. In addition, there would be an open forum on the current award-winning projects.[32]

In 1997 the highest design awards went to projects involving the reuse of developed land. Cornell, Bridgers, and Troller won the Classic Award for the Franklin D. Murphy Sculpture Garden (1963), which had replaced a parking lot at the University of California, Los Angeles. Martha Schwartz, Inc., received an honor award for the witty and exceedingly functional revision of Jacob Javits Plaza in New York, formerly the site of Richard Serra's controversial *Tilted Arc*. Peter Walker William Johnson and Partners won an honor award for the environmentally sensitive Longacres Park near Seattle—The Boeing Company's corporate campus that replaced an old racetrack. The public golf course in southeastern Wisconsin designed by landscape architects Kerry Mattingly and Gregg Kuehn did not involve reuse, but it, too, was praised for sensitivity to the environment as well as for a sculptural use of grasses.

In 1997 all the design jurors were landscape architects—Ed Black, principal of Land Studio; Mary Margaret Jones, principal of Hargreaves Associates; and William H. Roberts, a founding partner and practicing partner of Wallace Roberts and Todd. Their choice for the President's Award of Excellence was the reshaping of a one-acre suburban landscape into the Therapeutic Garden for Children by landscape architect Douglas Reed, who undertook this project while he was a principal at

Child Associates in Cambridge, Massachusetts. This garden at the Institute for Child and Adolescent Development, west of Boston, could be many things—a magical place of "worlds within worlds," as Alan Ward noted, or simply an invitation to stroll along a narrow, steel-sided rill of water that wound across open lawns, into the shadows and out again. The therapist could watch a child follow the rill into the unknown. The historian could trace the rill to William Kent's early-eighteenth-century curving rill at Rousham in Oxfordshire. The designer modestly gave credit to the director of the Institute, who had developed clear ideas about what a therapeutic garden should offer. "My role as the landscape architect was to give form to those theories and ideas," explained Reed. It could be Thomas Church speaking. Like Church, Reed was willing to listen.

Already intertwining, the main threads of these stories, from planning to design and art, and back again, begin to form a pattern—a figure in the carpet—as the final story of technology and the media is briefly sketched in.

Back in the early 1970s, when landscape architects found that process could be as intriguing as products, computers were still something of a novelty. In 1972, when Eckbo, Dean, Austin & Williams won a merit award for a study on the routing of transmission lines for a California utility company, the jury noted, "The way they use the computer made it possible to succinctly analyze their process. This is a much better presentation than any we have seen in this area."[33] By 1978, when ASLA

awards were first given for "research and analysis," landscape architects had used the computer extensively in several award-winning projects of environmental analysis. Often the client was an agency of the federal government. But with a change of administrations in 1981, as noted earlier, the wave of environmental planning, analysis, and research supported (or mandated) by the federal government subsided. In 1984 juror Carl D. Johnson observed of entries for planning and analysis, "We're state-of-the-art ten years ago. There was almost no response to high technology in these awards submissions. We have the ability to use computers, but applications are still limited."[34] Then, by the end of the 1980s opportunities to use increasingly powerful and affordable computers and other forms of electronic technology had multiplied for landscape architects. Computers had become familiar tools—not only for planning, analysis, and research, but also for design, information systems, office management, and financial planning. In this quick overview the use of sophisticated technology over two decades follows a familiar pattern. A challenge from some large entity—a governmental agency or the enemy in time of war—calls for a response that requires a new technology to be developed and controlled by a few highly trained specialists. In time, with many new commercial applications of that technology, new commodities are mass-produced and the costs of manufacturing are brought down. And as this technology frees manufacturers from their roots in a single community or nation they find cheaper labor in countries abroad, and costs go down even further. Before long, what was once a complex machine understood by a few becomes accessible to many. And so a computer becomes "just a tool," nothing remarkable.

This may help to explain why cutting-edge technologies attracted so little attention in the ASLA awards program of the 1990s. Research jurors have tended to ask not "how" a particular project was accomplished technically, but "why?" and "to what effect?" Thus honor awards for research have lately gone to two projects that explored qualitative factors without emphasizing technological tools: in 1991 a study of gardens and yards of African-Americans in the rural south by landscape architect Richard Westmacott, a professor at the University of Georgia, and in 1993 a collection of research studies and policy reports on "Wind Energy and the Landscape," submitted by a group headed by Professor Robert L. Thayer, Jr., of the University of California, Davis. Thayer's study did involve advanced technologies, but he and his group were mainly looking at public attitudes toward the siting of wind turbines. And the jury was interested in how their peer-reviewed publications might have influenced a utility company.[35]

An interest in the qualitative, long-term results of research, rather than in technical tools per se, might be expected in landscape architecture. And yet at some point it is worth looking at the tools themselves for their long-term effects. There is now a growing body of literature to suggest that the computer is much more than a tool, that it is only the latest in a long line of inventions that have inevitably shaped the thought processes of those who use them. While some writers are delighted with the prospects of new ways to perceive, communicate, and wield power and influence, others fear the loss of previous ways of thinking, perceiving, knowing, and communicating.[36] And in light of the foreseeable, long-term effects of modern technology—effects that may be both environmentally devastating and personally liberating—one recent study of tools ends on a cautiously optimistic note.

In *The Axemaker's Gift* (1995) James Burke and Robert Ornstein discuss the interactions that have led human beings to both enrich and endanger their physical environment by developing such tools as the ax, the alphabet, the printing press, and computers. In the 1970s in the Public Broadcasting Service (PBS) television series, *Connections*, Burke told stories of how, throughout human history, one tool, one calamity, one mistake, or one breakthrough has led to another. Later, he developed a darker view of humans' webs of invention in his PBS series, *The Day the Universe Changed*. Now, with coauthor Ornstein, who heads the Institute for the Study of Human Knowledge in Los Altos, California, Burke has shown how technological developments, largely unexamined for social, cultural, and environmental consequences, have already led to life-threatening conditions for plants, animals, and humans.

Quoting Thoreau ("men have become the tools of their tools"), Burke and Ornstein believe that this condition need not persist. As the computer's webs of information become more widely accessible, permeating the process of learning and discovery, "the skills of reading and writing may well become less important," they observe. Agility in visual, aural, and tactile skills may become more important. Once the information super-highway is in place, the abilities to make connections, to "think imaginatively," to see the larger relationships—that is, the abilities of the generalist—may become more valuable than those of a specialist. In the end the authors remain hopeful that the skills needed to navigate the coming information systems will allow humans to avoid the worst-case scenarios of uncontrolled technological development. Over millennia, in the development of certain tools that have nurtured certain human talents, they argue, a wealth of other human talent has been ignored. Harnessing this talent will thus require a nurturing of individual and cultural diversity—a celebration rather than a further suppression of differences.[37]

If this is true, then the prospects might seem bright for landscape architects, particularly those with strengths in design and visual thinking. The diversity that Burke and Ornstein anticipate is already thriving among landscape architects—although the lack of a single strong image of the profession still troubles some of them. Patrick Miller's recent survey of ASLA fellows, mentioned in the Introduction, does underscore a few other long-standing concerns: the lack of understanding of what landscape architects do, the absence of a common base of knowledge and philosophical tenets, and the tendency to defend professional turf from outsiders.[38] But even these issues may fade in an increasingly "wired" world of interconnections. And so, what is to prevent landscape architects from sharing in the power and influence enjoyed by those who can master the most advanced technological tools?

The flaw lies in the implication that reading and writing are skills that can lose importance, perhaps even wither away, without much cause for concern. An affinity for images, connections, and quick intuitive leaps of imagination may seem an attractive substitute for relatively slow linear thought. It may seem "democratic" to dispense with the intellectually demanding processes of learning to read and write. But we don't yet understand the long-term prospects for children who are exposed to computers and television at increasingly tender ages. We do know something about fragmentation in the postmodern world. We know the pressures to divide our attention among too many things, while trying to keep up with all the media that technology makes "essential." We know how to parcel out a grand enterprise into segments that a small army of workers can handle efficiently, if listlessly. And of all people, landscape architects know about the increasing fragmentation of the physical world—developed, redeveloped, overbuilt, abandoned, degraded, perhaps restored, yet never quite made whole. "Cut and control" is the phrase Burke and Ornstein use repeatedly to describe the tools of human conquest, including language itself. Yet language is one of the finest tools we will ever have to develop a vision of wholeness.

This is not to say that computers, CAD systems, geographic information systems, and all the other technological tools are in themselves suspect. Burke and Ornstein are probably justified in hoping that the wise use of these tools will help maintain the earth as a place for living organisms. But they may have underestimated the power of the very words that they themselves use so skillfully. Language is a power, a force that landscape architects have traditionally turned to their own advantage. If few of them could be considered literary artists, landscape architects have, nevertheless, used language to give meaning, sometimes several layers of meaning, to their visions of the landscape—which may itself be layered with geological strata, natural systems, and further layers of brick and stone, ground covers, and canopies. Without the abilities to read, write, speak, and draw with a skilled hand, landscape architects will become merely manipulators of things—or be manipulated. With these abilities they may be able to convey a vision of wholeness that the earth needs so badly. That is their figure in the carpet: the whole carpet, with all its richness of color, texture, thickness, and cultural meaning. It cannot, in the end, be cut up into bits and accessed on a computer screen. It can only be conveyed in the actual, living landscape, in free-hand drawings and renderings, through public speaking, and in the books and essays that landscape architects write themselves.

EDITORS' NOTE: It can be argued that in 1998 the awards represented the triumph of the art of design. Two firms known for their aesthetic concerns—Peter Walker and Partners (PWP), Berkeley, and Hargreaves Associates, San Francisco—between them won sixteen awards: PWP winning four honor and three merit awards as well as the Classic Award for the 1971 Weyerhaeuser Corporate Headquarters in Tacoma (a project Walker designed as a partner with Sasaki Walker and Associ-

ates); Hargreaves Associates, two honor and six merit awards. And other winners included practitioners known in the field as designers: for example, Mario Schjetnan, FASLA, and Jose Luis Perez of Grupo de Deseño Urbano, Mexico City, who won the President's Award of Excellence (for the second time) for Parque El Cedazo; and Michael Van Valkenburgh, FASLA, Cambridge, Massachusetts, who won a merit award for the courtyard of the New School in New York City. Awards also went to such younger designers as H. Keith Wagner, Burlington, Vermont, and Douglas Reed, Cambridge, who have been influenced by the aesthetic aspirations of the older designers.

On closer examination, however, these design projects as well as other award winners reveal no definite dividing line between art and environmental concerns. In the *Landscape Architecture* magazine article announcing the awards juror James Corner pointed out a design trend in the winning projects: "There's not a stylistic agenda either to make the whole site conform to a grid or to make the whole site look like some sort of ecological wetland. A single project can go from some highly formal conditions to some very raw aquatic conditions. This inviting of nature into the design is . . . a shift from ten years or so ago when designers liked a project to be one way—formal—or the other way—natural." Perhaps this shift is a response to such specific design questions as "What does nature look like in the age of fractals?" Or perhaps it suggests a long-awaited synthesis of the research, environmental, and design interests that have seemed antagonistic in previous decades.

"We liked the relationship between the architecture and the landscape,

the lookout plazas, and the simplicity and straightforwardness of

the waterfront furniture and railings."

Mario Schjetnan (1991)

Newcastle Beach park

Bellevue, Washington

Jones & Jones

Architects & Landscape Architects

1991 ASLA Honor Award Design

"Lacking modern machinery, all grading, site construction, and planting was carried

out by hand with the help of more than 1,000 local laborers. The result is a quiet,

hand-tooled museum sheathed in native cantera stone and native plants."

ASLA Jury (1991)

MEXICO'S MUSEUM OF ANTHROPOLOGY

XALAPA, MEXICO

EDWARD D. STONE, JR. & ASSOCIATES

PLANNERS AND LANDSCAPE ARCHITECTS

PHOTOGRAPH COURTESY OF EDSA

1991 ASLA HONOR AWARD DESIGN

"A powerful overlap of ecological diligence and picturesque composition.

At once a visual feast and a science lesson."

ALEX KRIEGER (1991)

CROSBY ARBORETUM

PICAYUNE, MISSISSIPPI

EDWARD L. BLAKE, JR., CAROL FRANKLIN,

AND ROLF SAUER, LANDSCAPE ARCHITECTS

ANDROPOGON ASSOCIATES, LTD., CONSULTANTS

JONES AND JENNINGS, ARCHITECTS

PHOTOGRAPH BY EDWARD L. BLAKE, JR., COURTESY OF THE ASLA

1991 ASLA HONOR AWARD DESIGN

293

"This hilltop garden combines ecological concern with the exuberance and

bravura of Roberto Burle-Marx."

PETER WALKER (1999)

VILLA ZAPU

NAPA VALLEY, CALIFORNIA

HARGREAVES ASSOCIATES

LANDSCAPE ARCHITECTS

PHOTOGRAPH COURTESY OF THE ASLA

1991 ASLA HONOR AWARD DESIGN

"We wanted to create a memorable series of spaces as you approach the park. You see the

screen, you hear the crack of the bat, maybe a home run bounces at your feet.

We wanted people to see, hear, and feel the park even if they weren't going to the game."

ALAN WARD (1997)

THE GATEWAY

CLEVELAND, OHIO

SASAKI ASSOCIATES, LANDSCAPE ARCHITECTS AND

URBAN DESIGNERS

PHOTOGRAPH BY SUSAN DUCA, COURTESY OF SASAKI ASSOCIATES

1991 ASLA HONOR AWARD PLANNING & URBAN DESIGN

"What the Initiative does seem to involve is a lot of definition and primary explanation,

much of it repetitious and some of it imbued with a stern voice; this is because at the

most basic level the Initiative is issuing a warning that we need to look at all landscapes

historically. [Charles] Birnbaum believes that the profession lost this historic eye . . .

during the period of the Modernist rejection of the Beaux Arts."

Jane Brown Gillette (1997)

HISTORIC LANDSCAPE INITIATIVE

National Park Service

Photograph at Wave Hill from The Flower Garden toward the Palisades

Courtesy of Wave Hill

1995 ASLA Presidential Award of Excellence

"This garden demonstrates a desert-derived alternative view of what

a man-made landscape can be."

George Hargreaves (1992)

Arid Zone Trees

Queen's Creek, Arizona

Steve Martino & Associates

Landscape Architects

Photograph by Steve Martino, Courtesy of the ASLA

1992 ASLA Honor Award Design

"It's a wonderful way to dramatize the power of a great river cutting

through that limestone."

Susan Child (1992)

RIVERFRONT PROMENADE

INDIANAPOLIS, INDIANA

DANADJIEVA & KOENIG ASSOCIATES

LANDSCAPE ARCHITECTS

ANGELA DANADJIEVA, PARTNER IN CHARGE

PHOTOGRAPH BY J. FRED HOUSEL. COURTESY OF DANADJIEVA & KOENIG ASSOCIATES

1992 ASLA HONOR AWARD DESIGN

"The founders of Mt. Auburn created a garden of graves. The enormous success of the cemetery and its imitators throughout the nation grew from the public's acceptance of the physical isolation of the dead from the living. The public accepted such a change only within the naturalistic landscape that the founders carefully created from the hills and valleys of the new cemetery. This landscape offered air and light, safety and nature, joy and optimism."

David Charles Sloane (1991)

MT. AUBURN MASTER PLAN

BOSTON, MASSACHUSETTS

THE HALVORSON COMPANY, INC.

PHOTOGRAPH BY ALAN WARD

1993 ASLA HONOR AWARD DESIGN

HARVARD YARD MASTER PLAN

Cambridge, Massachusetts

MICHAEL VAN VALKENBURGH ASSOCIATES

LANDSCAPE ARCHITECTS

Photograph by Alan Ward

1993 ASLA Merit Award Planning & Urban Design

"Many of those who have been intimately involved with Bryant Park's restoration

regard it as a monument to the vision of Holly Whyte. . . . For Laurie Olin, Whyte is quite simply 'our

patron saint. . . . We tried to give physical form to some of his ideas.'"

J. WILLIAM THOMPSON (1997)

BRYANT PARK RESTORATION

NEW YORK, NEW YORK

HANNA/OLIN, LTD., LANDSCAPE ARCHITECTS

PHOTOGRAPH BY ALEX MACLEAN, LANDSLIDES

1994 ASLA MERIT AWARD DESIGN

"The modern world has created a landscape which is a stage for the drama of two great protagonists, Nature and Technology.

The drama is especially dynamic, since Technology, like some mythic Jekyll and Hyde figure, has within itself two opposing faces and

contrasting personalities. The drama is performed in the landscapes we cherish and those we ignore or despise."

ROBERT L. THAYER, JR. (1994)

DURFEE GARDENS

UNIVERSITY OF MASSACHUSETTS AT AMHERST

DEAN CARDASIS AND ASSOCIATES

LANDSCAPE ARCHITECTS

PHOTOGRAPH BY DEAN CARDASIS

1995 ASLA HONOR AWARD DESIGN

"The original meaning of the word landscape . . . meant a collection, a 'sheaf' of lands, presumably interrelated and part of a system. A land was a defined piece of ground, and we can assume that in the medieval world it was most often used to indicate a patch of plowed or cultivated ground, that being the most valuable kind."

J. B. Jackson (1984)

THE VILLAGE OF YORKVILLE PARK

Toronto, Ontario, Canada

Schwartz Smith Meyer Landscape Architects

Ken Smith and David Meyer

Partners in Charge

Photograph by Ron Blunt

1996 ASLA Presidential Award of Excellence

"As with the architecture [of the Neurosciences Institute] the landscape

architecture combined a large-scale context with a more intimate process of discovery."

WILLIAM S. BURTON (1996)

THE NEUROSCIENCES INSTITUTE
———————————————————————
LA JOLLA, CALIFORNIA

BURTON ASSOCIATES
———————————————
LANDSCAPE ARCHITECTS
———————————————
TOD WILLIAMS BILLIE TSIEN & ASSOCIATES
———————————————————————————————
ARCHITECTS
——————————

PHOTOGRAPH COURTESY OF THE ASLA

1996 ASLA HONOR AWARD DESIGN

"With society's shift from belief in the new to its recognition of limits and interest in what exists, the stylistic explorations in postmodernist landscape architecture have just begun. Pluralism is appropriate. The expression of symbolism, mysticism, and humanism will become a preoccupation. Time, nature, and culture will serve as physical media and subject. . . . Where this will lead and what landscapes may come to look like is, of course, open ended."

GEORGE HARGREAVES (1983)

UNIVERSITY OF CINCINNATI MASTER PLAN

CINCINNATI, OHIO

HARGREAVES ASSOCIATES

LANDSCAPE ARCHITECTS AND PLANNERS

PHOTOGRAPH COURTESY OF THE ASLA

1996 ASLA HONOR AWARD PLANNING & URBAN DESIGN

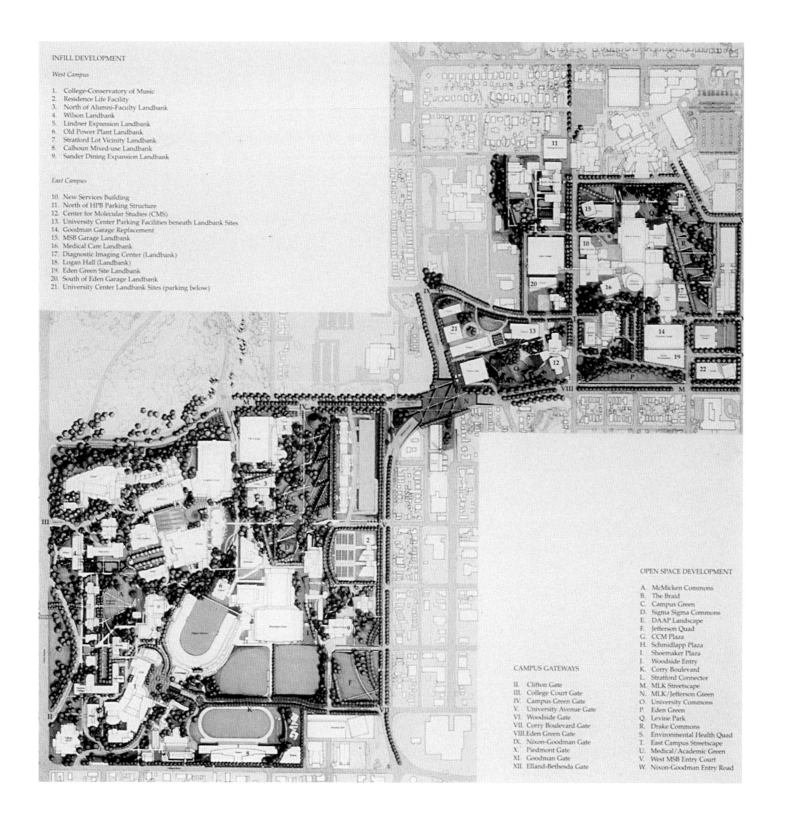

INFILL DEVELOPMENT

West Campus

1. College-Conservatory of Music
2. Residence Life Facility
3. North of Alumni-Faculty Landbank
4. Wilson Landbank
5. Lindner Expansion Landbank
6. Old Power Plant Landbank
7. Stratford Lot Vicinity Landbank
8. Calhoun Mixed-use Landbank
9. Sander Dining Expansion Landbank

East Campus

10. New Services Building
11. North of HPB Parking Structure
12. Center for Molecular Studies (CMS)
13. University Center Parking Facilities beneath Landbank Sites
14. Goodman Garage Replacement
15. MSB Garage Landbank
16. Medical Care Landbank
17. Diagnostic Imaging Center (Landbank)
18. Logan Hall (Landbank)
19. Eden Green Site Landbank
20. South of Eden Garage Landbank
21. University Center Landbank Sites (parking below)

CAMPUS GATEWAYS

II. Clifton Gate
III. College Court Gate
IV. Campus Green Gate
V. University Avenue Gate
VI. Woodside Gate
VII. Corry Boulevard Gate
VIII. Eden Green Gate
IX. Nixon-Goodman Gate
X. Piedmont Gate
XI. Goodman Gate
XII. Elland-Bethesda Gate

OPEN SPACE DEVELOPMENT

A. McMicken Commons
B. The Braid
C. Campus Green
D. Sigma Sigma Commons
E. DAAP Landscape
F. Jefferson Quad
G. CCM Plaza
H. Schmidlapp Plaza
I. Shoemaker Plaza
J. Woodside Entry
K. Corry Boulevard
L. Stratford Connector
M. MLK Streetscape
N. MLK/Jefferson Green
O. University Commons
P. Eden Green
Q. Levine Park
R. Drake Commons
S. Environmental Health Quad
T. East Campus Streetscape
U. Medical/Academic Green
V. West MSB Entry Court
W. Nixon-Goodman Entry Road

"Ever the provocateur, Schwartz contends that her use of such classic Olmstedian elements as Central Park lighting standards and benches—albeit in what she call 'tweaked' forms—offers a kind of wry commentary on the fact that 'while New York remains a cultural mecca for most art forms, exploration in landscape architecture receives little support.'"

Landscape Architecture Magazine, 1997

JACOB JAVITS PLAZA

New York City, New York

MARTHA SCHWARTZ, INC.

Photograph by Alan Ward

1997 ASLA Honor Award

318

"What could the child be about, loitering there upon the doorsteps in a vacant dream? . . .

A mazy paradise still lies ahead, before I shall have completed the circuit of the garden. And even as I

stand wavering, doubtful which delight to follow next, the bell rings out from the distant belfry of the

kitchen, and the endless morning has come to an end."

PERCY LUBBOCK (1922)

THERAPEUTIC GARDEN FOR CHILDREN

INSTITUTE FOR CHILD AND ADOLESCENT DEVELOPMENT, WELLESLEY, MASSACHUSETTS

DOUGLAS REED LANDSCAPE ARCHITECTURE, INC.

LANDSCAPE ARCHITECTS

CHILD ASSOCIATES, INC., SCHEMATIC/CONCEPTUAL DESIGN AND LANDFORM

PHOTOGRAPH BY DOUGLAS REED

1997 ASLA PRESIDENTIAL AWARD OF EXCELLENCE

"We intend that the design for the Franklin Delano Roosevelt Memorial be a more complete experience and, instead of one isolated symbol, that it emphasize the special qualities which only experience over time can create. Our intention is to make a memorial whose environmental qualities are primarily experiential rather than purely visual—one which is evocative, involving, and appropriate for all ages and all people."

Lawrence Halprin (1975)

FRANKLIN DELANO ROOSEVELT MEMORIAL

Washington, DC

THE OFFICE OF LAWRENCE HALPRIN

LANDSCAPE ARCHITECTS

Photograph by Alan Ward 1997

July 1997 *Landscape Architecture* cover story

"... a true university, a mirror of the world, accessible to all true seekers;

each institution a planet within the universe of the mind, creating and shedding light

upon a darker world which looks for it there, and would look for it elsewhere in vain."

JACQUES BARZUN (1944)

FRANKLIN D. MURPHY SCULPTURE GARDEN

UNIVERSITY OF CALIFORNIA AT LOS ANGELES

CORNELL, BRIDGERS, AND TROLLER

LANDSCAPE ARCHITECTS

PHOTOGRAPH BY RICHARD MAYER, COURTESY OF THE ASLA

1997 ASLA CLASSIC AWARD

"The design elevates the landscape to a national symbol."

ASLA Jury (1992)

NEW PARLIAMENT HOUSE

CANBERRA, AUSTRALIA

PETER ROLAND & ASSOCIATES

LANDSCAPE ARCHITECTS

Photograph courtesy of the ASLA

1992 ASLA Honor Award Design

"The golf course is placed, not imposed. When you drive by it,

you're not even aware that a golf course is there."

COUNTRY CLUB OF WISCONSIN

GRAFTON, WISCONSIN

MATTINGLY KUEHN GOLF DESIGN, INC.

PHOTOGRAPH COURTESY OF THE ASLA

1997 ASLA HONOR AWARD DESIGN

"This public landscape must function as a repository for memory, a manifesto

for contemporaneity, and a tool for education."

PETER WALKER (1997)

TOYOTA MUNICIPAL MUSEUM OF ART

TOYOTA CITY, AICHI PREFECTURE, JAPAN

PETER WALKER AND PARTNERS

LANDSCAPE ARCHITECTS

TANIGUCHI AND ASSOCIATES

ARCHITECTS

PHOTOGRAPH COURTESY OF PETER WALKER AND PARTNERS

1997 ASLA MERIT AWARD DESIGN

"What I like about it is the diverse range of conditions and programs it sets up—that

it's not just an open park as a vessel for escape from the city but an open park

that is very engaging of the city."

JAMES CORNER (1998)

PARQUE EL CEDAZO

MEXICO

GRUPO DE DESEÑO URBANO, SC

LANDSCAPE ARCHITECTS

PHOTOGRAPH COURTESY OF THE ASLA

1998 ASLA PRESIDENTIAL AWARD

"The Park throughout is a single work of art, and as such subject to the primary law of

every work of art, namely, that it shall be framed upon a single, noble motive, to which

the design of all its parts, in some more or less subtle way, shall be confluent and helpful. "

REPORT SUBMITTED WITH THE GREENSWARD PLAN, AWARDED FIRST PRIZE BY THE

BOARD OF COMMISSIONERS OF THE CENTRAL PARK (APRIL 28, 1858)

CENTRAL PARK

NEW YORK, NEW YORK

PHOTOGRAPH BY SARA CEDAR MILLER

RECONSTRUCTION OF THE SHEEP MEADOW

CENTRAL PARK CONSERVANCY

NEW YORK CITY DEPARTMENT OF RECREATION

1992 ASLA HONOR AWARD

RECONSTRUCTION OF THE GREAT LAWN AND

ADJACENT LANDSCAPES

CENTRAL PARK CONSERVANCY

VOLLMER ASSOCIATES

1998 ASLA HONOR AWARD DESIGN

PAST PRESENT AND FUTURE

SOME THOUGHTS ON THE PROFESSION OF LANDSCAPE

ARCHITECTURE BY ASLA MEDAL WINNERS

A.E. Bye

"How do you do it?" we are asked. It is not an easy question to answer. You do start out with an idea. When you work on the idea in the outdoors, progress on your design changes like the sculptor's efforts with clay, stone, wood, or metal. It evolves.

The creative landscape architect sculpting the land with bulldozers and graders finds that the light changes from moment to moment as the sun floats through the sky on a sunny day, transforming the look of mounds and valleys, the shadows in between, and the shadows of nearby vertical forms. We have to remember that what we see as landforms in the fall are different from what we see in winter, spring, or summer. Change animates the landscape, and it is fascinating to the interested observer to see the changes occur.

I was once asked by John Gaines of Gainesway Farm in Lexington, Kentucky, to design a lake along a local river that ran through his property. "You have the whole day to do it," he said. I didn't have a survey to use, so I got the idea of driving a pickup truck over the level land to appraise its suitability for a lake. Upon driving over the land I looked into the rearview mirror, and, lo and behold! I could see that the tires were making splendid impressions in the sod, and as I turned, the curves were without kinks and were smooth and even. "I'll design the shape of the lake with the tires," I thought. In an hour or so I came up with an outline appropriate for the need. I could easily see what I was doing. I needed to preserve the design, so I got tall stakes and with the help of Andy Dotsey, my liaison at Gainesway Farm, drove the stakes into the soft soil—close enough so that we could see what we were doing. By midafternoon we had it, and to make the design more visible from afar we flagged each stake with fluttering white ribbons. That evening when John Gaines returned from his office he asked to see the design. "I don't have one," I replied.

"What have you been doing all day?" he asked. I said, "Don't get into a big sweat. Come with me." I took him by the hand, and we shuffled our way down the stony slopes. Halfway down we stopped. "Look," I said. He could "see" the lake. "Wonderful," he proclaimed. "We dig tomorrow." After a whiskey and roast-beef dinner at his home, we went into the living room where there was a roaring fire on the hearth. As he stood before the fire he asked me what he could do for me. "Just step aside," I replied, "so that I can enjoy the fire.

On another occasion Janis Hall and I were asked by the client to design a long drive over their 500 acres of farmland located near the city of Louisville, Kentucky. They, too, did not have a land survey, but we said that we could locate their driveway with a pick-up truck. They were skeptical at first, but when we drove over the land they could see what we were doing. They said, "Go ahead." We drove over the hayfields, through groves of trees, down slopes, up over hills,

VIETNAM MEMORIAL, WASHINGTON, DC

MAYA LIN, ARTIST, HANNA/OLIN LTD. LANDSCAPE ARCHITECTS

PHOTOGRAPH BY ALAN WARD

along a pond, and then over some more hayfields to their front door. They were delighted with the results. "How about details?" "We don't need to draw any; the contractor knows how to build a driveway," we replied. And so without a lot of paperwork and supervision in the field, we got it done.

GARRETT ECKBO

In the roster of professional organizations the ASLA is small. We are vastly outnumbered by those with missions that are seen and felt to be closer to the vital centers of our society. But as a profession we are uniquely aware of the complexity of the environmental changes that mankind has persuaded old Mother Earth to allow us to make in her housekeeping since we first began to focus on sheltered living in caves and tree houses.

Shelter grew rapidly beyond security and weather protection to reflect the growth of family, tribal, local, area, national, religious, and geographical organization—the socio-political history of people. As it became richer and more complex it demanded greater technical and physical expression for both function and security.

Today, around the world on all continents and many an island, we

live in a complex network of national and local organizations that have taken over the patterns and forms of nature to replace them with structures that fulfill our own needs. Nature, originally composed of earth, rock, water, vegetation, and animal life, has been taken over in much of the world by the concrete, steel, wood, masonry, glass, and utilities needed by human society.

We are now closer to world urbanization than we have ever been. Politically this can only be brought about by world peace through world government—not necessarily through single concentrated power centers, but rather through nucleated, coordinated cooperative structures. Much hard work remains to be done to achieve world peace. But we will do it, because we must.

The nature of the design problem that urban society imposes on us is clearly exemplified in existing urbanization and in the complexities of proposals for new cities around the world. Historically the original existing landscape structure has been systematically, though irregularly, replaced by urban development, which has continuously increased in density, measured by numbers of people on the land. Science fiction has regularly presented us with warning visions of future supercities

that totally eliminate nature. The forces that accelerate this growth are basically economic and only partially democratic. The primary pressure is from expanding birth rates. Only China has attempted to reduce this pressure—with considerable resistance from its people. Growing populations are seen as symbols of success in spite of economic failure, perhaps because the growth areas benefit the sponsors and directors of growth.

Urban growth and the resource development that it demands are steadily and persistently eliminating natural landscapes and the processes that support their growth. Powerful movements for resource protection and growth control have slowed the devastation that seems to symbolize progress, but they have not stopped it or modified its basic attitudes and demands. At this late date in historical development we appear to be a society dedicated to urban development that leaves shrinking areas of intensive agriculture and resources for a future of continuing population growth.

World governments and the forces that dominate economic development seem determined to continue such development regardless of its impact on the basic natural world. The machinery of economic development—called "progress"—is unstoppable once its

carefully programmed rationale has begun to move. The program is based on the development and use of resources that are relevant to existing programs.

Old-fashioned resource-development programs, focused on extracting the most profit from nature for the least cost, have begun to encounter the outrage of societies that must deal with the vast devastation such programs leave behind. Dedicated, thoughtful programs focused on the preservation and renewal of devastated areas may require compensation and reconstruction from the exploiters. The problems may become infinitely more complex. Conservation programs, originally responsible for nature parks and the preservation of wilderness areas around the world, now must interlock in cooperation with the exploiters to block the genteel devastation that they perpetuate, to rebuild a natural world in which resource use and preservation by redevelopment can function cooperatively.

We can envision a future world that integrates the construction industry with ecological-preservation concepts and processes—a whole new resource for civilized environmental design.

Perhaps at this particular time in history what is most important is to reconstruct the connections between man and nature that the Industrial

Revolution so widely shattered and scattered.

Man is a product of nature, beginning as an animal.

Nature is world and universe, the total material complex that houses us. To separate it for various conquests may be the most incredible stupidity we have perpetrated.

But how does it all fit together now?

What we now need is a total review of all landscapes in the world, from primitive, original, natural to hi-tech human construction for whatever purposes. A museum of world landscapes could become our guidebook for a coordinated, self-salvaging world. Salvation can grow from spiritual to realistic and from rhetoric to realism.

These are large words and bold statements. What, if we agree, can we actually do about the situation?

Certainly the ASLA has expanded its vision—and its programming and education—in recent years. This is apparent in the magazine and most of our educational programs. The spirit of Olmsted and his successors is alive and well among us. But where should we go?

A realistic survey among our fellow citizens would certainly reveal wide support for preservation and reconstruction of natural and historic landscapes. There is certainly great interest in, and support for, proposals that

reach beyond preservation into reconstruction, and even development, of landscapes; that reach toward new possibilities resulting from interaction between basic natural socioecological processes; that reach toward a cultural marriage between the nature that still exists around the world and the visions that are developing among all those citizens who are concerned with future environments. These can range from continuations of basic natural ecological processes through social and cultural development traditions as seen by architects, engineers, and other cultural leaders, into the exploration and development of new forms of urban, suburban, and mixed-use development springing from the widespread computerization of all of our work/production processes. This could lead to new urbanisms, suburbanisms, and even more open reintegration with nature. After all, it is now quite possible to visualize very elaborate developments in which architectural, engineering, and landscape concepts combine and interact. Some current electronic leaders are showing us the way. The twenty-first century may be more romantic and startling than we can even now imagine.

The computer certainly contains the potential for breaking down the habitual tendency to separate construc-

tion from nature conceptually. But current efforts to make use of Third World pools of cheap labor via computerized controls may be only the beginnings of very wide social rearrangements and reconstructions. Corporate management may remain in comfortable well-vegetated suburban hideouts, while labor is concentrated in new forms of factories with electronic management and control. Then, what price labor organization and control? And environmental design? Much depends on goals and objectives.

At first man emerged from nature, developing the skills and visions with which to conquer her. From the time the Egyptian pyramids were built to the present day man has developed his own cultural vocabulary with construction, mining, agriculture, and gardening—reshaping the landscape, building cities, roads, and so on. Now the world is largely humanized. The next period, beginning soon if not yet, offers us the ultimate choice: a total structural urbanization of the world, as science fiction and Hollywood generally expect, or the preservation of nature, taking cues from the eighteenth-century English romantics as well as from Japanese, Chinese, and other Asian and African sources that create a happy marriage between nature and human culture.

Of course, the basic resistance to such a harmonious development may come from certain dedicated architecture/engineering practitioners who think of the landscape as a setting for construction that must express its own formal and functional demands. Architecture and engineering are riding high today while the lesser arts (including landscape design) glorify construction without regard for its relationship with nature. That may be the great environmental debate of the twenty-first century.

JULIUS GY. FABOS

We have heard repeated claims in recent decades that landscape architecture is the fastest-growing profession among all design professions. According to the most recent salary survey published in 1998, our earnings surpassed the architects', by approximately twenty percent for the first time in history. Our numbers have also increased impressively. Landscape architects were counted only in the dozens at the end of the nineteenth century. The ASLA membership reached 1,000 by the early 1950s. Currently our membership is over 12,000, but according to rough estimates there may be 30,000 to 40,000 professionals in the United States working in many areas and sectors. Just during my professional career of a third of a century, we grew at least tenfold. We are certainly poised for continued growth in numbers and expansion in the new areas of practice.

Our impact on the larger landscape has increased even more than our professional demographics, and our potential is enormous. In this brief narrative I wish to focus on only one aspect of our broad-based profession, namely on how we came from park-making through open-space planning to greenway planning. This shift towards open-space planning and now greenway planning is clearly a response to the widespread decentralization of all human activities. Our society is increasingly making decisions outside of core urban areas to develop low-density housing, industries, and all other uses. Landscape architecture has emerged as the profession that can creatively and successfully balance complex natural and cultural issues better than our sister design and planning professions.

The new greenway movement is expected to help landscape architects focus their attention on the areas of the larger landscape and especially on those areas that are the most sensitive from the environmental and historical/cultural points of view. A network of greenways provides appropriate uses in these sensitive areas, which could be easily accessible to the populations wherever they live or work. Let me explain how these changes—decentralization and the greenway movement—could help to strengthen the contribution of landscape architects to the "society" at large, but first a bit of history is in order.

Population movement toward cities has continued throughout human history. Cities meant culture and opportunity to most people. During the nineteenth century, for example, these population centers provided the majority of the work for the small profession of landscape architects and the pathfinders of our profession, primarily in the design of public parks. The first work of Olmsted and Vaux was Central Park for New York City. While Olmsted and his contemporaries engaged other work, their major energy was directed toward the planning and design of urban parks.

In September 1864 Olmsted supervised the preparation of an influential policy report to the California legislature defining the duties and responsibilities of administering Yosemite Park, an early precedent for the national parks movement. With this work Olmsted clearly expressed a concern for the larger landscape around cities, including wilderness. During the 1870s Olmsted also experimented successfully with the creation of the first park system along the Muddy River of Boston, which became known as the Emerald Necklace. Today, the majority of authors of the greenway literature refer to Olmsted's Boston Park System as the first successful greenway. Olmsted's vision for Boston was greatly expanded by his protégé, Charles Eliot, whose Metropolitan Park System provided a greenway network for the rapidly growing Boston Metropolitan Region covering some 250 square miles in 1899.

Less than three decades later, in 1928, Charles Eliot's nephew, Charles Eliot II, drew up the first statewide open-space plan for the Commonwealth of Massachusetts. With that, he reestablished the role for landscape architects as visionaries and stewards for landscape preservation and use. Open-space planning has become a movement that has continued ever since. The result of this movement is that many states and large numbers of cities or towns now have public open spaces that constitute from ten percent to even fifty percent or more of their land area. These public open spaces often have the dual functions of providing recreation and nature protection.

An important contribution of landscape architects has been the development of powerful assessment procedures to map environmentally and culturally sensitive areas that ought to be protected from development or restored. These landscape units are appropriate for inclusion into the greenway/green-space network. The greenway movement, indeed, has spread all over the United States during the last dozen years. During this time, the definition of greenways has expanded to include: (1) ecologically significant corridors and natural systems; (2) recreational greenways, mostly along rivers, lake and ocean fronts, and ridge lines; and, (3) greenways with historical and cultural/heritage values. Our initial studies suggest that when the average landscape is assessed, almost one third of the landscapes are sensitive from the environmental or from the historical/cultural points of view. These areas are ideal for inclusion into the network of greenway corridors.

Landscape architects have continued their involvement in open-space planning; our role, however, has become less clear as state organizations took over the coordination of planning of open spaces. Landscape architecture is the ideal profession to help the society at large ensure that the sensitive areas along river corridors, coastlines, and ridgelines are used wisely. And if we do so, we will have an enormous impact. A greenway/green-space network of this magnitude would ensure the appropriate use of more than 700 million acres, one third of the United States! Such a system would help us to maintain environmental quality and would also aid economic development and tourism.

Ecological sensitivity should be the baseline to determine the level of use, if any, within these areas. Previous studies have also concluded that more than ninety percent of valuable historical/cultural resources are within these corridors. Hence, landscape architects are ideal for facilitating the balancing act between the protection of nature and cultural and recreational uses.

In conclusion, the profession of landscape architecture has made huge strides during the last 150 years. Its potential contribution to American society is enormous. Our education and training make us highly qualified to be leaders of the greenway movement of the twenty-first century. I invite and urge all of my professional colleagues to join this movement and promote its planning and implementation—not only nationally but globally. If so, our profession would help make decisions about the areas that are most environmentally sensitive while improving environmental quality and economic potential.

RAYMOND L. FREEMAN

I graduated in 1942 and went directly into the military for four years during World War II. Consequently, I had very little time to consider my profession. My experience in landscape architecture began in July 1946.

When in school I was most interested in the conservation of natural resources and primarily the public practice of the profession. I have always felt that the profession has produced many very talented people in private practice and the academic field. Landscape architecture must have talented professionals in meaningful positions in the public fields—in charge of bureaus of local, state, and federal governments.

Just think! If talented landscape architects were in the highest decision-making positions, the quality of living would be better for everyone.

In the last ten years the profession has begun to recognize the real importance of public service and involvement. Of course, to carry out this phase of the profession's work takes talented members. In 1971, when I was president of ASLA, I proudly told the annual-meeting delegates that we had 4,000 members. However, many were delinquent in paying dues so actual dues-paying members numbered about 3,000. Today, the dues-paying members total 12,300, and the number is growing. We now have many forms of practice and are moving into new types of single and cooperative practice with other professions.

Can you imagine what our country would be like if we didn't have the Blue Ridge National Parkway, the Westchester County Parkway, and the Natchez Trace and Colonial parkways? These are products of landscape architects, and we must be proud of them. The contributions of landscape architects in developing and managing the world-famous National Park Service have been outstanding. This is because we have had landscape architects in high decision-making positions.

Don't you think that our cities and freeways would be better planned if landscape architects were chairmen of planning commissions and directors of state, county, and federal agencies?

Landscape architects must get involved with the political field at all levels. We have one member of the U.S. Congress doing a great job. Don't you think five members would be great?

The ASLA has provided the leadership for the profession, to move the profession into a position to continue the growth and the value of our work. Over the years the ASLA has provided a great deal of information for the members.

We have produced many publications of all kinds. Today, we receive a state-of-the-art monthly magazine, an excellent *Land* newsletter, and ASLA convention communications.

We are on a roll. We get as many people to attend our annual meetings as we had total membership back in the 1970s.

It takes hard work and more members to move the profession to the level that people deserve. We need to get in the driver's seat to make our talents recognized. This can be done by strengthening our educational system—by including fields of study to broaden the practice of landscape architecture. In this day of more education, perhaps some landscape architects should do further studies toward master's degrees in management and political science. Take a page from the engineering field! They are getting law degrees and working in the patent field.

Remember that Frederick Law Olmsted, the founder of landscape architecture in the United States, was more than a landscape architect. He was a social scientist, a journalist, a manager, and a leader in helping people to attain a high quality of life. Get active in your community, volunteer to help, and be sure everyone knows who you are and what your profession is and how it can benefit all concerned.

LAWRENCE HALPRIN

Ours is potentially a great profession, one that is based inevitably on the assignments we take. As we approach the millennium we should reflect upon the manner in which the products of our profession have always been an expression of the times. It is important to recognize the synergy between culture and landscape design both as it reflects civilization historically and as it influences the future symbolically and subliminally.

In the past pharaohs, kings, and princes built palaces and grand gardens in an attempt to reinforce their political and social positions. At that time society's noble elite determined the physical image of civilization. Throughout the seventeenth century this elite built constructions in which the disciplined order of a classical vocabulary provided a powerful visual metaphor of social hierarchies. Versailles's remarkable garden echoes this elite view of the world.

Shifts of power have always affected architectural styles. The nineteenth century brought about a significant profession in which the rich elite came to be included among the noble patrons of the arts. The second half of that century brought about the collision of two schools of romanticism and

was dominated by Lancelot (Capability) Brown, who was architecturally minded and preoccupied with form. His work was particularly significant in the transformation of noble classical into romantic landscapes.

As in the past the arts will continue to be an expression of current human needs and desires. Today much of our work deals with shopping centers, golf courses, corporate headquarters, large private gardens, and the edges of highways. Whether we feel this is of importance or not is irrelevant. What is important is how we echo and guide our society and culture. This is one of the great contributions that Olmsted left to our profession at the end of the century. In order for landscape architecture to more greatly affect our culture we need landscape architects who will become deeply involved in their communities and provide insightful and meaningful reflections of the best we have to offer.

At the core of my approach is the examination of the landscape art form. As landscape architects we need to work with an incredible range of sensibilities. We start with land and nature (and all that implies) and also with the knowledge of how people respond to this matrix. All of these considerations need to function together. We design communities where people

live, where they work, recreate, and interact with one another. We need to design, protect, and conserve open spaces that encourage this synergy for communities.

For us to do this well we must know everything we can about our planet as well as understand as much as possible about the human condition: its sources, its need for myths and rituals, its need for health and dreams and relationships. We need to understand what makes life rich and viable. And we need to understand the importance of culture and the expressive means people have developed since primitive times to speak to each other about the important things in life.

I realize that I am proposing a large and complex role for our profession. To accomplish this in our current democratic society a major task is to educate people about their roles. Beginning with preschool, children need to be taught to appreciate their physical environment and recognize how it affects their lives. In different societies land plays varying roles in its relationship to individuals. In some cultures land is owned by the state or community. In our society land is a valuable commodity. How our children understand this relationship may change their lives.

More immediately our future lies in educating our clients about real issues

and about getting involved at the onset of projects when basic decisions are made. By "client" I hope you understand that I am not only talking about politicians and developers but about our larger constituency, those who will use the projects we design. As professionals we must not lecture people but allow them to learn through guidance, such as in participatory workshops. We must encourage our clients to have visionary ideas that can in turn inspire us. And we must embrace this involvement because often such inclusion has significant impact on people's lives and on their relationships to nature and to community.

In my Taking Part workshops I have for years been searching for archetypal relationships. These workshops primarily take place in the landscape and allow participants the opportunity to discover and articulate their own needs and desires. They discover creative new ways to communicate with one another. Since both clients and community members work together they arrive at collective decisions based on multiple inputs. This sort of collaboration leads to both client and community empowerment.

As I see it, part of our art form is to open up perceptions and sensitivities. In this way we can bring more variety to the value judgments and life experiences reflected in our work. Our profession is multifaceted. It deals with the ineffable as well as the known. If it has reason for being it is to make life more liveable, both spiritually and physically. It is my hope that through this process of understanding and design we can create a landscape that nurtures a human ecosystem in ways that are both biologically and emotionally satisfying. We must continue to press for this delicate balance in harmony if we are to ensure our place within it for the future.

CAROL R. JOHNSON

From the point of view of one who has practiced landscape architecture for more than forty years the profession has provided a lifelong adventure and an endless learning experience, from the first introductory design programs that began to reveal this almost completely unknown discipline to yesterday's challenges, problems, and solutions. Landscape architecture has been taught as problem solving in the outdoor environment. Its practitioners need to be thinkers as well as doers, and the best work in the profession reflects this. What has been missing is the evolution of landscape architecture practitioners from the monocultural founders to reflect the multicultural population of present-day America.

Is monocultural the opposite of multicultural? Landscape architecture was founded by a group of not very culturally diverse men from the northeastern United States. Just as landscape architects have always protected the diversity of our natural environments so does the future of the profession lie in its ability to attract students of various cultural and racial backgrounds so that landscape architects represent and serve the diverse cultural mix that enriches American society.

When the profession was founded, a balance of agriculture and trade automatically gave the built landscape its physical form. As manufacturing created an imbalance in the quality of habitation and the environment for living in cities, landscape architects came on the scene to restore the balance with parks and other amenities of social and physical importance.

When, as Norman T. Newton writes, the American economy went into a "coma" in the 1930s, landscape architects prepared plans and programs for large-scale conservation and recreation. These were called "emergency" programs at the time, not so much because of the erosion problems they solved or the recreational opportunities they provided, but because they gave employment to people out of

work. Extraordinary progress was made in land and water conservation, recreation, and the documentation of historic resources. War and a renewed economy ended the program.

Today road systems and tracts of individual dwellings give the built landscape its form. Landscape architects have struggled to mitigate the impacts of such development, but the scale and the social and physical impact of this imbalance are far greater than the earlier imbalances that development created in the landscape. The public areas that remain have greater and greater intensity of use and less and less management and maintenance. Without an economic "coma" nothing major is done. This is, however, just as great an emergency for the landscape as the emergency of the New Deal era. A new Civilian Conservation Corps, with the dedication of the original, is needed to attack the land and water and community problems with which we are now faced. A cadre of well-trained, skillful, thoughtful, and diverse landscape architects could influence those whose support is needed for such a program and could oversee it. Only with a truly broad base will landscape architects be a key factor in the urgently needed rebalance of the American social and physical environment—as they were when the profession was founded.

WILLIAM JOHNSON

As I consider my professional activity over the past forty years I cannot think of any other work I could have chosen that would have provided more interest, more challenge, or been so fitting to who I was and still am. Although landscape architecture continues to seem narrow and limited to many who observe the field from a distance it is difficult to do it justice without touching upon how at least a dozen allied fields relate. Work is as simple at times as the design of a garden corner, at other times as complex as helping to resolve development issues with global implications. It is in this context that I highlight a few thoughts about the continuing strength and influence of this small, yet important profession. These points concern scale and the way we work.

I recall the discussions around scale that Hideo Sasaki engendered among students at Harvard in the mid-1950s. He often pointed out that if our process principles were sound about fitting people appropriately into their environment, we could approach any kind of development issue at any scale and expect a responsible outcome. Our debates on this matter came at a time when the practice of landscape architecture was encountering a whole new set of development challenges. I recall how energizing our discussions were.

My professional work started in the late 1950s, when the Beaux Arts design tradition, then still relevant to architects, city planners, and landscape architects, was fading in response to baby-boom growth and development. In the ensuing years landscape architects would lead and participate in an unprecedented range of design and planning projects. This great range has made it important for me to periodically remind myself that landscape architecture is a design profession. It is not a natural science. It is not a public policy field, nor is it an engineering field. Giving frequent emphasis to this point seems important because many of our professional assignments call on the sciences and other allied professions so heavily that the focus can shift away from design creativity. It happens a lot, and at times it takes a good deal of determination to avoid it.

The focus of landscape architecture is to shape the physical world in which we live, giving particular attention to the use of natural materials in addition to the bricks and mortar of architecture. Materials such as vegetation, terrain, water, and even open space need to be understood in the context of extensive natural systems highly affected by the constructed world.

Therefore, seeking how to best design with natural materials inevitably draws us into an ever-broadening series of related associations, urban systems, historic values, resource economics, and public policy, to name but a few. The scale always bumps up. The important process of understanding the context of a given problem is one of the most intriguing and compelling challenges a designer in landscape architecture faces. Ian McHarg has taught us much about that phenomenon.

This may explain in part the tendency during the 1960s and 1970s for many landscape architects with strong design motivations to move from the tradition of detailed design to broader-scale environmental and urban-development issues. Here they perceived, for good reason, their design influence could be greater. To be sure, their integrative skill as designers could be very beneficial at a planning or policy level. But they tended to be drawn away from their design focus into a more policy-oriented focus. In design endeavors, when the "overview mindset" disengages from the "detail mindset" much creativity can be lost. It is my observation that the more effective designers today range across the scale spectrum with ease, relating their detailed design moves to a greater sense of the whole.

Certainly the process of design can be overworked, and in excess it can be an actual deterrent to fresh and creative results. But I believe that one of the great strengths of this profession is tied up in the way we are inclined to go about our work. The basic premise is this: Inherent in the circumstances in which a development or preservation problem arises lies an answer to that problem, unique in form, character, and significance.

Accordingly, if we can understand enough about the people of a place and the physical attributes of that place, then ideas about a solution will abound. We need only to go about our work in such a way that these ideas emerge. In the hundreds of projects I have experienced that premise has proven to be a sound expectation.

There are many good models in the profession. I only want to point out here the key attributes of the process when it is at its best: inclusive, integrative, and idea-oriented.

Inclusive: A most significant development in the profession over the course of my career is the increasing skill with which professional designers bring "outsiders" into the process. It once was innovative to organize on-site work sessions with local residents or potential users, working in con-

cert to develop the first notions of how a problem could be solved. Not anymore. Today the art of creative process is well advanced and getting better. The effective designers are particularly skillful at leading an unfolding design process wherein the many participants become involved with a solution that is "built" with their inputs. When people see an inspiring idea emerge in their presence from roots with which they are familiar, they become more effective advocates of the initiative than even the designer.

Integrative: One of the great frustrations I experience is the number of people, groups, agencies, and programs in our society willing to be single-purpose-oriented. We suffer greatly by the resulting "bits and pieces development syndrome." The designer's way of working is inherently integrative, relating relevant information about a problem with the kind of balanced decision-making that can only come from an informed overview. Integrative thinking is a significant and important contribution of professional designers, and I am impressed with the increasing number of architects and landscape architects who recognize that role and play it out with great skill.

Idea-oriented: It may be that the most important product of the design mind is an idea, a vision, a dream. The complex analyses we put ourselves through are primarily mechanisms to discover a fitting way to solve a problem. Problems regarding community and the environment are often so full of issues that people can lose their way without a compelling vision to sustain their energy and drive. It continues to be a great satisfaction for me to watch effective designers extract potential solutions out of an array of data and analyses that most others see as merely information. I like the idea that the effective designers can be the "keepers of the vision." It's a natural role and certainly a worthy one.

PHILIP H. LEWIS, JR.

Here is a recipe for Centennial Year Landscape Care.

First, start with what you know best—for me, landscape design concepts initiated and documented in the Midwest.

Second, set forth some directions about how landscape architecture as a regional design profession can provide a model for any other state or region.

Put the fermenting mixture in a favorable political climate. For action, an environmentally oriented president and governors are needed, as well as legislatures that favor environmental as well as social justice in order to pre-

serve the physical, social, and economic fabric of our society. The public must be involved in the political process by voting, informing candidates, and educating legislators and executives in office. Particularly desirable is a governor like Gaylord Nelson, the "Father of Earth Day," who succinctly summarized the consequences of the population explosion to the legislature: "Cities are becoming larger, busier, and more crowded. Population densities are increasing, traffic is growing, and satellite bedroom communities are eating up nearby countrysides. . . . The Great Outdoors is shrinking!"

Now add the basic ingredients, i.e., the necessary budget and staff. In 1960 Governor Nelson proposed a one-cent sales tax per pack of cigarettes to raise $50 million with which to purchase natural and cultural landscapes, the basis of our life-support system and Wisconsin's multimillion-dollar recreation and tourism business. The tax was adopted, and I served on a creative planning and design team to interpret the physical features that make Wisconsin an outstanding state for recreation. The team was headed by Dr. David Carley, a political scientist, with among others Harold Jordahl, who dealt with planning and land easements, and Jake Beuscher, who contributed expertise in land-use controls

and water law. An environmental governor, a budget for staffing and implementation, and a sound planning and design team are necessary to preserve and enhance any regional landscape.

From earlier studies in Illinois and Indiana I had developed the environmental-corridor concept that was applied in Wisconsin. In these corridors occur most of the important natural and cultural resources. The combined mapping of water, wetland, and steep topography patterns included as many as 220 additional physical values held in high esteem by the public. The plan assured protection of roughly 33,000 acres of choice landscapes each year of the ten-year program. I was assisted by eighteen part-time students in landscape architecture who worked days, nights, and weekends for a year. (The recipe was facilitated by the fact that the school of landscape architecture, the state university, and the state capital are in the same city.)

Once identified, protection must be assured for the outstanding landscape patterns. The $50-million program and the more recent $250-million Stewardship Fund certainly have gone a long way, but many features are still threatened by sprawling urbanization.

Well-informed legislators come and go every few years, and a centennial recipe demands a continuing-educa-

tion program for all newcomers to lengthen their attention span to more than a year or two of foresight. My recipe for education called for an environmental-corridor demonstration in Madison for the legislature, the thousands of students, and the citizens of the urban region. Twenty-eight years later, with the investment of $5 million by Dane County, we have a twenty-four-mile urban/rural corridor designated as an E-Way, (E as in educational, ecological, environmental, and exercise). A surfaced bicycle trail (the Capital City Trail) connects most of the E-Way to the university campus, the state legislature, and downtown.

Any corridor requires a buffer zone and ordinances guiding adjacent development. Massive proposed and ongoing development is occurring in Fitchburg along the E-Way's south boundary. An advisory committee that I cochaired presented Fitchburg's mayor with a sixty-five-page set of recommendations for various actions and ordinances to manage storm-water run-off in the E-Way corridor, recommendations on which he has agreed to move promptly.

What becomes obvious in such studies is the need for three-dimensional design guidelines for all land uses (residential, commercial, industrial, institutional) adjacent to these fragile corridors, a challenge our profession must meet.

Our twenty-one-mile E-Way also provides outstanding educational opportunities in some forty-six museums or institutions that are on or near the E-Way, "educational jewels" on the E-Way emerald necklace. I am working with the State Department of Education to create an Internet virtual museum to convey the exhibits and resources of these facilities to teachers planning field trips (especially for fourth-graders, who are beginning conservation and state-history study).

In Wisconsin the emphasis has been on demonstrating and educating about where to build and where not to build and what to build in relation to environmental corridors.

Our recipe must also include designing new urban infill for creating higher liveable densities in our cities and slowing unguided rural sprawl. The Madison and Dane County historical rail network fans out from the capital like an octopus to all communities but two small villages. Plans are under way for a series of design conferences in 1999 to develop new urban forms around an integrated transit, utility, and fiber-optic communication system. Based on this information, an Urban Form Charrette

will be held in Madison in the year 2000 to launch the new millennium, before or after LABash, at which 400 to 500 students from the United States and Canada will meet in Madison.

In forty-five years of educational experience I have stressed the urgent need to build interdisciplinary centers where adequately trained personnel and commensurate facilities are available in every region, metropolis, and urban constellation on the globe.

I envision the new urban form for Madison to contain such an interdisciplinary facility—designated The Wisconsin Idea Center—using the latest technologies to present holistic and sustainable futures.

My charge to the profession is to exert leadership to make every capital city and surrounds a model for the future. Our great range of professionals could make all capitals models for the world. They could convey the uniqueness of regional diversity and show how, with an interdisciplinary team, our profession can identify, protect, restore, and enhance these life-giving resources.

JOHN LYLE

(John Lyle passed away shortly before writing an essay for this volume. As his contribution we have included a shortened version of an address that Lyle delivered to the Federal University of Rio Grande de Sul in Canela, Brazil, on November 14, 1997.)

Over the past century of industrial development we have created a world that is simultaneously growing out of control and progressively destroying itself. This world of human devising is superimposed on the living earth that evolved over the last 4.6 billion years. The human world takes energy and materials in great quantities from the natural world but refuses to participate fully in the evolved processes that support and sustain life. More than sixty percent of the earth's land surface is used by humans to produce energy and materials for human consumption. Most of that sixty percent is in a state of degeneration; that is, its ability to support life is declining because humans are taking more from the land than they give in return; they are failing to foster nature's evolved processes of regeneration. Most of the materials taken from the land eventually show up somewhere else as pollution.

Let us imagine a diagram that describes the general operation of the global industrial system that we have imposed upon the earth. On the left-hand side of the diagram are the sources of energy and materials that supply the human population with the necessities and the luxuries of life. These are spread out over the surface of the earth and include farms and grazing lands, forests, mines, and oil and gas fields. Energy and materials move from these to the places—on the right-hand side of the imaginary diagram—where they are converted into useful forms and then consumed. In our increasingly urbanized world the conversion and consumption occur mostly in cities. At a fundamental level our cities are rarely sources; they produce nothing at a fundamental level within their own boundaries; rather, they consume. In the ecological sense their relationship with the natural world is a parasitic one.

After consumption, which generally takes a very short time, the energy and materials leave the city as wastes. The resulting global problems of air and water pollution are well known; there is no need to elaborate here. What this means is that the deterioration of the earth's ability to support life is built into the global industrial system of energy and material flows. It is essentially a linear throughput system, moving resources from source to use to sink in an ongoing pattern. With its ever-growing appetites for energy and materials and its increasingly massive apparatus for producing, transporting, and processing them, this pattern of flow is not sustainable. With ongoing depletion on the source side, sooner or later, the energy and materials will run out, and with increasing pollution on the sink side, sooner or later the overloading reaches a stage of system dysfunction and eventually the stage of sickness and death. Over the past few years we have seen increasing numbers of examples of the dysfunctional stage and occasional examples of the stages of sickness and death.

All of us alive today have spent most or all of our lives in this degenerative world; we are all part of it, and we are also its victims. Since we have known nothing else we tend to think of the environment of steel and concrete simply as the way things are—like rivers and seashores and blue skies. But in fact it is a world designed by humans—albeit with little conscious forethought or intent—and built by humans, mostly over the past century. What humans designed, we can redesign, and what humans built, we can rebuild. This will be the great challenge for the design professions in the next

century: to lead the way in achieving a sustainable future, that is, in reshaping a world that can provide healthy and fulfilling lives for all of its residents through future centuries.

Although right now we do not fully know how to accomplish this, we do have some sense of direction and a few promising examples. The only reliable model for sustainability that we have is the naturally evolved ecosystem. We know that nature achieves sustainability not by refusing to change but through dynamic ongoing processes of regeneration. Nature's major energy source is the sun, which continuously renews the earth's energy supply day after day. Materials are not resupplied from outside as energy is, but are continuously used, reassimilated through biological processes, and reused. Thus, natural systems sustain themselves through regenerative processes of ongoing self-renewal. We can draw upon these same regenerative processes in the design of the human environment and thus shape buildings, cities, and landscapes—and even an economy and systems of production—that are integrated and in harmony with nature's processes. A global regenerative system would work in contrast with the degenerative throughput system of the industrial age.

In a regenerative system some of the sun's energy is used directly as heat, but most is converted by various means to useful forms, including biomass materials. After initial use it is often possible to reuse some small portion of energy, but with each use most of it is dissipated as unusable heat. Materials, by contrast, do not dissipate but continuously recycle. Some are reused in essentially their original form, while others are broken down through biological processes into their component elements and later reassembled through photosynthesis or other processes into usable forms. The breaking down is accomplished by microorganisms, mostly bacteria. Achieving sustainability will require that humans form a partnership with bacteria, nurture and protect them, and make good use of their services. Our waste is their food.

In the operation of the industrial system sources and sinks are highly concentrated and centralized, as are the areas of processing and consumption. The channels of movement linking them are essential to the operation of the system. These include pipes, high-tension lines, highways, channels, shipping lanes, and related port facilities, airports, and other routes and modes of movement. This infrastructure is generally massive in scale, constructed

of steel and concrete, enormously expensive, and ecologically damaging. It is fueled by vast quantities of petroleum and probably could not function if petroleum were not available at prices far below its real cost. For the time being, however, it is available. So making use of underpriced petroleum, industrial infrastructure continues to expand, increasingly forming a girdle of steel and concrete enveloping the earth.

The infrastructure of regenerative systems is quite different in character and extent. Embedded in the local landscape and drawing as much as possible on natural resources, regenerative systems rely far less on moving large quantities of energy and materials. Rather than being concentrated and centralized, regenerative systems tend to be dispersed and decentralized. This is because the sun's energy is dispersed, and natural resources tend to be spread out in varied patterns. Regenerative systems tend to seek out local conditions suitable for their operation to adapt to local landscapes. Being rooted in natural processes, regenerative infrastructure is integrated with the land; indeed, much of it is quite literally landscape. Thus, we can call it green infrastructure as compared to the gray infrastructure of industrial systems.

To explain what I mean by this and to demonstrate that these are useful and practical technologies, proven in practice, I will describe a few examples of green infrastructure in operation. To show how these technologies can serve our most fundamental needs I will concentrate on systems for supplying energy, water, and food. For contrast and to make clear the differences between green and gray I will also show examples of industrial infrastructure serving the same human needs.

Because the stored energy in fossil fuels is at the operational core of the industrial world I will begin by describing the infrastructure of energy with the emphasis on electricity. Most of our electricity is produced by fossil-fuel-driven generating plants. Typical of such plants is one that stands in the Mojave Desert of California, distant from any community, far out of view for the vast majority of the population. Through high-tension lines it feeds electricity into a grid that serves all of the western United States, including cities more than a thousand miles away.

Now consider the Lug generating plant, which is also located in the Mojave Desert near the gas-fired plant mentioned above. The Luz plant is a solar-thermal facility that uses solar radiation to generate electricity and therefore qualifies as

regenerative technology. In this facility rows of long trough-shaped reflectors track the sun, reflect solar rays onto a pipe, and heat the fluids in the pipe to levels above 400 degrees centigrade. The superheated fluid is then used to make the steam that drives the turbines. The Luz plant, while it produces renewable energy and is regenerative in character, is a centralized facility that, like the nearby gas-fired plant, is connected to the grid and uses high-tension lines for distribution.

In contrast to this centralized facility there is, at the Center for Regenerative Studies in Pomona, California, a small Dish-Sterling solar-thermal converter that generates only 8.5 kilowatts peak. This is a little less than half the amount needed to serve the electrical needs of the small Center community. But it is even more efficient in converting solar energy than the much larger Luz plant. In this case there is no economy of scale. The Dish-Sterling unit fits comfortably into its knolltop setting within the Center's landscape, an integral part of the surrounding suburban area. Its land requirement is minimal. All around it, people go about their daily tasks. It requires no high-tension lines and no grid, and it can easily be operated by residents of the community.

Using such devices, a city might provide for its electrical needs within the city itself. In this case the massive infrastructure of the distribution grid might eventually disappear, eliminating the high-tension lines with their potentially damaging electro-magnetic fields and their high cost, which is estimated to be thirty to forty percent of the cost of electricity to consumers.

In some cases, green infrastructure can be so thoroughly integrated with other functions that it no longer exists as separate structure. This is the case with solar heating and natural cooling. In the buildings of the Center for Regenerative Studies, south-facing glass admits solar radiation during the winters. The sun heats the air within the building along with some thermal-mass materials such as concrete floors and walls and a few large tanks of water. The thermal-mass materials absorb heat and release it as the building begins to cool at night and on cloudy days. Grapevines mounted on trellises shade the glass during the summer to prevent overheating.

Thus, by making use of the solar radiation available on the site, by careful design, and with the thoughtful participation of residents it is possible to serve most or all of the energy needs of a community with little or no consumption of fossil fuels. Fol-

lowing this approach every site is different and requires different forms that underscore the uniqueness of place. Industrial infrastructure, in contrast, supplies energy and materials more or less of equal quality and quantity everywhere and thus illuminates local differences. Industrial infrastructure homogenizes the world; green infrastructure regionalizes.

The control of water has been a major factor in the growth of civilization. Over the past century the control has become virtually complete with most of the world's rivers dammed at least at one point and most of the world's cities drained by concrete channels that once were streams and rivers. Many cities now depend for their water supplies on distant watersheds, sometimes more than a thousand kilometers away. This extreme state of water control has greatly reduced the biological richness and diversity of streams and rivers and their riparian banks and floodplains, has actually increased flooding in many places, has created water-quality problems, and has depleted groundwater supplies.

Through the industrial era the control of water has been accomplished primarily by massive concrete structures that simply overpower the water, including dams, channels, aqueducts, seawalls, and other rigid forms.

For example, in most cities after water falls as rain it is concentrated in pipes, channels, or ditches and rushed off the site, fed into larger flood-control channels, and rushed to the nearest ocean, river, or bay. Almost none makes its way down into groundwater storage as it did before such flood-control systems were built. Meanwhile, the water supply for most cities is brought in from distant watersheds.

The drainage system for the Center for Regenerative Studies follows a quite different approach. Only a very small portion of the rainfall drains into the storm-drain system. Most of the runoff water is guided into retention basins and slowly infiltrates into underground storage where it is available later to be pumped back up and used to supply local needs. In the retention basins the water is treated by aquatic plants, primarily water hyacinth and duckweed. Bacteria growing on the roots and stems draw out excess nutrients that have accumulated in the water on its overland journey and use them in their own growth processes. The bacteria also take up most other pollutants, so the water is relatively pure before it soaks into the ground. However, the soil also acts as a filter as the water moves down into the aquifer, removing whatever materials may not have been taken out by

the plants and bacteria. The retention basins are part ponds and part wetlands and thus provide ideal habitat for diverse populations of birds and small mammals. Egrets, herons, cormorants, and many duck species are often seen in the basins. As with solar architecture the green infrastructure of water varies greatly in form depending on local conditions.

Another important component of the infrastructure of water is the treatment of sewage. The treatment plants of the industrial age use energy-intensive mechanical processes in factorylike facilities of steel and concrete. Their purposes are to separate water from solids and then dispose of them, usually by discharging into rivers, oceans, or large lakes. Regenerative treatment, in contrast, uses living plants and their related microorganisms in settings that are essentially landscapes very much like those in nature. Its purpose is to prepare the water and solid material for reintroduction into the environment where they can continue playing their roles in supporting life. The processes of treatment take place in ponds and wetlands that feature little or no steel or concrete, consume little or no energy, and cost about half as much as conventional treatment plants

During the industrial era farms have become horizontal factories that con-

vert petroleum into food. They are concentrated in a few regions, and the food they produce is moved around the world through a vast infrastructure of highways, railroads, airplanes, ships, and automated ports. A major portion of our food cost in both money and energy goes for shipping and distribution. This global infrastructure of food is entirely dependent on large supplies of petroleum and natural gas, which we know will not always be available.

Regenerative agriculture uses good soil to produce food, uses few or no chemicals either as fertilizers or pesticides, and moves most of its products only short distances because they are grown near where they are consumed. The city itself is a good place to grow food because it can provide so many of the resources essential to agriculture. Most of these resources are commonly considered as wastes that present disposal problems. Reclaimed water produced by natural treatment systems, if treated to an advanced level, can be used for irrigation. Composted sewage sludge is an ideal soil amendment. Ground-up tree trimmings from urban landscapes make good mulch. And labor is usually available from the city's surplus.

The Center for Regenerative Studies demonstrates a number of ways that

growing food can be integrated into urban landscapes. At the Center most of the plants growing between and around buildings, which would be ornamentals in most cities, produce food. Deciduous fruit trees grow on trellises extending over the south-facing glass to provide shade during the summer as well as food. Herbs and vegetable gardens grow on the ground around the buildings and in planter boxes on the flat roofs. Aquaculture ponds produce several species of fish, also quite near the buildings. Chickens and ducks are housed in small pens within the core area. There is no reason why most cities cannot incorporate food production into their urban fabric in similar ways to provide most of the fruits, herbs, and vegetables as well as a large portion of the protein consumed by their populations.

As green infrastructure grows and, over time, at least partially replaces the steel and concrete of industrial infrastructure we can expect far-reaching changes in the environment. Green infrastructure returns to the landscape the life-support functions that have been usurped over the past century by inert infrastructure of steel and concrete. Thus, over time, we will have more living green landscape and less hard structure. Most of the landscape of green infrastructure will be where people live:

in towns and cities. And this land will serve a multiplicity of uses. Flood-control basins and solar-conversion areas will also be parks. Sewage-treatment plants will also be water gardens and wildlife habitat. All of these and urban farms as well will produce oxygen, absorb carbon dioxide, and help to ameliorate the extremes of urban climate.

Green infrastructure will also bring change in the larger landscape. As pipes, channels, powerlines, and even industrial farms are abandoned in rural areas, much of the land they now occupy can return to its naturally evolved state, a state that helps to enrich and restore natural communities.

Whatever the benefits, however, we should not expect that the transitions to green infrastructure will come easily. Enormous amounts of money are invested in industrial infrastructure, and those investments cannot simply be abandoned. But even steel and concrete wear out, deteriorate, and become obsolete. This is happening now with much of the infrastructure developed during the boom following World War II. To renew and rebuild these facilities without very careful consideration of green alternatives would be a serious mistake, with a high likelihood of projecting obsolete technologies into an era when the dysfunctions of their operation become in-

creasingly damaging and obvious. Nevertheless, we can expect that resistance to green infrastructure will be determined, perhaps overwhelming, in a great many situations. Just as green infrastructure tends by its nature to disperse and decentralize functions and facilities, it tends to deconcentrate wealth. Industrial infrastructure, in contrast, tends to concentrate wealth. A great many people now in positions of power have benefited enormously from this concentration of wealth. Whatever the benefits of green infrastructure to the larger society and natural communities, resistance to change is likely to be powerful.

IAN McHARG

The twenty-first century offers an unparalleled challenge and opportunity for the profession of landscape architecture. Can it fulfill the promise of its history? Make no mistake: There is no comparable profession. Nevertheless, its extraordinary thrust faltered in the twentieth century, which saw a contraction of scale, a diminution in social purpose, a preoccupation with small decorations only rarely redeemed. The landscape shrank in importance. Its role in the twentieth century was to host the rape of resources, environmental pollution, diminished

biodiversity, and atmospheric dis-equilibrium. The centuries-old preoccupation with nature was supplanted by wars: World War I and II, Korea, and Vietnam. In this sad catalog there is a single huge exception: the unilateral disarmament by Mikhail Gorbachev and the end to the threat of nuclear cataclysm. This is surely the most important event of the century for society and nature. There is reason to believe that the world could never have recovered from such an event. It has been averted, thank God.

This paper begins with the assertion that the forthcoming century offers powerful challenges and opportunities for the profession. Certainly a new confluence of trends offers an enlarged future.

The first of these trends is a profound increase in knowledge of the natural environment—for which landscape architects should be clear beneficiaries. Next is the advent of world warming, whereby catastrophes have increased in frequency and ferocity. Landscape architecture should be trained to provide guidance on this subject and practice avoidance and mitigation. World warming has exerted a profound effect on the inversion of values whereby "improved" accelerates energy consumption and pollution (including an increase in car-

bon dioxide) and contributes little or nothing to photosynthesis and carbon-fixing. In contrast, "unimproved" lands contribute no pollution, do not consume energy, and are the major contributors to carbon-fixing. The remedy for world warming is carbon-fixing, most necessary in megacities and urban places. The basis of the remedy is greening, for which landscape architects have unique qualifications.

These factors are interdependent: the appreciation of nature, the consequences of world warming, the consequent inversion of values, and the necessity, not only of reducing energy consumption and pollution, but also of enhancing carbon-fixing, particularly in cities. Together they provide great new opportunities for the profession.

Understanding nature: As interest in nature increases, landscape architects can become major beneficiaries, particularly if they assume the role of defenders of nature and perform felicitous and appropriate adaptations. Increased interest is evidenced in magazines and books and particularly on television.

World warming: I well recall the event only a decade ago when a distinguished meteorologist averred that it was preposterous to believe that human interventions could have any effect upon that huge heat engine, the sun and atmosphere. It is not so today. In the greenhouse effect the gases of pollution are trapped within the earth's atmosphere and obstruct the normal escape of energy to space. This energy thereby abnormally heats the earth. Water expands when heated, ice melts, and warm air transports more vapor. Hence violent climatic events have quite measurably increased, silencing the skeptics. In addition, there is a hypothesis that suggests that increased global temperatures will exacerbate vulcanism and earthquakes and the tsunamis that accompany them. Clearly there is an important role for those who understand climatic, geological, hydrological, and ecological processes and can advise society where not to build and where and how to build. Landscape architects should seize this role.

Inversion of values: From mother's milk, mother's knees, kindergarten, grade school, and college we have acquired an implicit value system: Man is the apex of evolution. He has dominion over all matter and life and has been enjoined to subdue the earth. This value system is epitomized by two terms, "unimproved" and "improved." The former describes "wild" lands having negligible value. In contrast, "improvements" reflect a sequence of events that lead to an urban or indus-

trial presence—planning, roads, curbs, sewers, water and telephone lines, electricity, storm drains, and buildings. Generally the higher the density, the greater the value of "improved" land.

In global warming the "improved" properties are the culprits. There may well be value in urbanization, but the costs are high, for urbanization is the major consumer of energy and emitter of transportation pollution and greenhouse gases. Moreover, highly urbanized land provides little photosynthesis and carbon-fixing. It is then doubly culpable, the major miscreant that contributes massively to the problem and does nothing to alleviate it. "Unimproved" land, in contrast, contributes nothing to the problem but provides the major remedy of carbon-fixing. Hence, the necessary inversion of values. We need to recognize the unparalleled value of rain forest, boreal forest, savanna, prairie, coral reef—indeed, of wild land wherever it exists and diminishes the damaging effects of urbanization.

Global greening: The last factor involves a global program of greening, notably tree planting, to compensate for carbon-dioxide imbalance. This should involve recognizing those regions that now perform this role—the great forests, coral reefs, wild lands, oceans, and estuaries.

The program should also identify the culprits, the generators of the major pollutants, the gluttons of energy and resource exploitation. Among these, megacities loom large. The objective here should be to green them, to green every brown field, plant every vacant space, roof, and wall, and thereby respond to the carbon-dioxide crisis while making cities more salubrious and habitable. Shades of Olmsted.

These are the confluent factors offering great promise to the profession—a wider understanding and concern for nature, an appreciation of the processes that have contributed to global warming and climatic perturbation, a recognition of the significance of an inversion of values, and, last but not least, the extraordinary challenge to the profession to lead in the greening of cities and towns worldwide. Note that this is moral leadership.

Two comments can close this piece. Leslie Jones Sauer entitled the book she wrote with Andropogon *The Once and Future Forests: Let Us Make a Habit of Restoration.*

And on the occasion of awarding me the National Medal of Art President George Bush said, "It is my earnest hope, Mr. McHarg, that the art (and science) of the twenty-first century will be devoted to the restoration of the land."

So be it. May landscape architects prepare to meet the challenge and perform a unique and invaluable role for the United States and human kind in the twenty-first century.

THEODORE OSMUNDSON

As a fellow and past president of the ASLA I feel that I can speak of the ASLA from my chapter base in the San Francisco Bay Area and also from more than a half century of experience at state and national levels.

When I entered the American Society of Landscape Architects from Iowa State College (now University) in 1943 as a junior associate, the ASLA and the profession were still in another world. After a devastating depression and an ongoing world war the members of the ASLA totaled a little more than 400 and there were only twelve schools throughout the country. My wife Lorraine and I were married when I graduated, and we moved to San Diego, then Oakland/Berkeley. With a mitral deficiency of the heart caused by two near-fatal bouts with rheumatic fever, I was given a permanent deferment. I worked first with Garrett Eckbo, then with Thomas Church, and finally for a large nursery as landscape superintendent for a year before starting my own office in 1946.

In 1947 landscape architects returning from the war were looking for professional cohesion through a new organization of landscape architects. From the beginning I realized that the profession was at the bottom of a long climb upward and resolved to do whatever I could to advance our organization as the instrument for progress. The ASLA nationally was a nonentity, with the exception of the indomitable Bradford Williams at 9 Park Street, Boston, who never lost faith and almost single-handedly held it together.

The Northern California Chapter of the ASLA had a membership of about ten souls with no chapter structure and no prospects of gaining new members. The ASLA was locked into complicated and burdensome entry rules that blocked growth, and those in control were not yet ready to change. Based on the ASLA's longstanding policy that all applicants for membership be in private practice or have served time in it in order to ensure professionalism, sets of actual working drawings of projects prepared by the applicant were required to be submitted and judged by a committee in the East. This eliminated most teachers as a source of new members and also students, who without their teacher's help were not encouraged to join the ASLA.

In the Bay Area with some of the most active members of the profession both in landscape design and organization activities a new broad-based group was formed, the Association of Landscape Architects (ALA), later to become the California Association of Landscape Architects (CALA). This organization was the most progressive in the country and represented landscape architects until it was absorbed into the ASLA after entrance applications had been changed to nearly their present form. Meetings drew from thirty to fifty members. There remained, however, the "private-practice-only" rule, not removed until, as president of the ASLA, I proposed and the trustees agreed to drop this requirement allowing educators without practice experience to become members in 1967 to 1969. Membership began to grow. Today there are sixty-four student chapters from which to draw new members, and our chapter alone has more than 400 members.

These early and critical postwar years were characterized by a constant effort to define and explain the unique and many-faceted nature of landscape architecture and the development of a better trained and housed educational structure throughout the United States in our

major universities. Today we have fifty-nine accredited schools throughout the country and a public much better informed about our mission.

During the 1940s the idea of state licensing, following the lead of the architects and engineers, emerged and through the leadership of members such as Lynn M.F. Harris, Raymond Page, Arthur Barton, Harry Shepherd, Alfred Kuehl, George Huntington, and others in California came to fruition in 1953 with the passing of the first licensing of landscape architects in the United States. The older men were the leaders, but we younger men were always ready to help them, and we did. From that point on there followed a biannual legislative attack on the board in which I and others were closely involved. CALA, and later the ASLA Northern California Chapter, and the Southern California Chapter of the ASLA and the International Institute of Landscape Architects (now defunct), formed the California Council of Landscape Architects to coordinate the protection of licensing. It has been constantly involved with fund raising, meetings with legislators, letter writing to constituents, and other time- and money-consuming activities. This constant conflict has continued for forty-five odd years ending in 1998 when our

independent board was "sunsetted" and became an adjunct of the architects' board, a result with mixed blessings. The efforts to establish state licensing of landscape architects has continued to this day with a few losses and many successes throughout the country. Today, with forty-six chapters, forty-six states have licensing of landscape architects.

With the idea of raising the consciousness of others about the ASLA, the decision was made in 1959 to move the national office from Boston to Washington, D.C., to place it within taxi distance of the major professional, conservation, and governmental organizations. This has been of great importance, drawing upon talented people in the nation's capital and providing a sense of pride in the staff and all who come to the ASLA offices. Lynn Harris was the first executive director. We now have our own building there.

Nationally the ASLA had grown to some 3,000 to 3,500 members with an annual budget of around $110,000 by the late 1960s when I was ASLA president. With the good efforts of the new assistant director, Gary Robinette, we raised more money for special projects in the Foundation than from ASLA dues. Today, the total annual budget of ASLA is over $7 million, and the Landscape Architecture Foundation has raised more than $2 million in its current ongoing drive.

The ASLA joined the International Federation of Landscape Architects in the early 1950s and sent a delegate each year to its annual Grand Council meeting and Congress. By the early 1970s the ASLA had grown so large compared to other national organizations that dues, based on each member, became also disproportionate to all other countries. In 1980 delegate Campbell Miller negotiated a dues structure in which ASLA would pay no more than twenty-five percent of all the other nations' combined dues. A second dues schedule was made in Jamaica in 1983. Despite the ASLA's protests the Grand Council in 1989 at Bogotá, Colombia, voted to revert the ASLA's dues to the original system by 1998. Shortly thereafter, ASLA resigned along with the United Kingdom, Australia, Canada, and Japan. To date, after seven years of negotiation by our appointed representative Robert Mortensen, who has done yeoman service to settle the differences, they remain unresolved.

What does this portend for the future? During the twentieth century we slowly built a solid foundation under our profession, one that places it in a position to become a "household term" in the next century. We now have licensing in forty-six states, fifty-nine accredited schools, a strong financial base with which to further our goals, a well-run staff of thirty-five in the Washington office, and excellent publications. We also now have a well-financed Landscape Architecture Foundation to enter into effort-sharing programs in the public interest, to further our publications, student assistance, and our currently flagging efforts in research. With a growing membership of more than 11,000 from which to draw even better leadership talent we are now ready to make huge strides in advancing landscape architecture in the twenty-first century. In the next one hundred years I foresee that land will become a very rare commodity and that every development of land of any kind in the United States will require the services of a landscape architect by public law. We will be ready when that happens.

MEADE PALMER

When I graduated from Cornell in 1939 I was able to get a job with the Arlington County, Virginia, planning department as their first landscape architect. I was given a variety of jobs that my Cornell education had not covered, such as reviewing subdivision plans and searching the land records for park lands.

After two years I was offered a job in Richmond, Virginia, at $90 per month, $10 more than the county was paying me. With some hesitation I accepted the Richmond offer since it included an apartment over the office. The offer came from Charles Gillette, a well-known landscape architect with an established practice in Virginia and nearby states.

Gillette's practice was an outgrowth of his having been sent to Richmond by the Manning firm in 1911 to supervise the development of the master plan for the University of Richmond. He grew fond of Richmond and decided to stay and open an office. His office was in a renovated townhouse in downtown Richmond with a charming garden in the rear. His practice consisted of a variety of projects, not unlike a similarly situated office today: private estates, historic homes, schools, colleges, cemeteries, subdivisions, commercial properties, and parks.

Gillette had a vast knowledge of plant materials, and his work reflected that knowledge. Having seen the results of his many projects and from my own experience, I am convinced that the creative use of plants is fundamental to the practice of landscape architecture. We are the sole design profession that integrates living, growing material as one of the elements of our work.

Over the past few decades I have noticed an increased use of plants in public and private enterprises. I remember when fast-food restaurants and shopping centers (now malls) were minimalist structures surrounded by acres of black asphalt with no plants in sight. A major task confronting the profession is convincing the public and the related professions that our knowledge of plants is coupled with the unique ability to relate an assortment of land-use problems into an integrated whole, and I believe that we are making strides in this direction. During the fifty years that I have been practicing I have seen our profession grow from a few individuals in the larger metropolitan areas to large corporations and small firms and individuals practicing in every state and many foreign countries.

ROBERT REICH

My primary contribution to the profession has been in the area of education. So my comments are slanted that way.

In the 1930s, when I first became involved with the profession, the emphasis was upon parks, Reptonian-type subdivisions, and large private estates. With the Depression the number of estate projects rapidly declined, but due to WPA programs, public-park projects expanded rapidly. These changes filtered down to teaching.

By the 1940s estate work was pretty well gone, but emphasis was now beginning to be placed upon small residential grounds in which detailed planting plans were very important. By the 1950s most landscape architects were largely involved with these types of projects. This was evidenced in the writings of such leaders in the profession as Garrett Eckbo and Jim Rose.

Until that time the eclectic approach to design was commonly practiced and taught in the colleges: This method left little need for creativity. Eckbo, Rose, and Kiley rebelled against eclecticism. To them every design was different, to be creatively fitted to user needs and site conditions.

During the past two decades there has been a gradual expansion of the profession. Today the scope is so wide that it becomes very difficult to be an expert in all aspects of the profession. In fact, schools are experiencing great difficulty in determining what to cut in order to add what appear to be very important new phases of the profession.

One other factor has to be considered: More and more people are going into landscape architecture as a second profession. They are coming with previous degrees in a wide assortment of areas. For most of those people the graduate program is three years in duration, the first year being a concentrated coverage of the essential undergraduate subjects.

Over the years educators have found that their efforts could not be limited to the training of professionals. Education of the general public concerning the profession and its significance has been of critical importance.

My personal approach to this problem started with active participation in men's and women's garden clubs. That led to my being placed on city and state park boards, which in turn led to working with the beautification commission and city and state political organizations. All of those activities resulted in greater and greater public understanding of the significance of the profession. In 1965 we were responsible for creation by the Louisiana State Parks of a staff position of landscape architect. Today there are four landscape architects on the staff. In addition practicing professional landscape architects are employed in the design of every new state park.

An even better example of the value of garden clubs in stimulating a college program in landscape architecture can be found in the development of the program at the University of Georgia. Hubert Owens set a fine example for other schools to follow, LSU included.

Until I started teaching at LSU in 1941 there was only one landscape architect in the entire state of Louisiana, and most of his work was in the Northeast. And for years it was much more difficult to find employment for college graduates in landscape architecture than in related fields. Today there are 331 landscape architects registered in the state. With the greatly increased public understanding of the profession, the number of job opportunities in landscape architecture relative to those in related professions has shown a marked increase. This increase in the understanding of and demand for landscape architecture in Louisiana seems to be typical of what has been happening all over the country and even in many other parts of the world.

We landscape architects must recognize our own significance. Over the years we have been given and/or have taken secondary places on collaborative teams and have developed a feeling of inferiority to architects, engineers, and others. This should no longer be the case. Educators must impress our graduates with the tremendous breadth and importance of our profession. We need to develop confidence in their value to society. However, to support this attitude we must be certain that the students we graduate are of the highest quality, prepared to be leaders in the preservation and development of the environment.

ROBERT N. ROYSTON

Sixty-two years ago I began my studies at the University of California in Berkeley, California. If someone at that time had told me what the nature of my work in my chosen profession, landscape architecture, would be, this is what I might have been told:

You will be a visiting professor at more than twenty-six universities, each assignment ranging from three days to a month. There you will teach the challenge and importance and excitement of design in all that you do.

You will participate in planning open-space and recreation potentials for thousands of acres within cities, counties, and states. This understanding of design method and process will lead to the design of new towns, communities, and resorts.

You will work with planning and recreation staffs in various cities and help guide the use, form, and quality of open spaces.

In your professional life you will work with and for talented architects, planners, and engineers. You will design and administrate projects with economists, biologists, geologists, meteorologists, traffic engineers, soil engineers, structural engineers, recreational specialists, and others.

You will design children's playgrounds, park systems, movement systems, and bicycle and pedestrian paths; make parks out of garbage and solid waste areas; recover quarries; and restore the marshlands.

You will be involved with urban parks, urban design, street systems, the landscape of transportation corridors, pedestrian systems, and flood-control systems.

You will design golf courses, business parks, subdivisions, housing projects, small communities, large neighborhoods, school grounds, university master plans, and resorts.

You will provide land-management studies; locate rights-of-way; and propose secondary uses for rights-of-way, airport environments, and amenities.

You will design new towns and prepare master plans for river systems, main streets, and historic-neighborhood rehabilitation as well as environmental-assessment and visual-analysis studies.

You will advocate landscape as the structure and green lungs of high-density communities and prepare master plans for research and development complexes and for private and national laboratories.

You will teach the ways that the structure of society can consume the land in gentle ways.

You will suggest alternatives to environmental pollution and advocate sustainable environments.

You will bridge the gap between the natural landscape and structure and property lines.

You will know the cost of development, and you will work to put dollar value to human amenities.

Cemeteries, by your hand, will become beautiful spaces in the city with a new respect for the past.

Designing and preserving the water's edge will be within your scope of services for nature and for people.

Some of your open-space studies will include entire states and entire countries.

Your wider understanding of method and process will allow you to see and to recommend land use over thousands of square miles.

To your students, your clients, your staff, and all those concerned in the community you will teach the importance of design in all you do.

You will work for the National Park Service and the Forest Service. You will champion the work of better form when working with the Corps of Army Engineers.

You will take your knowledge abroad. You will work with other countries. To other cultures you will export expertise with knowledge and, hopefully, with humility. You will learn to listen and participate in a team effort with communities.

You will become more self-confident in your professional ability to design this land for people. You will care about people. You will deal with living things. The walls and the feeling of our spaces are constantly changing, and we are aware of those changes—although often constrained in area and often by spaces that are left over from development.

We as a civilized nation must always remember that landscape architecture, this great profession, is to be nurtured as an activist profession in the quest and struggle for work, health, and survival. Landscape architects are the people who day by day are designing and building the existing spaces.

Ours are the only consistently trained and practicing professionals whose entire lifetime is spent in a small or large way in the design and stewardship of places for people, between structure and structure, and between structure and nature.

This profession is consistently concerned about physical well-being based on the health and pleasure in a sustained landscape, and the world needs us. Our work is largely preventive medicine.

In retrospect, I would never have believed in 1936 that my life as a professional would be challenged by such a variety of projects, problems, and possibilities.

We, as landscape architects, will become more and more aware of other form determinants that will involve us as we face local and global challenges that are brought on by expanding populations, scarcity of water, growing pollution, contaminated waste (nuclear or other), and the shrinking habitat for all living things.

As a group we must look with trust and faith toward an expanding sphere of influence. Let us go for it!

JOHN O. SIMONDS

The intent of this brief commentary is to underscore the telling contribution by American landscape architects to our national well-being.

For starters, let it be proposed that over the past one hundred years no single group of professionals has done more, or as much, to protect our living landscape and give it meaningful form. Nor does any group hold forth such promise for the creation of a more desirable living environment in the years ahead. These are broad statements demanding tangible proof. By way of substantiation let us consider the key elements of responsible landscape evolution. They are preservation, conservation, and sound development.

There are areas of the Earth's land and water surface that should be left undisturbed: the ecologically sensitive tracts vital to the food chain and the continuity of such natural systems as woodlands, wetlands, and waterways. There are also highly productive farmlands and scenic / historic areas deserving almost total protection. Early on, the first American landscape architects, imbued with the thinking of such writ-ers as Henry David Thoreau, George Perkins Marsh, and Aldo Leopold, made preservation a central thesis of their guiding credo. So strong has been this commitment that a first step in all thoughtful landscape planning has now become that of defining those landscape areas to be preserved intact.

The term "conservation" has often been woefully misconstrued. To many misguided zealots it has come to mean unconditioned continuation of the status quo. Wiser heads have long realized that true dynamic conservation is better defined as the wise use and management of our natural resources. Conservation lands, with limited uses, are often conceived as protective sheaths beside or around an area or feature to be preserved. Typically a conservation area is planned to respond sensitively to its landscape character while serving one or more compatible functions such as open-space uses including farmlands, forest, gamelands, parks, and parkways. At a lesser scale a conservation area may be a natural drainageway incorporating a foot or bicycle path or no more than a patch of natural cover for birds.

When most land owners acquire property they have things other than preservation or conservation in mind. Be they individuals, corporations, or public agencies they usually have plans to develop and use their property for human activities of one kind or another. The uses may be of an infinite variety, but as in preservation and conservation the landscape architect has much to contribute in the process of land planning. In most land development the input of the landscape architect is essential. Commonly the need is so obvious and demanding that the landscape architect is elected to lead the team. Here follow examples of the types of projects in which landscape architects have played the leading role.

Parks and recreation areas: Perhaps the best-known works of landscape architecture are the national, state, and regional parks. They have conserved and made available for public use and enjoyment hundreds of thousands of acres of the natural rural and wilderness landscape. Towns and cities throughout the length and breadth of our land have taken form around parks and recreation areas. These have been augmented by a myriad of school athletic fields and playgrounds as well as neighborhood and community open spaces.

Planned neighborhoods, communities, and new towns: These have long been a specialized field of the larger interdisciplinary landscape architecture firms. In such planned commu-nities homes are clustered around open-space preserves that follow the natural drainageways and are interlaced with traffic-free foot and bicycle paths connecting to schools, playfields, shopping compounds, and business offices. Other firms have focused upon such components as institutional grounds and campuses, commercial compounds, industrial parks, botanic gardens, and golf courses. Other diverse projects requiring an understanding of topography and natural processes include military installations, resorts, marinas, forest lands, gamelands, and wildlife sanctuaries. By tradition the emphasis has been on environmental fit and empathy for the users.

Residential: In the minds of many people the practice of landscape architecture is limited to residential planning. This is far from the fact. Homesite and garden design probably comprise less than five percent of the work of the average office. Well-planned homesites, however, do much to enhance the American scene. In the aggregate they brighten our communities and individually serve our neighborhoods as models. They demonstrate clearly the need for and benefits of larger-scale landscape planning.

Transportation: Few realize the immense impact of landscape architects in the field of transportation planning. Clarke + Rapuano were the fathers of such national parkways as the Taconic, Palisades, Blue Ridge, Great Smokies, George Washington, and Yorktown-Jamestown. Landscape architects were also the early proponents of the non-frontage, controlled-access interstate freeways and integrated transmission-transit corridors.

Historic preservation: As works of landscape architecture these can range from the protection of an ancient burial ground to the restoration of a canal, battlefield, whaling port, or historic village.

Environmental improvement: The expanding demand for a more workable and desirable living environment has led landscape architects into such new directions as water-resource management; river-basin planning; coastal and marine bottomland protection; land reclamation, as of denuded forest slopes, depleted and eroding farmlands, and polluted wetlands; reversal of the blight of urban sprawl; growth management; education of the public about the necessity for comprehensive landscape planning; and the preparation for each region and state and the nation of a guiding land-use plan.

What qualifies the landscape architect for this vital role in the protection and evolution of the Ameri-

can landscape? Without question it is our core curriculum in the natural sciences. Beyond physics and chemistry it is the study of geology, biology, ecology, and botany that engenders a feel for the workings of the natural world. These courses are supplemented with study in the humanities, liberal arts, communications, and a thorough grounding in design. Aside from these, many accredited schools give emphasis to such varied aspects of land planning as forestry, recreation, or urban studies—depending upon their resources and locale. From this unique and central base in the natural sciences the graduate landscape architect can move out in many directions. It is our common denominator.

A second common denominator is a sense of mission. And what is that? It has been told that in medieval times a traveler approached the construction site of a new cathedral. Inquisitive, he asked a workman what he was doing. The reply, "Can't you see? I'm sawing a board." A second workman replied, "I'm making a window frame." A third, a stone mason, laid his hammer and chisel aside and, squaring his shoulders with pride, said, "I'm building a cathedral." A sense of mission! In working with students and confreres for more than fifty years the

author has found this compelling sense of mission to be so strong that without it, it could be believed, a person is in the wrong profession.

What then is this sense of mission that has guided us for the past one hundred years and into the next generation? It is the belief that the work of the landscape architect is to help bring the things people do, the structures they build, and the way they live into a more compatible and rewarding relationship with the living landscape of planet Earth.

EDWARD D. STONE, JR.

I came to Florida in the summer of 1959 as a newly minted MLA from Harvard. I had applied for and was subsequently awarded a Fulbright Fellowship to study garden design in Mexico, but the bureaucratic process didn't advise me of the award until after I had accepted employment with the late Frederick Stresau. Fred was a man of great good humor, a very knowledgeable plantsman, and a serious landscape architect who did not take himself seriously.

When I arrived at Fred's office in June of 1959 I became the tenth landscape architect in the State of Florida, which enabled us to then form a chapter. Previously we had been a sec-

tion of the Southeast Chapter, headquartered in Atlanta. I have subsequently attended executive committee meetings of the Florida Chapter at which there were probably some twenty landscape architects in attendance. This is eloquent testimony to the growth of our profession.

Fred's practice was fairly typical of the smaller landscape architecture offices of the time with the work consisting principally of residential projects, plus an occasional hotel, primarily due to our location near Miami. The jet age made it feasible for people to easily vacation, not only in South Florida, but also in the neighboring Caribbean. Fred was beginning to be active throughout the region, and it was an exciting opportunity.

After a year of apprenticeship with Fred I was a bit restless for larger assignments. I had seen the work done in the only two large offices that I knew of at the time, the Clarke + Rapuano office in New York and Hideo Sasaki's practice in Watertown, Massachusetts, which was gaining much acclaim.

At the time I had a developer friend, Jeff VanderWolk, whom I had met during pilot training in Big Spring, Texas. Jeff had sufficient confidence to allow me some planning assignments. Happily my early neat, very polished efforts did not ruin our friendship.

The office struggled in the early years, but ultimately we were successful in building a practice that has a happy balance of planning assignments and project design. I am personally now turning the practice over to my very talented and motivated partners and associates. I think our office and the profession at large are in good hands. And I think the profession is well positioned for the new millennium.

Concern for the environment has made the general public, governmental agencies, and the development community increasingly aware of landscape architects' unique skills and abilities to assist in development with respect for ecosystems. The landscape architects' unique understanding of ecosystems makes them particularly well-qualified to lead multidisciplinary teams in large and complex planning undertakings. Similarly, landscape architects are much in demand and will continue to be in demand for enriching our urban environment through community design and the creation of parks and open spaces in our cities, helping communities develop a real sense of community. Much has been written recently about the emergence of tourism and leisure as the largest global industry. Here again, landscape architects are uniquely qualified to par-

ticipate in this growing international arena, which, of necessity, requires resource preservation and enhancement.

Not only is the scope of the assignments for landscape architects growing, but so are the landscape architects' skills and abilities. The profession has been blessed to have excellent educators and a growing number of schools, with ever improving students.

I am optimistic that the next one hundred years for our profession can be a time of even more expansion numerically and hopefully expansion economically. In order to continue to prosper as a profession we must continue to be able to attract the best and the brightest. This will be an increasing challenge as the lure of exciting opportunities in other businesses, coupled with compensation not dreamed of in the design professions, will tempt all but the most committed. Nevertheless, I remain optimistic.

WILLIAM G. SWAIN

What one does vocationally is of greater importance than what one does in professional service: I believe that volunteer service to one's community is a lifetime obligation. This is paramount. The central theme of my life is a sense of loyalty to those for whom

I've worked or served in a professional capacity. These two principles are all one needs. I have always considered myself privileged to be a landscape architect. At the same time that I was being educated at Carnegie Tech as an architect I was working in a landscape studio under the direction of Ralph E. Griswold, who, along with Margaret Winters, entered a partnership with me in 1957. Bill Mullin, our first employee, joined later. We continued to follow the tradition of being a teaching office. Later, we incorporated and became GWSM Inc., and the library continued to grow. Many of our "alumni" drifted off to form their practices. Great! The more folks doing good landscape architecture, the better. Members of the firm, including stockholders Tom Borellis and Leland Bull, serve on various boards or participate in church work. All voluntary!

ERVIN H. ZUBE

Contemplating the future of landscape architecture can be both challenging and fascinating. My first attempt was more than thirty years ago when asked by landscape architecture students at the University of California, Berkeley, to write an article for their magazine *Landmark 65*. It was titled "What's in a Word?"

and addressed the adequacy of current curricula for the environmental focus then gaining currency across the nation. Also addressed was the adequacy of curricula for preparing students for future roles in designing and planning landscapes for culturally and economically heterogeneous populations. Another issue was the need for a research base to support the profession and provide the knowledge required to responsibly address growing concerns for design and planning solutions that were ecologically and culturally responsive. Information to support such solutions was, however, frequently conspicuous by its absence.

Even today our profession can learn important lessons from the evolution of the traditional professions of the clergy, medicine, law, and education. The studies of Abraham Flexner in the late nineteenth and early twentieth centuries were instrumental in developing a definition of a profession. In 1915 Flexner, following his studies of education in England, medicine in the United States and Canada and a number of other occupations that were then labeled by their practitioners as professions, produced a set of criteria for defining a profession. Among the stimuli that prompted him to develop that definition was his finding that it was less demanding to earn a medical degree in more than fifty percent of the existing academic programs for medicine in the United States and Canada than it was to earn a typical bachelor's degree. As a result of Flexner's work more than fifty percent of those programs were closed. In addition, Flexner also reacted to many occupations calling themselves professions that he firmly believed did not merit that title. The definition that Flexner developed addressed issues of content, process, ethics, and values. They are, I believe, as valid today as they were when he first drafted them. He suggested that a profession is essentially an intellectual operation with high individual responsibilities, has a content derived from science and learning that is particular to the occupation, involves a set of teachable skills, has a self-policing organization, has a philosophy of education, has a social function, exists to serve society, and has recognized autonomy for the practitioner.

In other words, professions have what is basically a legalized monopoly to provide specific services for the public because they address issues of public health, safety, and welfare. And society then provides for the licensing of qualified individuals via examination. Also embedded in that definition is the implicit understanding that a

profession is based on knowledge. This base calls for research support and the application of intellect over emotion.

Such professions as education, engineering, law, and medicine have long histories and, to some degree, share the attribute of having initially served individuals of wealth and power. There are several attributes of their histories, however, that set some of them apart from landscape architecture—namely, practice specialization, educational requirements for entry into the profession, and institutionalized research support.

For metropolitan Tucson, an area with a population of approximately 818,000, the telephone-directory yellow pages indicate thirty-three specializations for engineers; for attorneys fifty-four "Types of Practice" are listed; and for physicians and surgeons the list extends to seventy-six areas of specialization. In contrast, for both landscape architects and architects, there is only one heading—the name of the profession. (Note, the listing for planning is "Planners—City, Regional, Etc.")

Educational programs differ markedly: for example, engineering is still primarily undergraduate for the first professional degree while law and medicine are graduate-degree programs. These three profes-

sions do, however, share a long and strong tradition of scholarly and/or scientific research in their support, the kind of support that is fundamental to intellectual growth as well as to theory development, an activity that was long absent from landscape architecture.

Today, in each of these areas—specialization, education, and research—there are signs that bode well for the future of our profession. The market for landscape architects is considerably more diverse today than it was at the midpoint of the twentieth century. Programs from recent ASLA annual meetings give evidence of both established and emerging areas of specialization in practice, areas that are also found in the curricula of a number of academic programs across the country. Notable among these are landscape planning, based on ecology, cultural-landscape studies, historic landscape preservation and restoration, public-land planning and design, urban design, wildlands planning, landscape history, landscape perceptions and values, the concept of sustainability, computer applications ranging from data management and analysis to modelling and graphics, and the projects that have been the traditional focus of the profession for more than a century.

Another bright light on the hori-

zon is the increasing emphasis on scholarly and scientific research related to all dimensions of the profession, from history to application of the principles of ecology to post-construction evaluations of built projects and the development of theories in support of landscape design, planning, and teaching. While research is not a strong component of many academic programs it appears to be expanding nationwide. The goal should be to have a significant research activity in every region of the country.

Finally, I believe that there will be a growing recognition of the fact that landscape architects must be broadly educated before they receive intensive professional training and education. The model followed in law and medicine should be the model for landscape architects. The knowledge base required to be a truly competent professional cannot be adequately addressed at the undergraduate level. A graduate-level professional degree will also enhance the public image and prestige of, as well as respect for, the profession.

COURTESY OF
JOT DAVID CARPENTER, FASLA

12 FOUNDERS [1899]
NATHAN FRANKLIN BARRETT
ELIZABETH BULLARD
BEATRIX C.J. FARRAND
DANIEL WEBSTER LANGTON
CHARLES NASSAU LOWRIE
WARREN H. MANNING
JOHN CHARLES OLMSTED
FREDERICK LAW OLMSTED, JR.
SAMUEL PARSONS
GEORGE F. PENTACOST, JR.
OSSIAN COLE SIMONDS
DOWNING VAUX

1904
JAMES LEAL GREENLEAF
CHARLES WELLFORD LEAVITT

1906
JAMES STURGIS PRAY
FREDERICK G. TODD

1908
JOHN ROWLETT BRINLEY
HAROLD RHYS CAPARN
ALLING STEPHEN DEFOREST
CARL RUST PARKER
FERRUCCIO VITALE

1910
FRANK M. BUTTON
PERCIVAL GALLAGHER
HENRY VINCENT HUBBARD

1911
BRYANT FLEMING

1912
STEPHEN CHILD
HERBERT JOHN KELLAWAY
CARL F. PILAT
AUBREY TEALDI
LORING UNDERWOOD
ALANSON PHELPS WYMAN

1913
FRANKLIN NATHAN BRETT
ARTHUR FREEMAN BRINCKERHOFF

1914
JAMES FREDERICK DAWSON
RICHARD SCHERMERHORN, JR.

1915
ARTHUR RICHARDSON NICHOLS
T. GLENN PHILLIPS

1916
CHARLES HENRY RAMSDELL
RALPH MORNINGTON WEINRICHTER

1918
EMMANUEL T. MISCHE
JOHN FLETCHER STEELE

1919
GEORGE GIBBS
GEORGE E. KESSLER
ALBERT DAVIS TAYLOR

1920
ARTHUR COLEMAN COMEY

1921
BREMER WHIDDEN POND
WAYNE E. STILES

1923
CLARENCE FOWLER
ALFRED GEIFFERT, JR.

1924
ARTHUR M. KRUSE

1925
HAROLD HILL BLOSSOM

1926
FREDERICK N. EVANS
HERBERT LINCOLN FLINT

1927
PHILIP HOMER ELWOOD, JR.

1929
NOEL CHAMBERLIN

1930
HALLAM LEONARD MOVIUS
EDWARD CLARK WHITING

1932
ARTHUR HADDEN ALEXANDER
RALPH DALTON CORNELL

1933
ARMAND RHODES TIBBITTS
LEON DEMING TILTON
ROBERT WHEELWRIGHT

1934
WALTER LOUIS CHAMBERS
LAURIE DAVIDSON COX
MARTHA BROOKS HUTCHESON

1936
KATHERINE BASHFORD
ROSE GREELY
JOHN NOYES
JAMES ROY WEST
BRADFORD WILLIAMS

1938
RUSSELL VAN NEST BLACK
GORDON D. COOPER
CHARLES WILLIAM ELIOT II
LEON HENRY ZACH

1939
LAWRENCE V. SHERIDAN
WILLIAM AUGUSTUS STRONG
FRANK ALBERT WAUGH

1940
JOHN WILLIAM GREGG
NORMAN THOMAS NEWTON
MICHAEL RAPUANO
WILBUR H. SIMONSON

1942
ANNETTE HOYT FLANDERS

1943
OTTO GEORGE SCHAFFER
RICHARD K. WEBEL

1945
CLARENCE CORNELIUS COMBS

1946
HUGH FINDLAY
EMERSON KNIGHT
MARKLEY STEVENSON

1948
FRANCIS CORMIER
CONRAD LOUIS WIRTH

1950
JUSTIN R. HARTZOG
THOMAS C. JEFFERS, SR.
SIDNEY NICHOLS SHURCLIFF

1951
WILLIAM LYMAN PHILLIPS
CHARLES REUEL SUTTON

1952
STANLEY WILLIAM ABBOTT
FRED BARLOW, JR.
CLARENCE WAYNE BAUGHMAN
ALFRED L. BOERNER
AGNES SELKIRK CLARK
CORNELIUS EARL MORROW
ARTHUR L. MUNSON
CHARLES GOODWIN SAUERS
ROBERT OLIVER THOMPSON

1953
PRENTISS FRENCH
L. GLENN HALL
HELEN SWIFT JONES RICE

1954
JOHN ROBERT BRACKEN
OLIVER MICHAEL FANNING

EDWARD HARRY LAIRD
RUSSELL H. RILEY
H. LELAND VAUGHAN
HARLOW O. WHITTEMORE

1955
THOMAS H. JONES
KARL BAPTISTE LOHMANN
HARRY WHITCOMB SHEPHERD

1956
MALCOLM KIRKPATRICK
HENRY SCHULTHEIS

1957
REGINALD DRURY TILLSON
RICHARD KENNETH DEE
WALTER A.J. EWALD
FREDERIC A. FAY
JOE WALTER LANGRAN
ELDRIDGE H. LOVELACE
VINCENT NICHOLAS MERRILL
HALE WALKER
CARL WILLIAM WILD

1958
ALDEN HOPKINS
ALFRED CARLTON KUEHL
RUSSELL L. MCKOWN
THOMAS J. NELSON
MILTON MEADE PALMER
MORRIS E. TROTTER, JR.
BROOKS EDWARD WIGGINTON

1959
WOLCOTT ERSKINE ANDREWS
ARTHUR S. BERGER
ERNEST L. DEWALD
RICHARD C. MURDOCK
HAROLD STANLEY WAGNER
NELSON MILLER WELLS
DONALD HENRY WOLBRINK

1960
IRIS ASHWELL
WALLACE GORDON ATKINSON
EUGENE R. DESILETS, JR.

RAYMOND E. PAGE
WILLIAM WIDNEY WELLS

1961
CHARLES ALVIN DETURK
RICHARD CLAY GUTHRIDGE
EUGENE RICHARD MARTINI
STUART MOULTON MERTZ
ELIZABETH GREENLEAF PATTEE
NOREDA ANTHONY ROTUNNO

1962
GEORGE J. ALBRECHT
GARRETT ECKBO
ARTHUR FITZGERALD
SAM LESLIE HUDDLESTON
HAROLD WILLIAM LAUTNER

1963
ARTHUR GIPSON BARTON
FREDERICK ALEXANDER CUTHBERT
ARMISTEAD FITZHUGH
DOROTHEA KATHARINE HARRISON
THEODORE OSMUNDSON
NEIL HAMILL PARK

1964
ROBERT WINIFIELD ANDREWS
VINCENT CHARLES CERASI
LESTER ALBERTSON COLLINS
ALBE E. MUNSON
JOHN ORMSBEE SIMONDS
HELENE BLISS WARNER

1965
EDWARD BROOKS BALLARD
DEAN NEWTON GLICK
EARL C. GREVER
LYNN M.F. HARRISS
LAVAL SIDNEY MORRIS
CARY MILLHOLLAND PARKER
WILLIAM C. PAULEY
JANE SILVERSTEIN RIES

1966
JAMES BUSH-BROWN
CLARENCE ELLIOT HAMMOND

GEORGE ERWIN PATTON
CATHERINE JONES THOMPSON

1967
RAYMOND LEE FREEMAN
CARL STEFFENS GERLACH
ROBERT WILLLIAM PIERSON
ROBERT F. WHITE
GEORGE WILLIAM WICKSTEAD

1968
DOMENICO ANNESE
KENNETH I. HELPHAND
STEWART EDMUND KING
MARGARET WINTERS
ROBERT LEWIS ZION

1969
SAMUEL WILLIAM BRIDGERS
LAWRENCE HALPRIN
MARION V. PACKARD
HIDEO SASAKI
JOHN DUDLEY SCRUGGS
STANLEY HART WHITE

1970
MILTON BARON
GEORGE COOPER HUNTINGTON
DONALD HOWARD PARKER
RUBEE JEFFREY PEARSE
KATHERINE F. WILSON RAHN
ROBERT SIGMUND REICH

1971
ARTHUR EDWIN BYE, JR.
EDWARD LAWTON DAUGHERTY
WARREN E. LAUESON
AARON LEVINE
RUTH PATRICIA SHELLHORN
PHILIP DOUGLAS SIMONDS
DAVID E. THOMPSON

1972
JAMES BECKHAM GODWIN
IAN LENNOX MCHARG
OWEN HARLEY PETERS
HELMUT H. SCHMITZ

GERALDINE KNIGHT SCOTT
BRADFORD G. SEARS
WILLIAM GRANT SWAIN

1973
R. D'ARCY BONNET
HAROLD A. BREEN, JR.
WILLIAM J. JOHNSON
ARTEMAS PARTRIDGE RICHARDSON
DONALD M. ROBERTS
WILLIAM E. ROSE
ROBERT N. ROYSTON
GUNTER ARTHUR SCHOCH

1974
LLOYD M. BOND
BRADFORD MARSON GREENE
BYRON R. HANKE
ALFRED BASIL LAGASSE, JR.
FRANCIS JOHN MACDONALD
ALICE ORME SMITH
EDWARD DURELL STONE, JR.

1975
WILLIAM ALFRED BEHNKE
ALEXANDER BUDREVICS
PASCHALL CAMPBELL
CARLTON TYLER DODGE
THOMAS JOSEPH KANE
R. BURTON LITTON, JR.
PAUL M. SAITO
EDWARD H. STONE II
PETER EDWIN WALKER

1976
RICHARD MATHER BOWE
ROBERT P. EALY
LAWRENCE ALBERT ENERSEN
JACK O. HOLMES
ROBERT B. WALKER
GEORGE S. WALTERS
HENRY GORDON WHIFFEN
HARRIET BARNHARDT WIMMER

1977
YOSHIRO BEFU
JOHN WILLIS BRIGHT

SPENCER PERCY ELLIS
MORGAN BILL EVANS
BENJAMIN W. GARY, JR.
JAMES E. GLAVIN
EDWIN GILBERT THURLOW
RICHARD C. TONGG

1978
CALVIN THOMAS BISHOP
JOT DAVID CARPENTER
CLARA STIMSON COFFEY
FRANCIS HILL DEAN
ALICE RECKNAGEL IREYS
LANE L. MARSHALL
PAUL WILBUR MCCLOUD
ROBERT MERRILL O'DONNELL
LOUIS JOSEPH PERRON
RICHARD A. WILSON
THEODORE JULIAN WIRTH
ROBERT LESTER WOERNER

1979
HOWARD R. BAUMGARTEN
M. PAUL FRIEDBERG
CALVIN SARGENT HAMILTON
CARL DAVID JOHNSON
RICHARD B. MYRICK
EDWARD LYONS PRYCE
JOHN EDWARD RAHENKAMP
KENJI SHIOZAWA
DAVID G. WRIGHT
JOSEPH Y. YAMADA
DAVID LINCOLN YOUNG

1980
RICHARD CHEVALIER BELL
BAILEY O. BREEDLOVE
DAVID BARROW CARRUTH
LEWIS JAMES CLARKE
JACK ROBERT DAFT
S.R. DEBOER
DONOVAN EARL HOWER
GLEN H. HUNT
GRANT RICHARD JONES
ROBERT HENRY MORTENSEN
ROBERT LEWIS STEENHAGEN
NELVA MARGARET WEBER

1981
JAMES H. BASSETT
FRANK BERNARD BURGGRAF
ROBERT R. CARDOZA
LAURENCE E. COFFIN, JR.
JAMES FREDERICK FONDREN
DONALD FRANKLIN HILDERBRANT
BENJAMIN CREGAN HOWLAND, JR.
ROGER BOND MARTIN
WILLIAM ROBERT NELSON, JR.
HELEN M. QUACKENBUSH
OLLIE EUGENE SCHRICKEL, JR.
JOHN L. WACKER

1982
MYLES G. BOYLAN
RAYMOND F. CAIN
PAUL GARDESCU
CAROL ROXANNE JOHNSON
WARREN D. JONES
DARREL GENE MORRISON
DARWINA L. NEAL
WARREN J. OBLINGER
COURTLAND P. PAUL
PETER G. ROLLAND

1983
DERR A. CARPENTER
CLIFFORD WARTHEN COLLIER, JR.
RICHARD LEWIS HAAG
DEAN ADAMS JOHNSON
ROBERT LINWOOD O'BOYLE
J. STEVE OWNBY
PAUL N. PROCOPIO
ROBERT G. REIMANN
ROBERT H. RUCKER
HERRICK HAYNER SMITH

1984
HARRY J. BALDWIN
CLAIRE R. BENNETT
GEORGE EDWARD CREED
ASA HANAMOTO
JAMES E. KEETER
RAY O. KUSCHE
JACK ERVIN LEAMAN
JOSEPH H. LINESCH

JOHN GILMAN PARSONS
JOHN EDWARD PINCKNEY
CLARENCE ROY
WILLIAM SCATCHARD, JR.
ERVIN H. ZUBE

1985
ELEANOR A. CHRISTIE
JULIUS GYULA FABOS
BARBARA VORSE FEALY
ROBERT TRENT JONES
CAMERON R.J. MAN
EDWARD C. MARTIN, JR.
WILLIAM A. O'LEARY
THEODORE D. WALKER

1986
D. LYLE ATEN
CHARLES W. CARES
C. CHRISTOPHER DEGENHARDT
PHILIP E. FLORES
JERE STUART FRENCH
TERRY CLARK GERRARD
CLARE A. GUNN
WAYNE DAHL IVERSON
WALTER H. KEHM
MICHAEL LAURIE
THOMAS P. PAPANDREW
GERALD D. PATTEN
HARRY W. PORTER, JR.
ALBERT J. RUTLEDGE
THOMAS H. WALLIS, JR.

1987
DONALD B. AUSTIN
STUART O. DAWSON
E. ROBERT GREGAN
KARSTEN HANSEN
CHARLES WARD HARRIS
KENNETH R. KRABBENHOFT
RICHARD A. MOORE
MICHAEL PAINTER
TITO PATRI
NEIL H. PORTERFIELD
NICHOLAS QUENNELL
SALLY SCHAUMAN
RAYMOND L. UECKER, JR.

KENT E. WATSON

1988
DAVID E. ARBEGAST
JAMES E. CHRISTMAN
ROY J. DUNN
ANTHONY M. GUZZARDO
NANCY M. HARDESTY
GLENN O. HENDRIX
BRIAN S. KUBOTA
DONALD W. LESLIE
KENNETH J. POLAKOWSKI
JOE A. PORTER
HORST SCHACH
JONATHAN GROVER SEYMOUR
ALLEN D. STOVALL
BARRY THALDEN
ARNOLD VOLLMER
MORGAN DIX WHEELOCK, JR.
LAURENCE W. ZUELKE

1989
ELDON W. BECK
VINCENT J. BELLAFIORE
E. LEROY BRADY
ANTHONY B. CASENDINO
ROGER D. CLEMENCE
DIRK JONGEJAN
GRACE H. KIRKWOOD
ROGER B. MCERLANE
SATORU NISHITA
JOHN J. REYNOLDS
JERROLD SOESBE
ROBERT L. THAYER, JR.
FLOYD W. ZIMMERMAN

1990
CHERYL BARTON
RONALD M. IZUMITA
PETER D.A. JACOBS
JOHN T. LYLE
ROBERT E. MARVIN
GARY W. MEISNER
HERBERT R. SCHAAL
ARNO S. SCHMID
BRUCE G. SHARKY
JOHN B. SLATER

R. MERRICK SMITH
JOHN GODFREY STODDART
ROGER TRANCIK

1991
WILLIAM H. BAKER
ARMAND BENEDEK
EUGENE CASEY BROCK
WAYNE L. BUGGENHAGEN
WILLARD CALVERT BYRD
WILLIAM H. HAVENS
GARY E. KARNER
MASAO KINOSHITA
RICHARD K. LAW
DONALD J. MOLNAR
WOLFGANG OEHME
DON H. OLSON
KENNETH RAITHEL, JR.
BARRY W. STARKE
WILLIAM H. TISHLER

1992
MARVIN I. ADLEMAN
RUSSELL A. ADSIT
ANTHONY M. BAUER
THEORE W. BRICKMAN, JR.
JOSEPH E. BROWN
ROY H. DEBOER
RUDY J. FAVRETTI
DONALD L. FERLOW
JOHN W. FREY
HARRY L. GARNHAM
ROBERT E. GOETZ
EDITH HARRISON HENDERSON
ALLEN W. HIXON, JR.
JOSEPH HUDAK
JOSEPH P. KARR
FRANK H. KAWASAKI
J. TIMOTHY KELLER
DAVID O. LOSE
KATHRYN E. MCKNIGHT
E. LYNN MILLER
DEBRA L. MITCHELL
JOAN I. NASSAUER
JOHN A. NELSON
THOMAS J. NIEMAN
CORNELIA HAHN OBERLANDER

DONALD C. RICHARDSON
WILLIAM H. ROBERTS
LESLEE A. TEMPLE
DONALD H. TOMPKINS
L. AZEO TORRE
HOWARD E. TROLLER
ALBERT R. VERI

1993
KENNETH E. BASSETT
ROBERT S. BUDZ
CRAIG S. CAMPBELL
DONALD RAY CARTER
EUGENE H. CARTER
ALAN B. CLARKE
JON CHARLES COE
JOHN F. COLLINS
FRED J. CORREALE
JOHN EARL CUTLER
ROGER ALAN DEWEESE
P. WOODWARD DIKE
FRANK R. DUNBAR
THOMAS R. DUNBAR
DONALD H. ENSIGN
WILLIAM L. FLOURNOY, JR.
DONALD MARK FOX
ROBERT L. FRAZER
LESLIE A. KERR
E. BYRON MCCULLEY
ROBERT Z. MELNICK
PETER J. OLIN
DENNIS Y. OTSUJI
PETER M. POLLACK
RAE L. PRICE
ROBERT BARTLETT RILEY
JAMES C. STANSBURY
STEPHEN J. TRUDNAK
JAMES ANTHONY VAN SWEDEN
LAWRENCE L. WALKER
ANTHONY WALMSLEY
V. MICHAEL WEINMAYR
PATRICK H. WYSS
ROBERT W. ZOLOMIJ

1994
ROBERT F. BRISTOL
WILLIAM BYRD CALLAWAY

SAMUEL CROZIER
KURT CULBERTSON
NICHOLAS T. DINES
DAN W. DONELIN
BRUCE K. FERGUSON
RICHARD V. GIAMBERDINE
TERENCE G. HARKNESS
LEONARD J. HOPPER
LINDA JEWELL
ILZE JONES
JOSEPH J. LALLI
J. ROLAND LIEBER
SUSAN P. LITTLE
THOMAS A. LOCKETT
RICHARD K. MARSHALL
PATRICK C. MOORE
ROBERT K. MURASE
MERLYN J. PAULSON
ROBERT PERRON
HARVEY M. RUBENSTEIN
J. KIPP SHRACK
RODNEY L. SWINK
MICHAEL A. THEILACKER
MICHAEL VAN VALKENBURGH
SCOTT S. WEINBERG
ROGER WELLS
J. DANIEL WOJCIK

1995
HOWARD G. ABEL
DWAYNE ADAMS, JR.
DAVID ARMBRUSTER
ROY O. ASHLEY
DENNIS R. BUETTNER
ANN E. CHRISTOPH
BEATRIZ DE WINTHUYSEN COFFIN
GEORGE W. CURRY
BRUCE DEES
DAMON FARBER
EVERETT L. FLY
EMILY GABEL-LUDDY
GEORGE G. GENTILE
JOHN N. GRISSIM
PERRY HOWARD
SUSAN B. JACOBSON
FREDERICK D. JARVIS
CHARLES L. KNIGHT

BRUCE KULIK
DONALD F. LEDERER
PHILIP H. LEWIS, JR.
J. MACK LITTLE
JERRY J. LOOMIS
STEVE MARTINO
DAVID A. MCNEAL
LUCIANO MICELI
LYNN A. MOORE
PATRICIA M. O'DONNELL
DAVID C. RACKER
WILLIAM D. SANDERS
TERRY W. SAVAGE
MARIO G. SCHJETNAN
JUANITA D. SHEARER-SWINK
KEN B. SIMMONS, JR.
JAMES R. TURNER
RONALD W. TUTTLE
WILLIAM E. WENK

1996
JOHN AHERN
CHARLES BIRNBAUM
JEFFREY BRUCE
FRANKLIN CLEMENTS
ROBERT DEERING
DAVID ENGEL
SUSAN EVERETT
BARBABRA FAGA
DAVID FASSER
MARK HUNNER
MARK JOHNSON
WILLIAM KUHL
FREDERICK LANG
DOUGLAS MACY
MICHAEL MALYN
LEWIS MAY
CAROL MAYER-REED
PATRICK MILLER
MICHAEL MIYABARA
THOMAS MUSIAK
JOSEPH NEVIUS
WILLIAM PRESSLEY
GARY ROBINETTE
GEORGE SASS
MARGARET SAND
JANICE SCHACH

PETER TROWBRIDGE
VICTOR WALKER
DWIGHT WEATHERFORD

1997
TED BAKER
W. FRANK BRANDT
DONALD CARL BRINKERHOFF
GEORGE GLENN COOK
KENNETH R. COULTER
ROBERT W. DYAS
RICHARD GEORGE GIBBONS
H. KENNETH CRASCO
PHILIP H. GRAHAM, JR.
KATHLEEN M. FOX
DONALD H. GODI
LEONARD GRASSLI
FREDERICK EDWARD HALBACK
RICHARD E. HANSON
RICHARD G. HAUTAU
ROBERT GRAHAM HEILIG
LEERIE T. JENKINS, JR.
NIMROD W. E. LONG III
PAUL C. K. LU
RICHARD E. MAYER
VINCENT C. MCDERMOTT
MARK K. MORRISON
KENNETH S. NAKABA
KENICHI NAKANO
NEIL ODENWALD
F. TRUITT RABUN, JR.
RICHARD H. ROGERS
VIRGINIA LOCKETT RUSSELL
TERRY WARRINER RYAN
JERRY MITCHELL TURNER
MARK J. ZARILLO

1998
J. ROBERT ANDERSON
ARTHUR BEGGS
JAMES BELL
DAVID BLAU
MARK BRINKLEY
BRYAN CARLSON
CARLOS CASHIO
VAN COX
NEIL DEAN
JOHN FURLONG
H. ROWLAND JACKSON
GARY KESLER
MARY ANN LASCH
MARK LINDHULT
LAWRENCE MOLINE
PAUL MORRIS
ROBERT PERRY
KAREN PHILLIPS
MARJORIE PITZ
MARION PRESSLEY
JEFFREY SIEGEL
STANLEY SPECHT
RICHARD STAUFFER
SHAVAUN TOWERS
JAMES URBAN
E. NEAL WEATHERLY
ROBERT WEYGAND
JAMES WHEAT

YEARS NOT AVAILABLE
TRACY HAYES ABELL
EDWARD R. BACHTLE
HARRIET RODES BAKEWELL
DOUGLAS G. BAYLIS
EARL BLAIR

JAMES HENRY BROOKS, JR.
DONALD WILLIAM BUSH
WILLIAM GRAY CARNES
RICHARD CAROTHERS
GILMORE DAVID CLARKE
CHARLES PRENTICE CLAYTON
MARIAN CRUGER COFFIN
THOMAS MICHAEL COLGROVE
WILBUR DAVID COOK, JR.
DENNIS DAY
OLIVER A. DEAKIN
ROBERT B. DEERING
ROBERT IRA DERCK
THOMAS HENRY DESMOND
CHARLES HAYES DIGGS
EARLE SUMNER DRAPER
JOHN R. FITZSIMMONS
ROBERT L. FOWLER, JR.
CHARLES FREEMAN GILLETTE
E. GENEVIEVE GILLETTE
RALPH ESTY GRISWOLD
S. HERBERT HARE
SIDNEY J. HARE
KENNETH F. HIGGINS
ROLAND S. HOYT
EDWARD HUNTSMAN-TROUT
UMBERTO INNOCENTI
ALLYN RYERSON JENNINGS
FREDERICK H. KENNARD
SIDNEY STILES KENNEDY
JAMES ARTHUR LABRENZ
EDWARD GODFREY LAWSON
CHARLES DOWNING LAY
EMMET JOHN LAYTON
LAWRENCE G. LINNARD
WILLIAM BELL MARQUIS

H. BOYER MARX
RICHARD JAMES MEYERS
CAMPBELL E. MILLER
EUGENE DAVIS MONTILLON
JOHN BARSTOW MORRILL
KENNETH H.N. NEWTON
JOHN NOLEN
RICKSON ALBERT OUTHET
HUBERT BOND OWENS
CLIFTON E. RODGERS
JOHN I. ROGERS
JOHN J. MCC. RYAN
MEREL SEAMAN SAGER
THOMAS SEARS
ARTHUR ASAHEL SHURCLIFF
KENNETH BOYD SIMMONS
F.A. CUSHING SMITH
SIBLEY C. SMITH
FREDERIC BARNES STRESAU
ROBERT JAMES TEMPLETON
THOMAS CHALMERS VINT
RONALD M. WALTERS
JANET DARLING WEBEL
EMMET L. WEMPLE
WILLIAM S. WIEDORN
EDWARD AUGUSTUS WILLIAMS
WAYNE HAYES WILSON
DAVID G. WYMAN
GEORGE ARTHUR YARWOOD
MAY ELIZABETH MCADAMS

NOTES

NOTES

INTRODUCTION

1. Charles W. Eliot, "Welfare and Happiness in Works of Landscape Architecture," *Landscape Architecture* (April 1911), 145–53. Eliot was made an honorary member of the ASLA in 1916.

2. Richard Norton Smith, *The Harvard Century: The Making of a University to a Nation* (New York: Simon and Schuster, 1986), 13.

3. Van Wyck Brooks, *New England: Indian Summer, 1865–1915* (New York: E.P. Dutton, 1940), 104.

4. For perspectives on Roosevelt, Wilson, and the Progressive movement, see Richard Hofstadter, ed., *The Progressive Movement, 1900– 1915* (Englewood Cliffs, N.J.: Prentice-Hall, Inc., 1963), and Arthur S. Link, *Woodrow Wilson and the Progressive Era* (New York: Harper & Row, 1954).

5. Walter Lippmann, *Drift and Mastery* (New York: Mitchell Kennerley, 1914), xx. See also Mel Scott, *American City Planning Since 1890* (Berkeley: University of California Press, 1969), 120.

6. Herbert Croly, *The Promise of American Life* [1909], reprinted with an introduction by John William Ward (New York: Bobbs-Merrill, 1965), 14. Croly was editor of *The Architectural Record* and, beginning in 1914, editor of *The New Republic.*

7. Joseph Fels, "Taxation, Housing, and Town Planning," *Landscape Architecture* (October 1913), 11.

8. William Allen White, *Autobiography* (New York: Macmillan, 1946), 428.

9. A classic study of the Progressive Era is Richard Hofstadter, *The Age of Reform: From Bryan to F.D.R.* (New York: Alfred A. Knopf, 1955). See also Christopher Lasch, *The New Radicalism in America, 1889–1963* (New York: Alfred A. Knopf, 1965).

10. Lawrence F. Abbott, *Impressions of Theodore Roosevelt* (Garden City, New York: Doubleday, Page & Co.,

1919), 122–26. See also Roderick Nash, *Wilderness and the American Mind* [1967], third edition (New Haven: Yale University Press, 1982).

11. Laurence R. Veysey, *The Emergence of the American University* (Chicago: University of Chicago Press, 1965). See also "Harvard Graduate School of Design," vol. 1, in Gary O. Robinette, *Landscape Architectural Education,* 2 vols. (Dubuque, Iowa: Kendall/Hunt Publishing Co., 1973); Norman T. Newton, *Design on the Land: The Development of Landscape Architecture* (Cambridge: Harvard University Press, 1971), 335–36; and Note 2, above.

12. See Eliot's letters and reports regarding the Charles River, 1891–1896, in *Charles Eliot, Landscape Architect,* ed. Charles W. Eliot (Boston: Houghton, Mifflin, 1902), 557–92.

13. Charles Eliot, "What Would be Fair Must First be Fit," *Garden and Forest* (April 1, 1896), reprinted in *Charles Eliot, Landscape Architect,* 549–53. "The greatest good for the greatest number" was a utilitarian principle that J.S. Mill had absorbed from reading Jeremy Bentham's works.

14. Charles Eliot to Warren Manning, March 8, 1897, in *Charles Eliot, Landscape Architect,* 703. This letter is quoted in part in "Historical View of ASLA," *ASLA Bulletin* (June 1969), unpaged; shorter excerpts appear in Newton, *Design on the Land,* 385–86.

15. J.C. Olmsted, undated letter in "Historical View of ASLA," unpaged.

16. Laura Wood Roper, *FLO: A Biography of Frederick Law Olmsted* (Baltimore: Johns Hopkins University Press, 1973), 475.

17. H.W.S. Cleveland, undated letter quoted in "Historical View of ASLA," unpaged.

18. Charles S. Sargent and O.C. Simonds, undated letters quoted in "Historical View of ASLA," unpaged.

19. L.H. Bailey and M.G. Van Renssalaer, undated letters quoted in "Historical View of ASLA," unpaged. Van

Renssalaer's profile of Olmsted in *The Century Magazine* (October 1893), 860–67, was recently reprinted in Van Renssalaer, *Accents as Well as Broad Effects: Writings on Architecture, Landscape, and the Environment, 1876– 1925,* ed. David Gebhard (Berkeley: University of California Press, 1996).

20. See *Transactions of the American Society of Landscape Architects* (hereafter, *Transactions, ASLA*), vol. 1 (1899– 1908). See also Chapter 1, below.

21. Samuel P. Hays, *Conservation and the Gospel of Efficiency* [1959], new edition (New York: Atheneum, 1969), Preface.

22. Daniel Burnham, quoted in Roper, *FLO,* 447.

23. Dan Kiley, who had a rewarding six-year apprenticeship with Manning in the 1930s, recalls that Manning tried to steer him away from both Harvard and the ASLA. See Peter Walker and Melanie Simo, *Invisible Gardens: The Search for Modernism in the American Landscape* (Cambridge: MIT Press, 1994), 181–82.

24. William Grundmann, "Warren H. Manning" in *American Landscape Architecture: Designers and Places,* ed. William H. Tishler (Washington, D.C.: National Trust for Historic Preservation/ASLA, 1989), 58.

25. Warren H. Manning, "The History of Village Improvement in the United States," *Craftsman* (February 1904), 423–32.

26. Manning, "National Parks, Monuments and Forests," *Landscape Architecture* (April 1916), 106–12, and "A National Plan Study Brief," a special supplement in *Landscape Architecture* (July 1923), 3–24. Charles Beveridge made this observation in conversation with the author. See also Roper, *FLO,* 324–26. The Staten Island plan of January 1871 was devised by a committee composed of Olmsted, H.H. Richardson, Dr. Elisha Harrison, and J.M. Trowbridge.

27. Ervin Zube, "The Advance of Ecol-

ogy," *Landscape Architecture* (March/ April 1986), 66–67. See also Carl Steinitz, Paul Parker, and Lawrie Jordan, "Hand Drawn Overlays: Their History and Prospective Uses," *Landscape Architecture* (September 1976), 444–55.

28. Ian McHarg, taped conversations with the author, May 20, 1987, in Berkeley, California; Heidi Landecker, "In Search of an Arbiter" [profile of Ian McHarg], *Landscape Architecture* (January 1990), 90.

29. Manning, "National Plan Study Brief," 4–23. Apparently Manning produced more than one version of his report on a national plan. Grundmann cites the full 900-page report in his article, "Warren H. Manning." Robin Karson refers to Manning's "National Plan" as a 427-page document. See Karson, *The Muses of Gwinn: Art and Nature in a Garden Designed by Warren H. Manning, Charles A. Platt & Ellen Biddle Shipman* (Sagaponack, New York: Sagapress/The Library of American Landscape History, 1995), 28.

30. Lippmann, *Drift and Mastery,* 165.

31. Arthur A. Shurtleff, "Annual Report of the President," *Landscape Architecture* (April 1930), 230.

32. Patrick A. Miller, "A Profession in Peril?" *Landscape Architecture* (August 1997), 66–71+.

33. William H. Roberts, quoted in Ibid.

34. Calvert Vaux to Frederick Law Olmsted, May 20, 1865, quoted in *The Papers of Frederick Law Olmsted,* vol. 5: *The California Frontier, 1863– 1865,* ed. Victoria Post Panney, Gerard J. Rauluk, and Carolyn F. Hoffman (Baltimore: Johns Hopkins University Press, 1990), 373–74; *The Papers of Frederick Law Olmsted,* vol. 3: *Creating Central Park, 1857–1861,* ed. Charles E. Beveridge and David Schuyler (1983), 267, Note 1.

35. *Papers of Frederick Law Olmsted,* vol. 5 (1990), 375, Note 7.

36. Peter Walker, quoted in Miller, "A Profession in Peril?" 69.

37. John O. Simonds and Rick G. Spalenka, letters to the editor, *Landscape Architecture* (October 1997), 52–54.

38. Henry Vincent Hubbard, "Annual Report of the President," *Landscape Architecture* (April 1934), 163.

CHAPTER I

1. For Nathan F. Barrett and J.C. Olmsted, see T*ransactions of the American Society of Landscape Architects* (hereafter, *Transactions, ASLA)*, vol. 2 (1909–21), 90–92, and 104–107.
   See also *Landscape Architecture* for the obituaries of O.C. Simonds (April 1932); Charles N. Lowrie (April 1940); Warren Manning (April 1938); and Samuel Parsons, Jr. (April 1923). For Farrand, see Robert W. Patterson, "Beatrix Farrand—1872–1959," *Landscape Architecture* (Summer 1959), 216–18, and Diana Balmori, Diane Kostial McGuire, and Eleanor M. McPeck, *Beatrix Farrand's American Landscapes: Her Gardens & Campuses* (Sagaponack, New York: Sagapress, 1985). Daniel W. Langton and George F. Pentecost, Jr., were also charter members of the ASLA. See *Transactions, ASLA,* vol. 1 (1899–1908); *ASLA Bulletin* (June 1969); and *Pioneers in American Landscape Design: An Annotated Bibliography,* ed. Charles A. Birnbaum and Lisa E. Crowder (Washington, D.C.: U.S. Government Printing Office, 1993).

2. Bremer W. Pond, "Fifty Years in Retrospect: Brief Account of the Origin and Development of the ASLA," *Landscape Architecture* (January 1950), 59; Norman T. Newton, *Design on the Land: The Development of Landscape Architecture* (Cambridge: Harvard University Press, 1971), 385–92.

3. Arthur A. Shurcliff, *Autobiography* [written 1943–1944, with additions in 1946 and 1947] privately printed. A copy is kept in the Frances Loeb

Library, Harvard University. See also obituaries in *Landscape Architecture* for Shurcliff (April 1958), Lay (April 1956), Hubbard (January 1948), Greenleaf (October 1933), and Vitale (July 1933).

4. Shurcliff, *Autobiography*, 16; Beatrix Jones, interview in *The New York Herald Tribune,* February 11, 1900, as quoted in Eleanor M. McPeck, "A Biographical Note," in Balmori, et al., *Beatrix Farrand's American Landscapes*, 22.

5. Bremer W. Pond, "Fifty Years in Retrospect," 59, and "Arthur Asahel Shurcliff," *Landscape Architecture* (April 1958), 183.

6. See T.J. Jackson Lears, *No Place of Grace: Antimodernism and the Transformation of American Culture, 1880–1920* (New York: Pantheon, 1981).

7. Robert Wheelwright, letter to the editor, *Landscape Architecture* (April 1955), 139.

8. George Santayana, *The Life of Reason* [1905–1906], excerpted in *The Philosophy of Santayana*, ed, Irwin Edman (New York: Modern Library, ca. 1936), 260, 332.

9. Ibid, 324. See also Santayana, "A Brief History of My Opinions" [1930], in the same work. For insights into emerging specialization in the sciences, see Alfred North Whitehead, *Science and the Modern World* [1925], new edition (New York: The Free Press, 1967), and James B. Conant, *My Several Lives: Memoirs of a Social Inventor* (New York: Harper & Row, 1970).

10. Hubbard and Kimball were quoting from Santayana's *Sense of Beauty* [1896]; see their book, *Introduction to the Study of Landscape Design* (New York: Macmillan, 1917), 20–21.

11. Santayana, *The Life of Reason*, excerpted in *The Philosophy of Santayana*, 254.

12. Ibid, 255.

13. See Frederick Law Olmsted, Jr., and Theodora Kimball, eds., *Forty Years of Landscape Architecture: Frederick Law Olmsted, Senior,* 2 vols. (New York: G.P. Putnam's Sons, 1922, 1928), and

Charles Eliot, Landscape Architect, ed. Charles W. Eliot, (Boston: Houghton Mifflin, 1902). Downing's *Treatise on the Theory and Practice of Landscape Gardening* (1841) went through at least nine editions through 1859 and had two supplements written by H.W. Sargent through 1875. Jacob Weidenmann's *Beautifying Country Homes* appeared in 1870, followed by H.W.S. Cleveland's *Landscape Architecture as Applied to the Wants of the West* (1873). *Landscape Gardening* (1891) by Samuel Parsons, Jr., was reprinted in 1900. In 1907 the ASLA began to sponsor a series of classics, beginning with an abridgment of Humphry Repton's works, edited by John Nolen. This was followed by Prince von Puckler–Muskau's *Hints on Landscape Gardening* [1834], translated from the German by Bernhard Sickert and edited by Samuel Parsons (1917), and Downing's *Treatise,* edited by Frank Waugh (1921).

14. Olmsted to Mrs. W.D. Whitney, December 16, 1890, quoted in Laura Wood Roper, *FLO: A Biography of Frederick Law Olmsted* (Baltimore: Johns Hopkins University Press, 1973), 420.

15. Eliot to Charles Francis Adams, December 12, 1896, in *Charles Eliot, Landscape Architect,* 630.

16. Charles W. Eliot, letter to the editor, dated September 24, 1910, in *Landscape Architecture* (October 1910), 40.

17. Warren Manning, "The Field of Landscape Design," *Landscape Architecture* (April 1912), 108.

18. H.V. Hubbard, editorial, *Landscape Architecture* (October 1910), 49.

19. Frank Waugh's *Landscape Beautiful,* reviewed in *Landscape Architecture* (January 1911), 100–102. See the obituary of Waugh in *Landscape Architecture* (October 1943), reprinted in Gary O. Robinette, *Landscape Architectural Education,* vol. 1 (Dubuque, Iowa: Kendall/Hunt Publishing Co., 1973), 133–34, and

Frederick R. Steiner, "Frank Albert Waugh," in *American Landscape Architecture: Designers and Places,* ed. William H. Tishler (Washington, D.C.: National Trust for Historic Preservation/ASLA, 1989), 100–103.

20. Harold A. Caparn, "Central Park, New York: A Work of Art," *Landscape Architecture* (July 1912), 167–76.

21. Ibid, 175–76.

22. Michael P. Cohen, *The History of the Sierra Club, 1892–1970* (San Francisco: Sierra Club Books, 1988), 31. See also Alfred Runte, *National Parks: The American Experience* (Lincoln: University of Nebraska Press, 1979); Samuel P. Hays, *Conservation and the Gospel of Efficiency* [1959], new edition (New York: Atheneum, 1969); and Michael P. Cohen, *The Pathless Way: John Muir and American Wilderness* (Madison: University of Wisconsin Press, 1984).

23. Frederick Law Olmsted, "Preliminary Report upon the Yosemite and Big Tree Grove" in *The Papers of Frederick Law Olmsted*, vol. 5: *The California Frontier, 1863–1865,* ed. Victoria Post Ranney, et al. (Baltimore: Johns Hopkins University Press, 1990), 488–511. In this volume see especially Charles E. Beveridge's "Introduction to the Landscape Design Reports" and Note 25 to Olmsted's report on Yosemite, p. 515. A version of this report was reprinted in *Landscape Architecture* (October 1952), and a portion was later quoted in Runte, *The National Parks*, 30–31.

24. Hays, *Conservation and the Gospel of Efficiency*, 194–95.

25. Frederick Law Olmsted (the younger), "Hetch Hetchy," *Boston Evening Transcript,* November 19, 1913, reprinted in *Landscape Architecture* (January 1914), 37–46.

26. Shary Page Berg, "Frederick Law Olmsted, Jr.," in *American Landscape Architecture,* ed. Tishler, 62.

27. Frederick Law Olmsted (the younger), quoted in Edward Clark

NOTES

Whiting and William Lyman Phillips, "Frederick Law Olmsted—1870–1957, An Appreciation of the Man and his Achievements," *Landscape Architecture* (April 1958), 155.

28. Mel Scott, *American City Planning Since 1890: A History Commemorating the Fiftieth Anniversary of the American Institute of Planners* (Berkeley: University of California Press, 1969), 170–72. See also Sam Bass Warner, Jr., *The Urban Wilderness* (New York: Harper & Row, 1972), 222–25, and Theodora Kimball, review of *Proceedings of the Ninth National Conference on City Planning*, Kansas City (May 7–9, 1917) in *Landscape Architecture* (April 1918), 155.

29. "War Records of Those Who were Fellows and Members during the years 1917 and 1918," *Transactions, ASLA* vol. 2 (1909–1921), 75–80. Theodore Osmundson alerted the author to the role of P. H. Elwood, Jr., in the war.

30. Scott, *American City Planning Since 1890*, 163.

31. Ibid, 170–72, 121–23.

32. For Jens Jensen's and Frank Waugh's relations with the ASLA during the 1920s and 1930s, see Robert E. Grese, *Jens Jensen: Maker of Natural Parks and Gardens* (Baltimore: Johns Hopkins University Press, 1992). See also Elbert Peets, "The Landscape Priesthood," *American Mercury* (January 1927), 94–99.

33. Charles Francis Atkinson coined the term "megalopolitan" to translate the word "grossstadtisch" in Oswald Spengler's *The Decline of the West*, which first appeared in the original German, in two volumes, 1918 and 1922. See Atkinson's note to his translation (originally published in two volumes, 1926 and 1928) in the one-volume edition (New York: Alfred A. Knopf, 1939), 29.

34. Mel Scott, *The San Francisco Bay Area: A Metropolis in Perspective* [1959], new edition (Berkeley: University of

California Press, 1985), 101–107, and *American City Planning Since 1890*, 100–109.

35. Thomas Adams, "The Regional Survey as the Basis for the Regional Plan. . . ," *Landscape Architecture* (July 1919), 179.

36. Mumford, "The Plan of New York," in *The New Republic*, a two-part series (June 15, 1932 and June 22, 1932) reprinted as one long selection in *Planning the Fourth Migration: The Neglected Vision of the Regional Planning Association of America*, ed. Carl Sussman (Cambridge: MIT Press, 1976), 224–59.

37. See Clarence S. Stein, *Toward New Towns for America* (Liverpool: The University Press of Liverpool, 1951), and Lewis Mumford, "The Fate of Garden Cities," *Journal of the American Institute of Architects* (February 1927), 37–39.

38. Benton MacKaye, "Outdoor Culture, The Philosophy of Through Trails," *Landscape Architecture* (April 1927), 163–71. See also MacKaye, "The New Exploration: Charting the Industrial Wilderness," *Survey Graphic* (May 1925).

39. Frederick R. Karl, *Modern and Modernism: The Sovereignty of the Artist, 1885–1925* (New York: Atheneum, 1985), 7.

40. *Transactions, ASLA*, vol. 1 (1899–1908).

41. See Brooklyn Institute of Arts and Sciences, *The American Renaissance: 1876–1917*, catalog of the exhibition, October 13–December 30, 1979. (Brooklyn, New York: The Brooklyn Museum, 1979), and Barbara Rose, *American Art Since 1900: A Critical History* (New York: Frederick A. Praeger, 1967).

42. See Rudi Blesh, *Modern Art USA: Men, Rebellion, Conquest, 1900–1956* (New York: Alfred A. Knopf, 1956), and Rose, *American Art Since 1900*.

43. See Beatrix Jones, "The Garden as a Picture," *Scribner's Magazine* (July 1907), 2–11, and "Landscape Com-

position," in Hubbard and Kimball, *Introduction to Landscape Design*, 88–129.

44. Charles Downing Lay, "Space Composition," *Landscape Architecture* (January 1918), 77–86. The quotation from Santayana is from *The Sense of Beauty* [1896], Part II, "The Materials of Beauty." Lay may have been referring to Meier-Graefe and Hildebrand from memory because he misspelled their names.

45. Berenson's words are quoted from his *Central Italian Painters of the Renaissance* [1897], reissued in Berenson, *The Italian Painters of the Renaissance* (New York: Phaidon, 1952), 122. In formulating his concept of space composition Berenson was apparently influenced by German sculptor and critic Adolf von Hildebrand, whose *Das Problem der Form in der bildenden Kunst* (1893) made a deep impression on him. Berenson read the recently published book shortly after meeting the author in Italy. See Ernest Samuels, *Bernard Berenson: The Making of a Connoisseur* (Cambridge: Harvard University Press, 1979), 179.

46. Charles Downing Lay, "Art and the Landscape Architect," *Landscape Architecture* (April 1923), 161–67.

47. See, for example, Wheelwright's account of the founding of *Landscape Architecture* in that magazine (Winter 1959–1960), 110, and the obituary he wrote for his former employer, Charles Downing Lay, in *Landscape Architecture* (April 1956), 162–64.

48. P.H. Elwood, Jr., *American Landscape Architecture* (New York: The Architectural Book Publishing Co./Paul Wenzel & Maurice Krakow, 1924).

CHAPTER 2

1. Alfred North Whitehead, *Science in the Modern World* [1925], new edition (New York: The Free Press, 1967), 194–202. Most of this book was

based on Whitehead's Lowell Lectures, delivered at Harvard University in February 1925.

2. James L. Greenleaf, "Annual Report of the President of the ASLA," *Landscape Architecture* (April 1925), 205–209.

3. Coolidge's remark dates from an address he gave in December 1923. See Richard Hofstadter, *Anti-Intellectualism in American Life* (New York: Knopf, 1963), 237, Note 3.

4. Calvin Coolidge, quoted in Charles A. Beard and Mary R. Beard, *The Rise of American Civilization*, 2 vols. (New York: Macmillan, 1927), vol. 2, 700.

5. See Charles W. Eliot II, "Planning Washington and its Environs," *City Planning* (July 1927), 177–93, which includes excerpts from President Coolidge's letter to the National Conference on City Planning (undated). See also the obituary of Ferruccio Vitale in *Landscape Architecture* (July 1933), 219–20.

6. Arthur M. Schlesinger, Jr., *The Age of Roosevelt: The Crisis of the Old Order, 1919–1933* (Boston: Houghton, Mifflin, 1956), 71–82. See also Richard Hofstadter, *Social Darwinism in American Thought* (Philadelphia: University of Pennsylvania Press, 1944), and Frederick Lewis Allen, *The Big Change: America Transforms Itself, 1900–1950* (New York: Harper & Bros., 1952), 109–20.

7. Schlesinger, *Crisis of the Old Order*, 82–89.

8. Robin Karson, *The Muses of Gwinn: Art and Nature in a Garden Designed by Warren H. Manning, Charles A. Platt & Ellen Biddle Shipman* (Sagaponack, New York: Sagapress/ The Library of American Landscape History, 1995), 27.

9. Warren H. Manning, "A National Plan Study Brief," a special supplement in *Landscape Architecture* (July 1923), 21.

10. Frank A. Waugh, "American Ideals in Landscape Architecture," *Landscape Architecture* (April 1925), 151–54.

11. Arthur Shurtleff, "Park Scenery in Relation to the Fine Arts and to Physical Recreation," *American Magazine of Art* (August 1926), 391–402.

12. James L. Greenleaf, "Annual Report of the President of the ASLA," *Landscape Architecture* (April 1924), 210.

13. Clarence Fowler, "Is There an Overproduction of Landscape Architects?" *Landscape Architecture* (April 1928), 181. Fowler's figures for ASLA membership and the U.S. Census are gleaned from writings by Mariana Griswold Van Rensselaer, an ASLA honorary member. See her new chapter, "Changes," in the revised 1925 edition of her book, *Art-out-of-Doors*, reprinted in Van Rensselaer, *Accents as Well as Broad Effects: Writings on Architecture, Landscape, and the Environment, 1876–1925*, ed. David Gebhard (Berkeley: University of California Press, 1996).

14. James L. Greenleaf, "Annual Report of the President," *Landscape Architecture* (April 1927), 230–36.

15. See Robert E. Grese, *Jens Jensen: Maker of Natural Parks and Gardens* (Baltimore: Johns Hopkins University Press, 1992), and Leonard K. Eaton, *Landscape Artist in America: The Life and Work of Jens Jensen* (Chicago: University of Chicago Press, 1964). Jensen was subjected to compulsive military service after Germany had absorbed his homeland in southern Denmark.

16. Jens Jensen, "Roadside Planting," *Landscape Architecture* (April 1924), 186–87, and Jensen, "Novelty versus Nature," *Landscape Architecture* (October 1924), 44–45.

17. "ASLA Notes," *Landscape Architecture* (April 1926), 191.

18. Grese, *Jens Jensen*, 28.

19. See the review of Waugh's *Natural Style in Landscape Architecture* (January 1918), 102–104, and Otto G. Schaffer's review of Jensen's *Siftings* in *Landscape Architecture* (April 1940), 153–54.

20. Walter Prichard Eaton, "Guiding the Tramper: The Example of Mt. Everett Reservation in the Berkshires," *Landscape Architecture* (October 1926), 1–7, and "From a Berkshire Mountain Top: A Plea for the Planning of Holiday Regions," *Landscape Architecture* (January 1928), 93–105.

21. Walter Prichard Eaton, *Everybody's Garden* (New York: Knopf, 1932).

22. "Editorial Notes" in *Landscape Architecture* (April 1915), 151–52, and (October 1915), 57.

23. "The League Exhibit," *Landscape Architecture* (July 1937), 177; the obituary of Alfred Geiffert, Jr., in *Landscape Architecture* (October 1957), 48–49.

24. "Honors in Landscape Architecture to Gilmore D. Clarke," *Landscape Architecture* (July 1937). See also Note 24.

25. "A Solution to the Housing Problem in the United States," *Landscape Architecture* (January 1920), 98–100; "The Paris Competition," *Landscape Architecture* (July 1920), 211–13; and "Recent Competitions," *Landscape Architecture* (April 1921), 151–52.

26. *Transactions ASLA*, vol. 2, 81–89.

27. E.S. Draper, "Shall the ASLA Undertake Publicity?" *Landscape Architecture* (January 1929), 126–28.

28. Arthur A. Shurtleff, "Annual Report of the President," *Landscape Architecture* (April 1930), 230–31.

29. Arthur A. Shurcliff, *New England Journal* (Boston: Houghton Mifflin, 1931), 8, 30. The formal change of name from Shurtleff to Shurcliff took place on April 17, 1930; see Shurcliff, *Autobiography* (privately printed, Cambridge, 1981), 1.

30. Henry Vincent Hubbard, "Annual Report of the President," *Landscape Architecture* (April 1932), 230–32.

31. Phoebe Cutler, *The Public Landscape of the New Deal* (New Haven: Yale University Press, 1985), 85. See also Norman T. Newton, *Design on the Land: The Development of Landscape Architecture* (Cambridge: Harvard University Press, 1971); Bruce Radde, *The Merritt Parkway* (New Haven:

Yale University Press, 1993); Mel Scott, *American City Planning Since 1890* (Berkeley: University of California Press, 1971); and Malcolm Cairns and Gary Kessler, "Stanley White, Teacher," *Landscape Architecture* (January/February 1985), 86–91.

32. A.D. Taylor, "Notes on Federal Activities Relating to Landscape Architecture," *Landscape Architecture* (April 1935), 164–71.

33. Henry Vincent Hubbard, "Annual Report of the President," *Landscape Architecture* (April 1935), 159–62.

34. Fletcher Steele, New Pioneering in Garden Design," *Landscape Architecture* (April 1930), 159–77.

35. See Charles Downing Lay, "Space Composition," *Landscape Architecture* (January 1918), 77–86, and Chapter 1, above.

36. See Fletcher Steele, *Gardens and People* (Boston: Houghton Mifflin, 1964), especially the final chapter, and Robin Karson, *Fletcher Steele, Landscape Architect* (New York: Harry N. Abrams/Sagapress, 1989).

37. Fletcher Steele, "Landscape Design of the Future," *Landscape Architecture* (July 1932), 299–302.

38. Malcolm H. Dill and Ralph E. Griswold, quoted in "Contemporary Trends and Future Possibilities in Landscape Design," *Landscape Architecture* (July 1932), 288–303.

39. Richard Schermerhorn, Jr., "Landscape Architecture—Its Future," *Landscape Architecture* (July 1932), 281–87.

40. Garrett Eckbo, "Small Gardens in the City," *Pencil Points* (September 1937), 573–86, and "Sculpture and Landscape Design," *Magazine of Art* (April 1938), 202–208+. See also a series of articles by James Rose, including "Why Not Try Science," *Pencil Points* (December 1939), 777, and "Gardens," *California Arts and Architecture* (May 1940). See also the series of articles by Eckbo, Rose, and Dan Kiley in *Architectural Record* (May 1939, August 1939, and February 1940). Some of

these articles are reprinted in *Modern Landscape Architecture: A Critical Review*, ed., Marc Treib (Cambridge: MIT Press, 1993).

41. See the response to Eckbo's article, with the author's reply, in *Magazine of Art* (June 1938), 370–71, and (July 1938), 431–32.

42. See the obituary of Henry Vincent Hubbard, *Landscape Architecture* (January 1948), 54, and "Editorial," *Landscape Architecture* (October 1935), 34.

43. Talbot F. Hamlin, "Farm Security Architecture: An Appraisal," *Pencil Points* (November 1941), 709–20.

44. Garrett Eckbo, typescript of an unpublished autobiography, written about 1971–1972, a copy of which Eckbo gave to the author.

45. "Landscape Architecture in Public Park Design," *Landscape Architecture* (April 1939), 103.

46. Arthur C. Comey, letter to the editor, *Landscape Architecture* (July 1944), 147–50; "Monkeying with the Name," *Landscape Architecture* (October 1942), 20–23.

47. *Official Guide Book: New York World's Fair, 1939* (New York: Exposition Publications, Inc., 1939); Eugen Neuhaus, *The Art of Treasure Island* (Berkeley: University of California Press, 1939); "New York World's Fair, 1939," *Magazine of Art* (May 1939); "Landscape Architecture at the New York World's Fair, I and II," *Landscape Architecture* (July 1939 and October 1939); and David Gelernter, *1939: The Lost World of the Fair* (New York: The Free Press, 1995).

48. Neuhaus, *Art of Treasure Island*, 63–80.

49. Arthur A. Shurcliff, "City Plan and Landscaping Problems," and William Graves Perry, "Notes on the Architecture" in the special issue on Colonial Williamsburg, *Architectural Record* (December 1935). For more on the Williamsburg restoration and collaboration, see *An Interview with Sidney N. Shurcliff on Arthur A. Shurcliff*, ed.

Karen Madsen (Watertown, Massachusetts: The Hubbard Educational Trust, 1992).

50. *Contemporary Landscape Architecture and its Sources*, catalogue of the exhibition at the San Francisco Museum of Art, February 12 to March 22, 1937.

51. "The ASLA in Detroit," *Landscape Architecture* (July 1946), 151; Edward H. Laird, "Electronics Park," *Landscape Architecture* (October 1946), 14–16.

52. John Ormsbee Simonds, *Landscape Architecture: The Shaping of Man's Natural Environment* (New York: McGraw-Hill, 1961), 221–25.

53. Vincent N. Merrill, "Wanted: A Sense of Professional Direction," *Landscape Architecture* (July 1941), 186–89.

CHAPTER 3

1. See, for example, Michael Elliott, *The Day Before Yesterday: Reconsidering America's Past, Rediscovering the Present* (New York: Simon & Schuster, 1996); Jeffrey Madrick, *The End of Affluence* (New York: Random House, 1995); Eric Hobsbawm, *The Age of Extremes: A History of the World, 1914–1991* [1994], new edition (New York: Vintage, 1996); William L. O'Neill, *American High: The Years of Confidence, 1945–1960* (New York: The Free Press, 1986); and Godfrey Hodgson, *America in Our Time* (Garden City, New York: Doubleday, 1976).

2. Gilmore D. Clarke, "A Challenge to the Landscape Architect," *Landscape Architecture* (July 1947), 140–41.

3. Bremer W. Pond, "Fifty Years in Retrospect," *Landscape Architecture* (January 1950), 66.

4. See *ASLA, Illustrations of Work of Members* (New York: Hayden Twiss, Publishers) for the years 1931 and 1932. See also "Code of Professional Ethics," *Landscape Architecture* (October 1940), 9–12, and "Landscape Architecture and the Landscape Architect: The Profession and its

Methods of Practice," *Landscape Architecture* (July 1940), 168–70. For Church's practice, see *Thomas Church, Landscape Architect*, 2 vols., interviews conducted by Suzanne B. Riess, Regional Oral History Office, Bancroft Library, University of California, Berkeley; and Pam-Anela Messenger, "The Art of Thomas Dolliver Church" (M.L.A. thesis, University of California at Berkeley, 1976).

5. James L. Greenleaf, "Annual Report of the President," *Landscape Architecture* (April 1927), 236.

6. See Christopher Tunnard, *Gardens in the Modern Landscape* (London: Architectural Press, 1938), and the series of three articles on urban, rural, and primeval environments by Garrett Eckbo, Daniel U. Kiley, and James C. Rose in *Architectural Record* (May 1939, August 1939, and February 1940).

7. Ervin Zube, "The Advance of Ecology," *Landscape Architecture* (March/April 1986), 59–60.

8. Barry Commoner, *The Closing Circle: Nature, Man, and Technology* (New York: Alfred A. Knopf, 1971), 21, 11–12.

9. The botanist Edith A. Roberts and landscape architect Elsa Rehmann co-authored several articles on plant ecology for *House Beautiful* that later formed their book, *American Plants for American Gardens: Plant Ecology— The Study of Plants in Relation to their Environment* (New York: Macmillan, 1929). See also Frank Waugh's articles in *Landscape Architecture*: "Ecology of the Roadside" (January 1931) and "Roadside Ecology—California Notes" (April 1936).

10. Jacob Bronowski, *Science and Human Values* [1956], new edition (New York: Harper & Bros., 1959), 13, 16.

11. See Arthur M. Schlesinger, Jr., *A Thousand Days: John F. Kennedy in the White House* (Boston: Houghton-Mifflin, 1965); *To Heal and to Build: The Programs of President Lyndon B. Johnson*, ed. James MacGregor Burns (New York: McGraw-Hill, 1968); and Alvin Toffler, *The Culture Consumers:*

Art and Affluence in America [1964], new edition (Baltimore: Penguin, 1965).

12. Richard Eells, *The Corporation and the Arts* (New York: MacMillan, 1967), 5, 14.

13. Toffler, *Culture Consumers*, 68.

14. Sidney Shurcliff and Campbell Miller, quoted in "Bay Area Landscape Architecture," *Landscape Architecture* (October 1957), 25–27. Sidney was the eldest son of former ASLA president Arthur A. Shurcliff and a partner in Shurcliff, Shurcliff and Merrill in Boston.

15. Stanley White, "Report from the Great Continental Divide," *Landscape Architecture* (Fall 1960), 48.

16. "What's Wrong with Landscape Architecture?" [excerpts gathered from Thomas A. Barton's survey], *Landscape Architecture* (July 1961), 254–55.

17. "Future of the Profession," *Landscape Architecture* (October 1962), 25–26.

18. Grady Clay, telephone interview with the author, May 21, 1997, and personal communication to the author, June 1997.

19. Norman T. Newton, obituary of Bradford Williams, *Landscape Architecture* (Spring 1960), 180–81.

20. Garrett Eckbo, "What Do We Mean by Modern Landscape Architecture?" *Journal of the Royal Architectural Institute of Canada* (August 1950), 268.

21. In 1987 Eckbo lent the author a copy of his Harvard textbook, *Introduction to the Study of Landscape Design* by H.V. Hubbard and Theodora Kimball (New York: Macmillan, 1917). See Melanie Simo, "The Education of a Modern Landscape Designer," *Pacific Horticulture* (Summer 1988), 19–30, and Reuben Rainey, " 'Organic Form in the Humanized Landscape': Garrett Eckbo's *Landscape for Living*," in *Modern Landscape Architecture: A Critical Review*, ed. Marc Treib (Cambridge: MIT Press, 1993).

22. Hideo Sasaki, "Thoughts on Education in Landscape Architecture: Some Comments on Today's Methodologies and Purposes," *Landscape Architecture* (July 1950), 158–60. See also Sasaki, "Landscape Architecture and the

Planning Effort," *Forsite* (1953), the annual students' publication of the department of city planning and landscape architecture, University of Illinois, Champaign-Urbana.

23. Grady Clay, telephone interview with the author, May 21, 1997.

24. Ian McHarg, "The Humane City: Must the Man of Distinction Always Move to the Suburbs?" *Landscape Architecture* (January 1958), 103–107.

25. Ian McHarg, "School News: A New Role for Landscape Architects," *Landscape Architecture* (April 1964), 227–28. See also McHarg and David A. Wallace, "Plan for the Valleys vs. Spectre of Uncontrolled Growth," *Landscape Architecture* (April 1965), 179–81.

26. "A Report on the Profession of Landscape Architecture" [abridged version of the full report], *Landscape Architecture* (October 1963), 34–37.

27. William J. Johnson, "Campus Planning for Growth," *Landscape Architecture* (April 1964), 208–16, and Philip H. Lewis, Jr., "Quality Corridors for Wisconsin," *Landscape Architecture* (January 1964), 100–107.

28. Albert Fein, "Parks in a Democratic Society," *Landscape Architecture* (October 1964), 24–31.

29. Garrett Eckbo, quoted in "ASLA Responds to 'Centennial Challenges,'" *Landscape Architecture* (October 1964), 12.

30. Garrett Eckbo, "Creative Design of the Landscape," *Landscape Architecture* (January 1965), 113–16.

31. Ibid. Eckbo served as chairman of the landscape architecture department at the University of California, Berkeley, from 1965 through 1969.

CHAPTER 4

1. Grady Clay, "Who Says 'Never Look Back'?" *Landscape Architecture* (January 1968), 111.

2. Edward Huntsman-Trout, letter to

NOTES

the editor, *Landscape Architecture* (July 1968), 268. For comments on Scripps College, see Michael Laurie, "The California Influence on Contemporary Landscape Architecture," *Landscape Architecture* (July 1966), 292–98.

3. Laura Wood Roper, *FLO: A Biography of Frederick Law Olmsted* (Baltimore: Johns Hopkins University Press, 1973), 282–85. See also Alfred Runte, *National Parks: The American Experience* (Lincoln: University of Nebraska Press, 1979), and Chapter One, above.

4. "New Missions for '66," *Landscape Architecture* (April 1966), 211–12.

5. "Exhibits: Atlanta Winners," *Landscape Architecture* (October 1967), 63. The 1967 award-winning projects were published in *Landscape Architecture* in April 1966, October 1967, and April 1968.

6. "Exhibits: Atlanta Winners," *Landscape Architecture* (October 1967), 63+.

7. Advertisement in *Landscape Architecture News Digest* (August 1974).

8. Raymond L. Freeman, "No Longer Weak and No Longer Small," *ASLA Bulletin* (September 1972), 4.

9. Theodore Osmundson, "Final Report . . . presented at the Annual Meeting, St. Louis, Missouri, June, 1969," *ASLA Bulletin* (August 1969), unpaged. Unfortunately, without acknowledging any abridgment, the editors of the *ASLA Bulletin* eliminated one entire paragraph of Osmundson's final report—the references to the "outstanding accomplishments" of Halprin, McHarg, Lewis, and the others. The omission tended to make the report seem more pessimistic than it actually was when it was presented in St. Louis. The author is indebted to Theodore Osmundson for sending a privately printed copy of his entire final report as ASLA president (1969).

10. Freeman, "No Longer Weak . . . ," 3–6.

11. "A New Form of Publication," *Landscape Architecture* (January 1971), 96; "An Evolving New Medium," *Landscape Architecture* (April 1971), 186;

and John Rahenkamp, Walter Sachs, and Roger Wells, "A Strategy for Watershed Development . . . ," *Landscape Architecture* (April 1971), 227–34.

12. Grady Clay, personal communication to the author, June 1997, and "Coming into its Own," *Landscape Architecture* (March 1982), 53–54.

13. Grady Clay, "Editorial Comment," *Landscape Architecture* (October 1972). See also *Beauty for America: Proceedings of the White House Conference on Natural Beauty* (Washington, D.C., May 24–25, 1965).

14. Mrs. Lyndon B. Johnson, letter to the editor, *Landscape Architecture* (April 1968), 176.

15. Campbell E. Miller, "Annual Report of the President," *ASLA Bulletin* (August 1971), 6; "The ASLA Today and Tomorrow," *ASLA Bulletin* (October 1974), unpaged, and Grady Clay, "The Readers Write . . . ," *Landscape Architecture* (January 1975), 127.

16. Campbell E. Miller, "This is ASLA . . . 1971," *ASLA Bulletin* (January 1971), 1–11.

17. "Professional Competition Winners," *Landscape Architecture* (October 1968), 75; see also projects published separately in this issue.

18. Karl Linn, "'White Solutions' won't work in black neighborhoods," and "Black energy," *Landscape Architecture* (October 1968), 23–25.

19. Ibid.

20. "Land, People and Plants," *Landscape Architecture* (April 1969), 207–208.

21. Ian McHarg, *Design with Nature* (Garden City, New York: The American Museum of Natural History/ The Natural History Press, 1969), 172–73, 196.

22. Neil Porterfield, "Ecological Basis for Planning a New Campus," *Landscape Architecture* (October 1969), 31–33.

23. Garrett Eckbo, letter to the editor, *Landscape Architecture* (April 1970), 200–201.

24. Neil Porterfield, letter to the editor, *Landscape Architecture* (April 1970),

201–202.

25. Garrett Eckbo, letter to the editor, *Landscape Architecture* (October 1970), 16.

26. Donald Appleyard, "Elitists versus the Public's Cry for Help," *Landscape Architecture* (October 1970), 25+, and "The Future of *Landscape Architecture* and Environmental Planning—A Personal View," *Landscape Architecture* (January 1971), 128–29. See also "New Emphasis on Evaluating Design," *Landscape Architecture* (January 1971), 102; Carl Steinitz and Peter Rogers, et al., *A Simulation Model of Urbanization and Change* (Cambridge: Harvard Graduate School of Design, 1968); and Steinitz, "Landscape Resource Analysis, The State of the Art," *Landscape Architecture* (January 1970), 101–105.

27. Donald Appleyard, "Elitists . . . ," 55, and "The Future . . . ," 129.

28. Peter G. Weisbrod, letter to the editor, *Landscape Architecture* (October 1968), 16.

29. Grady Clay, "Who Controls Neighborhood Open Space Design?" *Landscape Architecture* (July 1969), 282–83. For a distillation of the discussions, critiques, and final recommendations that emerged from this workshop, see *Workshop on Urban Open Space*, ed. Simpson F. Lawson (Washington, D.C.: U.S. Department of Housing and Urban Development, 1971). The author is indebted to Theodore Osmundson for sending a copy of this detailed report.

30. Denis R. Wilkinson, letter to the editor, *Landscape Architecture* (April 1970), 174.

31. Norman T. Newton, "Landscape Architecture: A Profession in Confusion?" *Landscape Architecture* (July 1974), 256–63.

32. "ASLA Awards Winners," *Landscape Architecture* (July 1971), 345.

33. Ian McHarg, conversation with the author, Berkeley, California, April 13, 1987.

34. See Franklin D. Becker, "A Class-Conscious Evaluation: Going Back to Sacramento's Pedestrian Mall," *Landscape Architecture* (October 1973), 448–57; Roger Martin, "Sites for the Hardy at 45° N," *Landscape Architecture* (January 1968), 124–29; and Clare C. Cooper, "Adventure Playgrounds," *Landscape Architecture* (October 1970), 18–29+.

35. Albert Fein, "Report on the Profession of Landscape Architecture," *Landscape Architecture* (October 1972), 37. See also Fein, "[Interim] Report on the Study of the Profession," *ASLA Bulletin* (August 1971), 12; "Priorities for ASLA: Final Report from the ASLA Task Force on the Study of the Profession," *ASLA Bulletin* (February 1974), 1–25; Peter Walker and Melanie Simo, *Invisible Gardens: The Search for Modernism in the American Landscape* (Cambridge: MIT Press, 1994, 287–91; and Note 36, below.

36. Norman T. Newton, "Landscape Architecture . . . ," *Landscape Architecture* (July 1974), 256–63; Garrett Eckbo, letter to the editor, *Landscape Architecture* (October 1974), 346–47; Ralph E. Griswold, letter to the editor, *Landscape Architecture* (October 1974), 438; and Theodore Osmundson, letter to the editor, *Landscape Architecture* (January 1975), 32.

37. Diane Kostial McGuire and Ann Satterthwaite, letters to the editor, *Landscape Architecture* (April 1968), 176. See Joseph H. Linesch, "Offshore innovation: Industrial camouflage for oil drillers," *Landscape Architecture* (October 1967), 33–36. See also "Report of the Task Force on Women in Landscape Architecture" (Darwina L. Neal, chair), *ASLA Bulletin* (July 1973), unpaged, and Raymond L. Freeman, "The Need for Black Landscape Architects," *ASLA Bulletin* (April 1973), 2.

38. Stanley White, "The Case for Landscape Architecture," *Forsite* (1952), a publication of students in the

NOTES

department of landscape architecture, University of Illinois, 27–29. See also Malcolm Cairns and Gary Kessler, "Stanley White, Teacher," *Landscape Architecture* (January/February 1985), 86–91, and Charles W. Harris, "The Affective Domain in Landscape Architecture Education," *HGSD News* (May 1977).

CHAPTER 5

1. See the jury's comments in *Landscape Architecture* (July 1971), 348, 357, and (July 1972), 340.
2. Lawrence Halprin, *The RSVP Cycles* (New York: Braziller, 1969), 2.
3. Theodore J. Wirth, letter to the editor, *Landscape Architecture* (January 1981), 37.
4. Sir Geoffrey Jellicoe, "Contemporary Meanings in the Landscape," *Landscape Architecture* (January 1980), 51–54.
5. Grady Clay, "Critics Wanted," *Landscape Architecture* (April 1958), 143.
6. Grady Clay, "The Planner and His Critics," *Journal of the American Institute of Architects* [hereafter, *AIA Journal*] (October 1960), 35.
7. C. McKim Norton and Ruben L. Parson, letters to the editor, *Landscape Architecture* (April 1961), 140.
8. Hideo Sasaki, "Thoughts on Education in Landscape Architecture: Some Comments on Today's Methodologies and Purpose," *Landscape Architecture* (July 1950), 160.
9. Hideo Sasaki, interview with the author, in Lafayette, California, May 18, 1996.
10. All quotations are from an article on the state of American college and university campuses in *The New York Times*, May 10, 1951, as quoted in William L. Shirer, *Midcentury Journey* (New York: Farrar, Straus and Young, 1952), 283–87.
11. Dan Kiley, "Nature: The Source of All Design," *Landscape Architecture* (January 1963), 127.
12. Richard A. Moore, "Objects? Today's

Students Couldn't Care Less," *Landscape Architecture* (April 1967), 229.
13. Ibid.
14. Anthony Walmsley, "Universities: On Teaching Design and Construction," *Landscape Architecture* (April 1967), 228–29+.
15. Carl Steinitz, "Landscape Resource Analysis: The State of the Art," *Landscape Architecture* (January 1970), 101–105.
16. Ian L. McHarg and Jonathan Sutton, "Ecological Plumbing for the Texas Coastal Plain," *Landscape Architecture* (January 1975), 78.
17. See, for example, Jeffrey Madrick, *The End of Affluence: The Causes and Consequences of America's Economic Dilemma* (New York: Random House, 1995); Robert C. Blattberg, ed., *The Economy in Transition* (New York: New York University Press, 1976); and Thomas Ferguson and Joel Rogers, *Right Turn: The Decline of the Democrats and the Future of American Politics* (New York: Hill and Wang, 1986).
18. A history of Sasaki Associates, The SWA Group, and Peter Walker and Partners by Melanie Simo is forthcoming from Spacemaker Press.
19. Grady Clay, "Winners in the 1978 Professional Design Competition of ASLA," *Landscape Architecture* (July 1978), 290.
20. Will Hooker, letter to the editor, *Landscape Architecture* (January 1979), 32. For Eckbo's and Porterfield's views, see Chapter 4.
21. Ralph E. Griswold, letter to the editor, *Landscape Architecture* (April 1974), 127.
22. "Winners . . . ," *Landscape Architecture* (July 1976).
23. "Winners . . . ," *Landscape Architecture* (July 1977).
24. Paul Goldberger, article in New York Times, March 30, 1978, reprinted, with afterthoughts circa 1983, in Goldberger, *On the Rise: Architecture and Design in a Postmodern Age* (New York: Viking Penguin, 1985), 107–10.

25. Ian McHarg, interview with the author, in Berkeley, California, April 13, 1987.
26. Warren Burgess, letter to the editor, *Landscape Architecture* (September 1976), 426.
27. Garrett Eckbo, "Suspended Between Ethics and Business: A View of the Professional's Obligations," *Landscape Architecture* (September 1978), 382–84. For Walker and The SWA Group in the 1970s, see *Process: Architecture 85: Peter Walker: Landscape as Art* (Tokyo, Japan: Process Architecture Publishing Company, October 1989).
28. Grady Clay, "Winners . . . ," *Landscape Architecture* (July 1978), 336–46.
29. Grady Clay, "Unlocking the Treasure House" and "The Competition," *Landscape Architecture* (July 1979), 376, 425–26.
30. "1980 ASLA Awards," *Landscape Architecture* (September 1980), 481–521.
31. "The 1981 ASLA Awards' New Meanings," *Landscape Architecture* (September 1981). See also Craig Campbell, "Seattle's Gas Plant Park," *Landscape Architecture* (July 1973), 338–42.
32. Marshall McLuhan, preface to the third printing, *Understanding Media: The Extensions of Man* (New York: McGraw-Hill, 1964), vii–viii.
33. See Joel Garreau, *Edge City: Life on the New Frontier* (New York: Doubleday, 1991).

CHAPTER 6

1. See Joel Garreau, *Edge City: Life on the New Frontier* (New York: Doubleday, 1991), and "Edge Cities: In Search of a Sense of Place," *Landscape Architecture* (December 1988), 48–54; Philip Langdon, *A Better Place to Live: Reshaping the American Suburb* (Amherst: University of Massachusetts Press, 1994); and Christopher B. Leinberger and Charles Lockwood, "How Business is Reshaping

America," *Atlantic* (October 1986), 43–52.
2. See John Kenneth Galbraith, *The Culture of Contentment* (Boston: Houghton Mifflin, 1992); Haynes Johnson, *Sleepwalking Through History: America in the Reagan Years* (New York: W. W. Norton, 1991); Robert Reich, *The Work of Nations: Preparing Ourselves for 21st-Century Capitalism* (New York: Alfred A. Knopf, 1993); and Kevin Phillips, *The Politics of Rich and Poor: Wealth and the American Electorate in the Reagan Aftermath* (New York: Random House, 1990).
3. Phillips, *Politics of Rich and Poor,* 183.
4. Stanley White, *The Teaching of Landscape Architecture* (East Lansing, Michigan, privately printed, June 25, 1953), 95. See above, Chapter 4.
5. Ervin H. Zube, James L. Sell, and Jonathan G. Taylor, quoted in "ASLA Honor Awards 1982," *Landscape Architecture* (September 1982), 86.
6. William Tucker, *Progress and Privilege: America in the Age of Environmentalism* (New York: Anchor Press/Doubleday, 1982), xii.
7. Mark Dowie, *Losing Ground: American Environmentalism at the Close of the Twentieth Century* (Cambridge: MIT Press, 1995), 67.
8. Ibid.
9. Thomas Ferguson and Joel Rogers, *Right Turn: The Decline of the Democrats and the Future of American Politics* (New York: Hill and Wang, 1986), 131–32.
10. "The 1983 ASLA Awards," *Landscape Architecture* (September/October 1983), 90.
11. Vincent Bellafiore and Neil H. Porterfield in "Jury Colloquy," *Landscape Architecture* (September/October 1983), 74.
12. John J. Reynolds and Thomas Zarfoss, in "1984 ASLA Awards," *Landscape Architecture* (September/October 1984), 44, 50–51.
13. John J. Reynolds, "Exalted Landscapes:

NOTES

A Charge to the Juries," *Landscape Architecture* (September/October 1985), 63.

14. John W. Simpson, "Environmental Planning in the Backwash," *Landscape Architecture* (January/February 1985), 72–77.

15. See letters to the editor of *Landscape Architecture* from Robert W. Ross, Jr., and William G. Swain (March/April 1985), 11,14, and from John T. Lyle and John W. Simpson (July/August 1985), 11, 14.

16. See Kevin Lynch, *The Image of the City* (Cambridge: MIT Press, 1960); Philip Lewis, Jr., "Quality Corridors for Wisconsin," *Landscape Architecture* (January 1964), 100–107; J. William Thompson, "Commonsense Visionary" [Profile of Philip Lewis], *Landscape Architecture* (July 1996), 67–71; and Chapter 3, above.

17. For further details of these projects, see Christopher Findlay, "A Model Resource for County Planning," and Stacey Freed, "Agent of Change," *Landscape Architecture* (September/October 1986), 82–91.

18. Charles W. Harris, "The Once–Lonely Turf: New directions for landscape architecture at Harvard from 1958 to 1970" in Margaret Henderson Floyd, *Architectural Education and Boston: Centennial Publication of the Boston Architectural Center, 1889–1989* (Boston: Boston Architectural Center, 1989), 105–107.

19. Norman T. Newton, *Design on the Land: The Development of Landscape Architecture* (Cambridge: Harvard University Press, 1971), xxi.

20. Grady Clay, "The Bagel Garden: Loud and Clear," *Landscape Architecture* (May 1980), 266.

21. Steven R. Krog, "Is it Art?" *Landscape Architecture* (May 1981), 373–76; letters to the editor in response (July 1981), 440–447+.

22. Walter Cudnohufsky, William Behnke, Garrett Eckbo, and J.B. Jackson, letters to the editor, *Landscape Archi-*

tecture (July 1981), 440–46.

23. Cheryl Barton, "Profile of the Profession," *Landscape Architecture* (September/October 1983), 50; "People," 17.

24. Cheryl Barton and William J. Johnson, in "1983 ASLA Awards," *Landscape Architecture* (September/October 1983), 50, 64–65.

25. Cheryl Barton, in "The Sum of the Parts," *Landscape Architecture* (September/October 1984), 50.

26. Carl D. Johnson, in Ibid, 50, 47.

27. "1985 ASLA Awards," *Landscape Architecture* (September/October 1985), 68–75.

28. "Awards 1986," *Landscape Architecture* (September/October 1986).

29. Richard Haag, quoted in Susan R. Frey, "A Series of Gardens," Ibid, 54–61+.

30. Richard Haag, "The Garden in the Collective Unconscious, or Design with DNA," in *Meanings of the Garden:* Proceedings of a Working Conference to Explore the Social, Psychological and Cultural Dimensions of Gardens, University of California, Davis, May 14–17, 1987, ed. Mark Francis and Randolph T. Hester, Jr., 47–49. Francis and Hester later revised these proceedings for the book, *The Meaning of Gardens* (Cambridge: MIT Press, 1990).

31. Jurors quoted (anonymously) in Susan R. Frey, "A Series of Gardens," *Landscape Architecture* (September/October 1986), 54–61+.

32. Bud Parker, letter to the editor, *Landscape Architecture* (January 1989), 10.

33. Joseph E. Brown and several others, letters to the editor, *Landscape Architecture* (February 1990), 10–12.

34. "Comments from the Juries," *Landscape Architecture* (November 1988), 99–108.

35. Ibid.

36. "1989 ASLA Awards," *Landscape Architecture* (November 1989).

37. Michael Van Valkenburgh, in Ibid, 119; John T. Lyle, "Prospect," *Landscape Architecture* (November 1989), 160.

38. For Darwin and Spencer, see Erich Harth, *Dawn of a Millennium: Beyond Evolution and Culture* (Boston: Little, Brown, 1990), 58–59.

39. See Lynn Margulis, "Early Life: The Microbes Have Priority," in *GAIA: A Way of Knowing: Political Implications of the New Biology*, ed. William Irwin Thompson (Great Barrington, Massachusetts: Lindisfarne Press, 1987), 98–109.

40. See Francisco Varela, "Laying Down a Path in Walking," in *GAIA*, 48–64.

41. Loren Eiseley, *The Unexpected Universe* (New York: Harcourt, Brace & World, 1969), 193. See especially 120–88.

CHAPTER 7

1. M. Paul Friedberg, "Out of the Woods, Into the Future," *Landscape Architecture* (December 1990), 53–54. Friedberg was surveying the ASLA's first annual competition, "Landscapes for the Twenty-first Century," later renamed "Visionary and Unbuilt Landscapes."

2. See the special issue devoted to landscape architecture history in *Landscape Architecture* (October 1990). Laurie Olin received one of the ASLA's Bradford Williams medals in 1991 for his article in this issue, "Wide Spaces and Widening Chaos."

3. Charles W. Eliot, letter to the editor, *Landscape Architecture* (October 1910), 40. See also Michael Leccese's article based on the LA Forum, "At the Beginning, Looking Back," *Landscape Architecture* (October 1990), 92.

4. Ervin Zube, "The Advance of Ecology," *Landscape Architecture* (March/April 1986), 66–67. See also Carl Steinitz, Paul Parker, and Lawrie Jordan, "Hand Drawn Overlays: Their History and Prospective Uses," *Landscape Architecture* (September 1976), 444–55. For Manning's work, see

Introduction and Chapter 1, above.

5. Grady Clay, telephone interview with the author, May 21, 1997.

6. John Rahenkamp, in LA Forum, "Rethinking Suburbia," *Landscape Architecture* (April 1991), 64; Ignacio Bunster-Ossa, in dialogue with Roger Wells, "Suburb vs. City," *Landscape Architecture* (June 1997), 89.

7. Randy Hester, quoted in Mac Griswold, "The Year of Living Responsibly," *Landscape Architecture* (November 1994), 52–55.

8. Reuben Rainey and Kenneth Helphand, quoted in Simpson Lawson, "An Enabling Body of Knowledge," *Landscape Architecture* (March 1992), 45.

9. For an unusually candid discussion by the founder and creator of LANDCADD, see Greg Jameson, "Technology: Are We Really Better Off?" *Landscape Architect and Specifier News* (December 1997), 72.

10. "1990 ASLA Awards," *Landscape Architecture* (November 1990), 60–63.

11. "1990 ASLA Awards," *Landscape Architecture* (November 1990), 50, and "1991 ASLA Awards," (November 1991), 66–69.

12. "1993 ASLA Awards," *Landscape Architecture* (November 1993), 60–62.

13. "1995 ASLA Awards," *Landscape Architecture* (November 1995), 54–56, and "1996 ASLA Awards," (November 1996), 84–86.

14. Mark Dowie, *Losing Ground: American Environmentalism at the Close of the Twentieth Century* (Cambridge: MIT Press, 1995).

15. "A Humanistic Design Manifesto," *Landscape Architecture* (November 1982), 41–44.

16. John T. Lyle, letter to the editor, *Landscape Architecture* (July/August 1985), 11.

17. Peter Walker, "A Levitation of Stones," *Landscape Architecture* (April 1990), 36–39. See also J. William Thompson, "A Passion for Restraint" [profile of Peter Walker], *Landscape Architecture* (December 1991), 61–67.

373

18. John Simonds, letter to the editor, *Landscape Architecture* (May 1990), 8–9. See the LA Forum on modernism, *Landscape Architecture* (January 1990); and Michael Leccese, "Mystical Pragmatist" [profile of John Simonds], *Landscape Architecture* (March 1990), 78–83.

19. J. William Thompson, "1990 ASLA Awards," *Landscape Architecture* (November 1990), 33–35.

20. Ervin H. Zube, letter to the editor, *Landscape Architecture* (February 1991).

21. Stuart O. Dawson, taped interviews with the author, December 13, 1988, and April 11, 1996, in Watertown, Massachusetts. See *Sasaki Associates: Integrated Environments*, text by Melanie Simo, dialogues by David Dillon (Washington, D.C.: Spacemaker Press, 1997).

22. George Bush, *Economic Report of the President Transmitted to the Congress, January 1993* (Washington, D.C.: U.S. Government Printing Office, 1993), 3.

23. William J. Johnson and Martha Schwartz, quoted in Benjamin Forgey, "We've got to get inside the system that builds America," and additional jurors' comments, *Landscape Architecture* (November 1992), 48–50, 56.

24. Mac Griswold, "New Clear Days," *Landscape Architecture* (November 1993), 43–47.

25. See the awards issues of *Landscape Architecture* (November 1992) and (November 1993).

26. Walter Hood, quoted in Mac Griswold, "The Year of Living Responsibly," *Landscape Architecture* (November 1994), 52–55.

27. Alan Ward, quoted in "1997 ASLA Awards," *Landscape Architecture* (November 1997), 41.

28. See Michel Foucault, "What is an Author?" in *Textual Strategies: Perspectives in Post-Structuralist Criticism*, ed. Josue V. Harari (Ithaca: Cornell University Press, 1979), 141–60, and Terry Eagleton, *Literary Theory: An Introduction* (Minneapolis: University of Minnesota Press, 1983).

29. James Atlas, *Battle of the Books: The Curriculum Debate in America* (New York: W.W. Norton, 1990), 76.

30. See awards issue of *Landscape Architecture* (November issues for 1994, 1995, and 1996).

31. Kurt Culbertson, quoted in "1996 ASLA Awards," *Landscape Architecture* (November 1996), 70.

32. "1997 ASLA Awards," *Landscape Architecture* (November 1997), 40–41.

33. "1972 Winners in ASLA Professional Competition," *Landscape Architecture* (July 1972), 340.

34. Carl D. Johnson, quoted in "1984 ASLA Awards," *Landscape Architecture* (September/October 1984), 50.

35. "1991 ASLA Awards," *Landscape Architecture* (November 1991), 76–77; "1993 ASLA Awards," (November 1993), 66–67.

36. For mainly positive views on emerging technologies, see *Technology 2001: The Future of Computing and Communications,* ed. Derek Leebaert (Cambridge: MIT Press, 1991) and William J. Mitchell, *City of Bits: Space, Place, and the Infobahn* (Cambridge: MIT Press, 1995). For negative views and ambivalence, see Sven Birkerts, *The Gutenberg Elegies: The Fate of Reading in an Electronic Age* (Boston: Faber and Faber, 1994); Stephen L. Talbott, *The Future Does Not Compute: Transcending the Machines in Our Midst* (Sebastopol, California: O'Reilly & Associates, 1995); and Jerry Mander, *In the Absence of the Sacred: The Failure of Technology & the Survival of the Indian Nations* (San Francisco: Sierra Club Books, 1991).

37. James Burke and Robert Ornstein, *The Axemaker's Gift: Technology's Capture and Control of Our Minds and Culture* [1995], new edition (New York: G.P. Putnam's Sons, 1997). See especially their concluding chapter, "Forward to the Past." Their quotation from Henry David Thoreau is from "Economy," the first chapter of *Walden* [1854], new edition (New York: The Modern Library, 1937), 33.

38. Patrick A. Miller, "A Profession in Peril?" *Landscape Architecture* (August 1997), 66–71+. See Introduction, above.